W9-CCE-315

WITHDRAWN

The Lost Way

The Lost Way

How Two Forgotten Gospels Are Rewriting
the Story of Christian Origins

Stephen J. Patterson

HarperOne
An Imprint of HarperCollinsPublishers

HarperOne

Scripture translations are the author's own unless otherwise noted.

THE LOST WAY: *How Two Forgotten Gospels Are Rewriting the Story of Christian Origins.* Copyright © 2014 by Stephen J. Patterson. All rights reserved. Printed in the United States of America. No part of this book may be used or reproduced in any manner whatsoever without written permission except in the case of brief quotations embodied in critical articles and reviews. For information address HarperCollins Publishers, 195 Broadway, New York, NY 10007.

HarperCollins books may be purchased for educational, business, or sales promotional use. For information please e-mail the Special Markets Department at SPsales@harpercollins.com.

HarperCollins website: http://www.harpercollins.com

HarperCollins®, 📕®, and HarperOne™ are trademarks of HarperCollins Publishers.

FIRST EDITION

Maps by Beehive Mapping

Library of Congress Cataloging-in-Publication Data is available upon request.

ISBN 978–0–06–233048–2

14 15 16 17 18 RRD(H) 10 9 8 7 6 5 4 3 2 1

For Marvin Meyer[†]

CONTENTS

ANOTHER GOSPEL

The Scotford Colony of the Hutterian Brethren is a vast farm thirty-five kilometers north of Edmonton, in Alberta. As we wander through the complex of buildings and yards, our host, Daniel (Danny) Hofer, explains to us, by turns, the basics of their sixteenth-century communal lifestyle and the workings of their new milk barn—an automated marvel in which hundreds of cows are milked by machines to which they attach *themselves*. As we contemplate the laser grid aligning robotic milkers to the teats of a restless cow, an old friend approaches. My wife knew many of these Hutterites forty years ago, when they wandered over from the colony to play together on the neighboring farm where she grew up. As she catches up with Susie, who wears a pleated, pressed, long-hemmed skirt, dark blue with polka dots, a white blouse, and a matching dark blue polka-dot head scarf, a robot wanders by and pushes hay closer to the pens, so the cows can reach it better.

"Z3PO," says my daughter.

My son corrects, "C3PO."

We are in a Star Wars dairy built by people who speak a dialect of German that has been dead for more than three centuries. As the robot scoots by, I notice that Susie's shoes are Keens. Later, in the school, Danny and Susie show us notebooks in which children have practiced writing this dialect in the most beautiful filigreed, cursive hand, filling pages with select passages of scripture. On Sundays, the colony gathers in this same room to hear sermons—the original sermons of their founder, Jacob Hutter, the South Tyrolean Anabaptist preacher who was burned at the stake in Innsbruck in 1536. A preacher reads them in Hochdeutsch, just as they were written in the sixteenth century, without alteration, to women sitting on the left and men on the right.

After the tour, we sit around the simple kitchen table of our host and enjoy freshly picked blueberries, tea, and cookies. The mood is friendly, but somber. The occasion for our visit is the impending death of my father-in-law, a neighbor well known to the colony and beloved by all present. Danny knows that I am a professor of religious studies and my wife is an ordained minister—an anomaly as strange to him as his milk barn is to us.

So he asks, "What is Christianity?"

Danny is very self-assured in all things. This is not the question of a seeker, but a quiz. He wants to know how close our answer will be to the right answer.

Normally I like to avoid the embarrassment of stammering at such questions by offering one of several stock answers I can live with without compromising too much integrity. But today I stammer. I have spent the afternoon working on a translation of Q, a lost gospel from the earliest years of Christianity—or what would become Christianity. I have been thinking too much. What *is* Christianity?

I knew this was going to be a conversation about origins. The Hutterites are all about origins. Their convictions about communal living are based on the Acts of the Apostles, the biblical account of Christian origins. And their pacifism, which I admire, is based on Jesus's Sermon on the Mount. But there is a lot more to the Christianity of Hutterites than this. Like most traditional Christians, they believe that Jesus is the Son of God, literally, and that his death was a blood sacrifice to atone for the sins of humanity. They believe that Jesus then rose from the dead, literally, and in this way conquered death, so that whoever believes in him might live on after death, in eternal life. These things are not incidental to the Hutterites. Indeed, they are quite central, under the present circumstances of our reunion. And Danny had every reason to expect that these fellow believers sitting at his table would share these traditional beliefs.

After a moment during which I must have had an odd, blank stare on my face, I say the wrong thing. "Christianity is many things."

I was thinking about origins and Q, that lost gospel I had been working on. Q was a text used by the authors of two biblical gospels, Matthew and Luke. It is, then, an earlier version of the gospel. In Q there is no account of Jesus's death and resurrection. And it is hard to tell if Jesus is even the Son of God. He might be the Son of Man, but in Q that is probably something different from Son of God. In Q Jesus seems to be on a par with John the Baptist, the teacher and prophet who baptized him in the Jordan. Like John he is a teacher and a prophet, a "child of Wisdom." His sayings are wise and clever, and often challenging. "Anyone who does not hate father and mother cannot be my disciple." Is *that* Christianity?

Sometimes he tells a story to illustrate his dominant theme: the kingdom of God, or, as I prefer to call it, the empire of God. In the empire of God people don't worry about what they shall wear or own— Danny would embrace this, I think. They share meals and care for one another in sickness—again, things my Hutterite friend would recognize. But then there is the story of a person who sows mustard—a weed—in his field. What has Christianity to do with weeds? Most of what Jesus teaches in Q is difficult for everyone: "Love your enemies." "Do not judge, lest you be judged." "Whoever strikes you on the cheek, turn to him the other as well." "To anyone who wants to take you to court to get your shirt, give him your coat as well." Is Christianity, then, simply difficult virtue? Admirable, but hardly unique.

As I sat contemplating what to say next, my thoughts turned also to the *Gospel of Thomas*. Here too was a very early expression of Christianity that had nothing to do with the central claims of traditional Christianity—that Jesus died for our sins and rose from the dead. In *Thomas*, Jesus never dies. He is the "living Jesus." Like Q, *Thomas* is a wisdom gospel, in which Jesus's wise sayings are offered with the promise, "Whoever finds the meaning of these sayings will not taste death." In this gospel too there are difficult sayings telling you to hate your mother and father, not to worry about what you will wear, and to give away your money. But there are also strange sayings, like the one that says you must "make the male and the female into a single one, so that the male will not be male and the female will not be female . . . then you will enter the empire (of God)." I think that Danny would like some of these sayings too though, especially one like "If you do not fast from the world, you will not find the empire (of God)." But these sayings and this gospel are not in the Bible. Could one trust a gospel that is not in the Bible to speak about the meaning of Jesus's teachings? And could salvation rest on a search to understand such odd, koanlike sayings? "If you bring forth what is within you, that which you have will save you." This is unique but odd. Was Jesus odd?

Christianity is indeed many things. Even today an enormous variety of beliefs and practices fit under the Christian umbrella. The Hutterites are part of that variety. But Christians in the modern West tend to think that the single thread running through all of these varieties must be the gospel—the gospel story of how Jesus died for our sins, but rose again to conquer death and offer us eternal life. Theologians of a previous generation even had a technical name for this story: the *kerygma*. The kerygma. Kerygma is just the Greek word for "preaching" or "message." This is and ever was the Christian gospel, from the first Christian communities to present-day Christianity in all its variety.

But the present generation of historians of earliest Christianity is not so sure. The study of Christian origins during the last fifty years has revealed a great deal more variety than our forebears ever thought possible. Texts like Q and the *Gospel of Thomas* represent a kind of

Christianity that is quite different, in fact. And these gospels are just a few of the many other gospels and writings, some lost, others now mostly forgotten to all but a handful of scholars. Why? How did it happen that the many versions of Christianity that existed in the beginning were eventually overshadowed by the one version we know as Christianity today—whether you're Catholic, Baptist, or Hutterite?

Four Gospels, No More, No Less

Near the end of the second century a church leader in the Roman provincial city of Lyon—modern Lyons, France—became concerned about a new prophecy that had recently come to his part of the world. He had even encountered its prophets in his own churches. Irenaeus of Lyon was worried. They claimed to speak in the spirit of the Lord. They brought to expression new ideas and claimed to have received secret, spiritual teachings from the *risen* Lord. They introduced new rituals to reflect these teachings. They interpreted the words of scripture, the apostle Paul, and even Jesus in ways that were consistent with their spiritual understanding, but that struck Irenaeus as odd and dangerous.

But Irenaeus had a problem. Not all of these new ideas were in fact new. The apostle Paul himself had spoken of secret and hidden teachings revealed to those who have the Spirit:

> But we teach a secret and hidden wisdom of God, which God announced before the ages for our glorification. . . . We teach this in words not taught by human wisdom, but taught by the Spirit, interpreting spiritual truths for those who have the Spirit. (1 Cor. 2:7, 13)

And one of the prize traditions of the new prophets was this saying of Jesus, found in both Matthew and Luke (see *Against Heresies* 1.20.3):

I thank you Father, Ruler of heaven and earth, that you have hidden these things from the wise and understanding and revealed them to babies; yes, Father, for this was your gracious will. All things have been given to me by my Father; and no one knows who the son is except the Father, or who the Father is except the son and any to whom the son chooses to reveal him. (Luke 10:21–22)

Such sayings seemed to open the floodgates, allowing prophets to say whatever they chose, no matter how odd or scandalous. Irenaeus felt he had to do something.

His urge to rein in the options and find a focus was perhaps motivated by the times. There had not yet been empire-wide, systematic persecution of Christians, but in local areas, especially where Christians had refused to participate in public rituals and sacrifices to the gods, imperial officials had begun to crack down. Christians were atheists by their lights and thus a threat to the *pax deorum,* the "peace of the gods." In Lyon, where Irenaeus lived, dozens of Christians had been thrown to the beasts to be ripped limb from limb. In the face of such danger, Irenaeus wanted solidarity. What little strength they had would be found in sticking together. The new prophets threatened to divide his house.

And so Irenaeus undertook the work for which he is primarily remembered by historians of early Christianity today, a treatise entitled *Against Heresies.* In it he describes and then refutes many early schools of thought that thrived in the first two centuries of Christianity, before there was any clear idea of what would become orthodox and what would be heterodox. In fact, Irenaeus's work went a long way toward establishing the notions of Christian orthodoxy and heresy. To refute the ideas of his opponents, he drew upon four gospels: Matthew, Mark, Luke, and John—gospels that Christians today recognize as the four canonical (biblical) gospels. But in Irenaeus's day, there were others as well—the *Gospel of the Hebrews,* the *Gospel of the*

Ebionites, the *Gospel of Truth,* the *Gospel of Mary,* the *Gospel of Peter,* and many others.

But Irenaeus decided to use only these four: Matthew, Mark, Luke, and John. He then made a statement that in hindsight can now be seen as quite historic. He said, "It is not possible that the gospels can be either more or fewer in number than they are." Why? His reasoning is, to ancient sensibilities, quite unimpeachable:

> For since there are four zones of the world in which we live, and four principal winds, while the Church is scattered throughout all the world, and the "pillar and ground" of the Church is the gospel and the spirit of life; it is fitting that she should have four pillars, breathing out immortality on every side, and enlivening people afresh. (*Against Heresies* 3.11.8)

Not only that, but the mythical cherubim who dwell in heaven have four faces, one a lion, one a calf, one human, and one an eagle. The Gospel of John to this day is symbolized as an eagle, Matthew a human face, Luke a calf, and Mark a lion—the lingering legacy of Irenaeus's logic. And finally, he argues, there are four principle covenants between God and the human race: Adam's, Noah's, Moses's, and the gospel's. Four winds, four faces, four covenants; therefore, there must be four gospels, no more, no less.

But what if Irenaeus had counted the covenant with Abraham too? Would he then have felt compelled to add a fifth gospel? Hardly. Irenaeus was not really interested in winds, cherubim, or covenants. He was interested in identifying a story around which he could rally his churches in the face of possible persecution and martyrdom. His choices reflect precisely that circumstance. The canonical four are all very similar. Each presents the story of Jesus as that of a martyr. In each, Jesus lives his life in faithfulness to his calling. In each, he is betrayed by a friend and suffers an unfair trial. In each, he is tortured and finally executed. And in each, God vindicates him by raising him from the dead. This is the story around which Irenaeus thought his people could rally.

The canonical gospels were not originally composed to satisfy Irenaeus's need, but they came by their martyrological focus honestly. They were all written near the end of the first century, during or in the immediate aftermath of an episode of great suffering and martyrdom among Jews living in the eastern Roman Empire. In the mid-60s CE the Jews in the Judean homeland rebelled against Roman rule and engaged in a great battle for freedom. But there would be no fairy-tale ending to this struggle. The rebellion was crushed by five Roman legions, the city of Jerusalem destroyed, and its great temple burned and desecrated. The dead could be counted in the hundreds of thousands; scores of slaves were marched off to Rome to be paraded before eager throngs gathered to see the vanquished Jews and their treasures. Today the scene stands immortalized on the inner panels of the Arch of Titus in Rome, the enduring monument to this great and shining moment in the emperor Titus's military career. In these early years there were not yet Christians, only Jews who believed Jesus to be the messiah. They looked upon this tragedy as other Jews did, with disbelief and horror. What was the meaning of the war? Was there a purpose to all the suffering and death? Why were the Jews so brutally vanquished?

The author of the Gospel of Mark chose to answer these questions by telling a story about Jesus's life. In this story, Jesus, the hidden messiah, goes to Jerusalem to bear witness to the coming reign of God. But there he is betrayed and killed. This, Mark thinks, explains the disastrous end to the war. Jerusalem was destroyed in the war, because thirty-five years earlier its leaders had rejected Jesus (12:1–12). That, for him, is the meaning of the war. What, then, should Jesus's followers do? Persevere. Just as Jesus persevered to the end, even accepting death, they too should persevere, even to the point of death. God had raised Jesus from the dead. God would do the same for them, if they remained faithful until the end (13:13). The war was just the beginning of a great apocalypse in which Jesus, the Son of Man, would soon return to punish the wicked and redeem the faithful (according to 13:14–37).

This, then, became the Christian story. Born in a time of great suffering, it would prove useful again and again in times of renewed suffering, including Irenaeus's time more than a century later. This story was not in the *Gospel of Truth* or the *Gospel of Philip* or the *Gospel of Mary*. Some of Irenaeus's foes, in fact, argued against martyrdom (see *Against Heresies* 3.18.5). The gospels that Irenaeus embraced were gospels that interpreted his own life and the martyrs he admired around him. In addition to Mark, there were Matthew and Luke, both of which used the Markan story as a template, and John, also a martyrdom story, though cut from somewhat different cloth. These were the four gospels Irenaeus chose to fill out his quartet. Jesus the martyr would inspire and unite his people as they faced persecution, suffering, and even death.

One day all of this would change. The world of Irenaeus, in which Christians were dissidents and sometimes persecuted, came to an end not with the apocalypse, but with another war. This was a civil war, pitting Roman against Roman. In October 312, Constantine the Great drove the army of his rival, Maxentius, into the Tiber River at the Milvian Bridge and thereby ended their long conflict. A legend says Constantine's victory came after a vision in which God showed him a sign, the chi-rho symbol used by Christians, and said to him, *in hoc signo vinces* ("by this sign you will conquer"; Eusebius, *Life of Constantine* 1.28). The legend says that he instructed his soldiers to put the mysterious sign on their shields before doing battle with Maxentius, and behold, it worked. That is the legend. The truth is more complicated. Nevertheless, when Constantine became emperor, he issued the Edict of Milan, and in 313 Christianity became a legal religion. Soon, Christians would no longer be the dissidents they had been for more than two centuries. Persecution, suffering, and martyrdom were no longer an issue.

But the four gospels lived on as the scriptural warrant for Christianity. Irenaeus's principle held: four gospels, no more, no less. Other gospels fell into disuse and disappeared, while the canonical gospels were repurposed. The necessity of faith gained a new context. Christians no longer faced persecution or expected the apocalypse, but they knew the day of reckoning that was universal to all—death. Faithfulness was now said to ensure survival beyond the grave. The gospels provided the theme of fidelity, but also the specific beliefs to which Christians were expected to remain true: Jesus's miraculous birth, the vicarious nature of his death, his resurrection, and his eventual return to judge "the quick and the dead." Christianity was now a religion about a dying and rising savior who conquered death and thereby gained immortality for those who believe in him.

ANCIENT GOSPELS IN A MODERN WORLD

And so it was for more than a thousand years. Christianity was a religion of beliefs. A common set of beliefs united the vast Holy Roman Empire under an emperor and a supreme spiritual leader, the Pope. Those who wandered from those beliefs were punished. Those who refused to accept them, like Jews, were persecuted. But the center could not hold forever. In the sixteenth century a German monk named Martin Luther led a rebellion against the Roman church and called for reform. Religious wars ensued, pitting Catholic against Protestant. The notion that a set of common beliefs could be the basis for a common community was proving to be calamitous. During the Thirty Years' War (1618–48) the population of Germany was reduced by half. It would take a century for the villages and towns of central Europe to recover. There were, however, no second thoughts yet about the religion that might have united, rather than divided, the warring parties. Catholics retrenched in new claims to authority, while Protestantism feathered into a myriad of sects, each with its own distinctive set of beliefs. When America became the destination for many of these groups, it soon became clear that our own experiment with a free and democratic society could only succeed if religious toleration were mandated and a "wall of separation" placed between government and religion, to the benefit of both. Today churches of every stripe continue to insist on right belief—*their* beliefs. Enlightenment extends only this far: dissenters are no longer burned at the stake.

Through all of this, Irenaeus's four-gospel canon remained. Matthew, Mark, Luke, and John were in the Bible. Their story of Jesus was *the* story of Jesus. The other gospels that had once vied for a voice in the early centuries of Christianity were forgotten by all but a few historians. But beginning in the eighteenth century, some scholars of the Bible began to wonder about the biblical gospels themselves. The faith they seemed to authorize—that Jesus was born miraculously, that he raised the dead, that he himself rose from the dead—now struck them as less than credible. Was religion, then, simply a matter of believing incredible things? This was the Age of Reason, the dawn of the modern era. Did Christianity have anything to offer modern people whose capacity to reason and think critically would not permit them to believe the unbelievable? Many said no. Christianity's days were numbered.

Thomas Jefferson was among those who decided that Christianity wasn't finished yet. When he read and studied the gospels, he noticed something obvious. Jesus was not just a miracle worker. He taught things. Before he died on the cross, Jesus lived for something worth dying for. Matthew, Mark, Luke, and John had not really neglected this. The form they chose—the martyr's story—had to include something of Jesus's life. After all, martyrs don't just die. They die for a cause—the thing they lived for before deciding finally to die for it. This is what Jefferson was interested in. What did *Jesus* believe? What did he teach? What did he say? What did he do, besides work miracles?

During the course of his life Jefferson returned to this question again and again and a little project we know today as the "Jefferson

Bible." Jefferson initially called it "The Philosophy of Jesus of Nazareth," with a subtitle suggesting the missionary purpose of using it to introduce Christianity to "the Indians." When he revised his work in 1819 he renamed it "The Life and Morals of Jesus of Nazareth." Jefferson never published the original work or the revision. He preferred to keep his personal beliefs private.

Or perhaps he just didn't want people to know what he had actually done. In 1804 he bought two copies of the King James Version of the New Testament published by Jacob Johnson of Philadelphia and commenced to cutting. Using a razor, he literally "cut and pasted" selections from the gospels into a kind of scrapbook. His cuttings were designed to omit anything of a miraculous, and therefore unbelievable, nature. He tinkered with the project for many years, finishing finally in 1813. But his original plan had been to include Greek and Latin texts alongside the English, so he began a revision of the work, now an elaborate thing containing parallel columns of English, Greek, Latin, and French texts. Jefferson was serious about his work. He did not trust the church and its theologians. But he trusted Jesus. He believed that what Jesus taught was worth saving.

Jefferson did not know that in creating his collection of Jesus's teachings he was actually returning to a gospel form that is very old, older, in fact, than the form in which we find our traditional four gospels. Before the author of Mark wrote his story of Jesus—and before Matthew, Luke, and John—there were collections of Jesus's sayings. The Gospel of Mark itself probably incorporates one in 4:1–32, which contains a group of seed-themed parables. Not all such collections were actually attributed to Jesus. One, the biblical Letter of James, is attributed to Jesus's brother, James. It is presently cast in the form of a letter, but it is actually a collection of wisdom sayings and apocalyptic warnings. Its history is unknown.

Also murky is the history of another early collection of teachings called "The Teaching of the Twelve Apostles," often referred to by its shortened Greek title, the *Didache*. The first six chapters of this text are instructional sayings cast within the framework of the "two ways," a common form in ancient Jewish moral instruction. Many of these sayings are later found in the gospels, especially Matthew, and attributed to Jesus. But in the *Didache* they belong to "the twelve apostles." In the *Didache* there is an especially interesting collection of wisdom sayings—a collection within the collection—each of which begins with the phrase "my child": "My child, flee from all evil and everything like it. . . . My child, do not be filled with passion, for passion leads to sex. . . . My child, do not practice divination, for this leads to idolatry. . . . My child, do not be a liar, for lying leads to robbery. . . . My child, do not be a complainer, for this leads to blasphemy. . . ." (3:1–6). The origin of this little collection is also unknown, but it most certainly predates the *Didache* itself.

These sayings collections are all very early—some earlier than the first biblical gospel, Mark. Where did they come from? What was happening in those early years among the followers of Jesus that prompted people to create these early collections of sayings?

If Jefferson had lived for another hundred years, his fascination with the sayings of Jesus would no doubt have deepened. In the 1830s he might have read an essay by the great German theologian Friedrich Schleiermacher suggesting that the author of Matthew may have used an earlier collection of Jesus's sayings to compose his gospel. Or perhaps he would have stumbled upon an obscure book by Christian Hermann Weisse that offered the first proof that Schleiermacher had been right, that Matthew's author had used such a collection, and moreover, that Luke's author had known and used that very same collection. In 1897 perhaps he would have read with excitement about two young British explorers, Bernard Grenfell and Arthur Hunt, who on their first expedition to Egypt had somehow stumbled across an ancient collection of Jesus's sayings, hitherto unknown. And just imagine Jefferson's excitement, sitting in his Philadelphia nursing home on October 27, 1959, and coming across this headline in his *New York Times:* "New 'Gospel' MS Being Published, Translation of 114 Sayings of Jesus Found in Egypt Will Be Out Saturday!" That would have set any 216-year-old heart to racing.

New Gospels from an Ancient Past

Thomas Jefferson did not live to see his vision of a sayings gospel come to life through scholarship and exciting archaeological discoveries. He was reticent even to admit to such a vision in his own day and time. In 1813 the world was not yet ready for his take on the Christian religion—or so he feared. But by 1959 it was. Or, one should say, the world was at least primed for a debate about the meaning and possible revolutionary implications of the discovery of the *Gospel of Thomas*, whose imminent arrival at bookstands the *New York Times* foretold on October 27 of that year. For the record, Jefferson himself would have been somewhat disappointed with the *Gospel of Thomas*. He despised miracles—which are indeed absent from *Thomas*—but also the "the Platonists and Plotinists, the Stagyrites and Gamalielites, the Eclectics, the Gnostics," and their various doctrines, some of which had indeed made quite a significant impact on the newly discovered gospel.

The debate that was to unfold in the 1960s, however, was more basic than all of this. Western Christendom was about to head into a period of doubt and reckoning the likes of which had not happened since the Reformation. Many were by now asking Jefferson's questions: What can moderns believe? Does Christianity consist merely in believing incredible things? Or is there more? Or better, is there less? If one no longer finds meaning in Jesus's death and resurrection; if one ceases to believe in his miraculous birth; if one no longer accepts as factual stories in which Jesus walks on water, heals the sick, and raises the dead, can one still find meaning in the Christian religion?

In the midst of this debate, many modern seekers were surprised to find that the biblical gospels were not the only gospels. Books with titles like *The Other Gospels, The Gnostic Gospels,* and *The Complete Gospels* became bestsellers. The new gospel announced by the *New York Times* in 1959 was part of a larger find, known today as the Nag Hammadi Library. In 1977 *The Nag Hammadi Library in English* was published to broad acclaim. Now, for the first time, people could read all of the texts for themselves. Most readers who dove into this work, however, found it to be rough sledding. Many of these texts were esoteric in the extreme and difficult to understand. It was perhaps becoming clear now why so many of them had disappeared in the first place—no one could remember what they meant!

But the *Gospel of Thomas* was different. To be sure, it had its share of strange sayings and baffling riddles. But more often, to read the *Gospel of Thomas* was to find oneself in strangely familiar territory. Here were dozens of sayings already familiar from Mark, Matthew, and Luke—even a few from John—but without the narrative framework of the biblical gospels. There were no birth stories, no miracles, no passion narrative in which Jesus is arrested and crucified, and no resurrection. How could one have a gospel with no resurrection?! Wasn't this, after all, what made Jesus matter to people? Critics argued that this gospel could not be early. It had to be late and derived from the canonical gospels themselves. Someone, they argued, must have deliberately altered both the form and the content of the gospel for their own perverse theological ends. But upon closer scrutiny some scholars began to notice that *Thomas*'s sayings were not obviously derived from the biblical four. To the contrary, many of them were cast in basic forms that seemed to predate their canonical parallels. Could there have been a gospel comprising only the sayings of Jesus?

This was a question that a small group of specialists had been asking for years. It arose in connection with the sayings collections mentioned above, and most particularly with the collection Christian Hermann Weisse had argued in the 1830s lay behind the gospels of Matthew and Luke. If Weisse was right, then one would have to posit *behind the canonical, biblical gospels* another, earlier gospel of quite a different sort. This would have been a gospel comprising mostly the sayings of Jesus. There are a few stories in Weisse's hypothetical source and even one miraculous healing story, but these tidbits could do little to address the doubts raised by the absence in the source of a passion narrative. Could there have been an earlier gospel in which these things had not been included?

Many found this to be a very troubling question, for the biblical story of Jesus had always been valued for its primacy. It was the first account, the apostolic account, and therefore the authoritative account. Irenaeus himself believed that the canonical four were the oldest and best gospels. They alone could be traced back to the apostles and their immediate followers. Weisse's hypothetical sayings gospel now appeared as an unwanted interloper. But those who opposed Weisse's theory had one very strong argument: no such sayings collection had ever been found. Weisse's hypothetical source was just a hypothesis—until the *Gospel of Thomas* was discovered.

The *Gospel of Thomas* is not the source Weisse had proposed, but it shares many sayings with Weisse's hypothetical source—about half of them, it turns out. But they are different collections. What they share with each other and with other early sayings collections is their *form*. This is not insignificant. Collecting the sayings of a famous person was quite a common activity in the ancient world. And it meant something. It meant that this person was a teacher, a sage, and more. He or she was a messenger from God. Wisdom, insight, prophetic sayings of public critique were all gifts from on high, shared through God's chosen sages and prophets. This is what *Thomas* and these other sayings collections represent.

Before Mark wrote his story interpreting Jesus as a martyr, other nascent Christians were already at work interpreting Jesus in another light—through the wisdom tradition. The idea is expressed beautifully in the contemporary Jewish wisdom book known as the Wisdom of Solomon, written about the time the followers of Jesus were assembling Jesus's parables, aphorisms, and prophetic sayings into collections. Here the sage speaks about Wisdom (Sophia), the person-ification of wisdom in divine form:

> Although she is but one, she can do all things,
> and while remaining in herself, she renews all things;
> in every generation she passes into holy souls
> and makes them friends of God, and prophets;
> for God loves nothing so much as the person who lives with
>   wisdom. (7:27–28, NRSV)

Those who created these early collections of sayings were thinking about Jesus and his followers in terms of early Jewish wisdom theology. If truth be told, wisdom theology was a very complex phenomenon, from which even the Markan story of Jesus's persecution, death, and resurrection could be derived. Wisdom theology is the font of many nascent Christian ideas. But the sayings collections express one of wisdom theology's most basic claims: wisdom and insight lie at the heart of the well-led life: "For God loves nothing so much as the person who lives with wisdom."

The sayings source behind Matthew and Luke is today known as "Q." Together with the *Gospel of Thomas*, it provides the best access to this early form of nascent Christian literature and its interpretation of Jesus. These two early Christian wisdom gospels are presented in this volume (Chapters 4 and 6) as an offering to an ongoing reassessment of the meaning of Jesus and the Christian tradition in the modern world. These texts are, of course, no less ancient than the canonical gospels, no less a product of the ancient world from which they come. But they are different. At a time when many wonder about the wisdom of martyr-dom, the glorification of suffering, or even the logic of vicarious death, it will be helpful to realize that this was not the only way that early fol-lowers of Jesus found meaning in his life. Many found meaning primar-ily in his sayings. This is the kind of nascent Christianity represented in Q and the *Gospel of Thomas*, Christianity's lost wisdom gospels.

For Further Study

On **Irenaeus**, the troubles in Lyons, martyrdom, and the preference for passion-centered gospels, see Elaine Pagels, "Gnostic and Orthodox Views of Christ's Passion: Paradigms for the Christian Response to Persecution," in Bentley Layton, ed., *The Rediscovery of Gnosticism,* 2 vols. (Leiden: Brill, 1979), 1:262–84. See also her treatment in *The Gnostic Gospels* (New York: Random House, Vintage 1981), 84–122.

For **the four-gospel canon** in the second century, see Lee Martin McDonald, *The Formation of the Christian Biblical Canon* (Nashville: Abingdon, 1988), 92–98. For Irenaeus's role in its creation, see especially the classic treatment by Hans von Campenhausen, *The Formation of the Christian Bible* (Philadelphia: Fortress, 1972), 182–206.

The **Judean revolt** and its consequences are the subject of Martin Goodman's *Rome and Jerusalem: The Clash of Ancient Civilizations* (New York: Random House, 2007). The primary witness to the revolt is the ancient historian Flavius Josephus (ca. 37–ca. 100 CE), a Jewish aristocrat who fought in the revolt. He was captured relatively early in the conflict, but survived when he predicted the Roman general in charge of the invading forces would become emperor—which he did. Josephus spent the rest of his life in Vespasian's Roman villa writing about the history of his people, including the multivolume *History of the Jewish War Against the Romans.* The standard edition of this work in English is *Josephus in Nine Volumes,* vols. 2–3: *The Jewish War,* trans. H. St. J. Thackeray, LCL 203, 210 (Cambridge, MA: Harvard Univ. Press, 1927–28). A new translation and critical commentary on Josephus's works is being prepared by Steven Mason, et al., *Flavius Josephus, Translation and Commentary* (Leiden: Brill, 2000–).

The story of Constantine is well told in James Carroll, *Constantine's Sword* (Boston: Houghton Mifflin, 2001), 165–94. A standard scholarly account is W. H. C. Frend, *The Rise of Christianity* (Philadelphia: Fortress, 1984), chap. 14, "The Constantinian Revolution."

The **Jefferson Bible**, which was not published until 1895, is available in many modern editions. The Smithsonian Institution published a full-color facsimile edition in 2011. It may be viewed and read on the Smithsonian's website at: http://americanhistory.si.edu/jeffersonbible/.

Early Christian sayings collections are discussed by James M. Robinson in "LOGOI SOPHON: On the Gattung of Q," reprinted in James M. Robinson and Helmut Koester, *Trajectories Through Early Christianity* (Philadelphia: Fortress, 1971), chap. 3.

For more on the *Didache,* see Kurt Niederwimmer, *The Didache: A Commentary,* Hermeneia (Minneapolis: Fortress, 1998); or the new introduction to this text by Clayton N. Jefford, *Didache: The Teaching of the Twelve Apostles* (Salem, OR: Polebridge, 2013).

The discovery of Q and the Gospel of *Thomas* will be treated in the next chapter.

Collections of other gospels mentioned in the chapter include: Ron Cameron, *The Other Gospels* (Nashville: Westminster, 1982); Robert Miller, ed., *The Complete Gospels,* 4th rev. ed. (Salem, OR: Polebridge Press, 2010); and Marvin Meyer, ed., *The Nag Hammadi Library in English,* rev. ed. (1977; San Francisco: HarperSanFrancisco, 2007). The standard collection scholars consult for these and other apocryphal texts is Edgar Hennecke and Wilhelm Schneemelcher, eds., *New Testament Apocrypha,* trans. R. McL. Wilson, 2 vols. (Cambridge: James Clarke; Louisville, KY: Westminster John Knox, 1991).

2

DISCOVERIES

No one really knows how the wisdom gospels came to be the lost gospels, but the story of their rediscovery is an extraordinary one. One of them, it turns out, was hiding in plain sight. Another lay still beneath the shifting sands of the Egyptian desert for more than fifteen hundred years, until, one day, two very young, very inexperienced archaeologists just got lucky, very lucky. That is where our story begins.

A MOST EXTRAORDINARY FIND

Bernard Pyne Grenfell and Arthur Surridge Hunt were in their early twenties when they set off for Egypt in 1895. Their destination was the Fayum district, where they would learn the basics of field archaeology by working with an experienced French team of excavators who had already spent several seasons in Egypt. Grenfell and Hunt, however, were neophytes. Pals throughout graduate school, they each now held a brand-new master's degree in Classics from Oxford. But they were young and tired of the musty stacks of the Bodleian Library. They wanted to get away. They wanted adventure. But more than this, they had a mission: to save the vast treasures of Egypt before they were all pillaged and sold for profit. Their sponsor was the Egypt Exploration Fund, organized for just this purpose.

Nineteenth-century Europeans were fascinated with Egypt. They were bowled over by its enormous antiquity—a civilization stretching back three thousand years before Christ. When Moses was thought to have sojourned there, Egyptian civilization had already existed for more than two millennia. The modern nation-states of Europe were mere infants by comparison. When Napoleon landed on Egypt's shores in 1798 with his Armée d'Orient, he also brought with him an army of scholars to study this strange land of dog-faced gods and inscrutable symbols carved in gigantic stone temples. Among their many finds was the Rosetta Stone, discovered by a French officer in 1799. With its inscriptions in Greek, Demotic, and the ancient hieroglyphic script of the pharaohs, scholars now had a chance to unlock the secrets of ancient Egypt by cracking the code that had long eluded them—they could now read the hieroglyphs. When the British defeated Napoleon's forces in 1801, one of their prizes was the Rosetta Stone, which they promptly spirited back to London and put on display in the British Museum—where it remains today, in spite of Egyptian efforts to get it back.

Londoners' interest in Egypt was piqued when the Egyptian Hall, a to-scale replica of the Temple of Dendera, was set up in Piccadilly in 1812. Scores of popular books appeared, picturing Egypt's ancient ruins and offering imaginative interpretations of what they might have been like. Europe acquired a taste for Egyptian style, which now inspired Egyptian-themed jewelry, furniture, and especially architecture, whose influence lasted well into the twentieth century. Then in 1873 the novelist and adventurer Amelia Edwards traveled to Egypt and ascended the Nile as far as Abu Simbel. Her account, *A Thousand Miles Up the Nile,* deepened Europe's fascination, but also sounded an alarm: Egypt's treasures were fast disappearing into the hands of grave robbers and unscrupulous antiquities dealers. Edwards herself helped to found the Egypt Exploration Fund, under whose auspices

Grenfell and Hunt now embarked on their mission to "rescue" some of these treasures for posterity.

In 1896 Grenfell and Hunt convinced the Egypt Exploration Fund that they were ready to excavate on their own. After spending the summer in Oxford, late that fall they boarded a steamer to Cairo to search on their own for the prize they coveted most as students of the classics: papyri. Papyrus was the "paper" on which most ancients committed their thoughts and records to writing. This ancient writing material was made from *Cyperus papyrus,* a reedlike plant that once grew abundantly in the lakes and marshlands of the Nile Valley. Papyrus was made by first cutting strips from the sinewy stems of this plant and laying them vertically side by side on a flat surface. A second layer of strips was then laid horizontally on top of the first, so it was at a 90-degree angle to the first layer. Then this double-layered stack was pounded with a broad mallet, so that the mushy, sticky pith emerged from the fibers to form a pasty surface reinforced by the fibers running beneath. Once it was dried, trimmed to size, and polished, the papyrus sheet was a convenient, if expensive, writing surface that could be used for any number of literary or utilitarian purposes.

But papyrus was fragile and subject to decay. Moisture is its enemy. Most Mediterranean climes are too wet to allow its long-term survival, and so papyrus was gradually replaced by vellum paper made from animal skins, which eventually became the standard for antique bookmaking. Papyrus books and scrolls were gradually replaced by vellum ones—that is, *many* of them were. Books and scrolls that failed to capture the interest of someone with the means to transfer their contents into the new medium of vellum simply decayed and turned to dust. That was the fate of most ancient writings. Except in Egypt. Here was a unique set of circumstances. The low-lying marshes of the Nile Valley produced an abundance of raw material for the manufacture of papyrus, and so there was lots of it around. The ancient library of Alexandria had by far the largest collection of books and scrolls in the ancient world. On the other hand, away from the actual floodplain itself, Egypt is extraordinarily dry—dry enough to preserve papyrus. That is why the Egypt Exploration Fund commissioned Grenfell and Hunt to go to Egypt in 1896 in search of papyri. What lost works of literary art might be discovered there before it was too late?

Grenfell and Hunt had in mind a place they had heard of in their previous season abroad: Oxyrhynchus. Oxyrhynchus—a city named for the "sharp-nosed fish" that once swam the nearby waters of the Nile—is located about a hundred miles south of present-day Cairo. In Roman times it was a significant administrative center, a place where people of means might have collected private libraries to help pass the time and bring culture to this remote outpost. The city itself was located on a rise about ten miles west of the Nile, high enough to ride out the annual flooding of the river that made possible Egypt's re-markable agricultural life. Because it was a Roman city, Oxyrhynchus held little interest for archaeologists fascinated with Egypt's most ancient past, the time of the pharaohs and their pyramids. Conse-quently, when Grenfell and Hunt arrived there in 1896, it had never been excavated.

Their first question was where to start. About the time Grenfell and Hunt became interested in Egyptian papyri, thousands of manu-scripts had made their way to England, Russia, and the United States from Cairo, where they had been discovered in the ancient *genizah*, or storage chamber, of a ninth-century synagogue in Old Cairo. In 1896 Solomon Schechter had just returned from Cairo with the first of what would eventually number more than a hundred thousand manuscripts carted away from the Cairo Genizah to become the pos-session of Cambridge University. Would they find a *genizah* in Oxy-rhynchus as well?

No. Grenfell and Hunt soon discovered that the ancient buildings of Roman Oxyrhynchus had long since fallen down; their stones had been used to build newer structures in later centuries. The next place to look was among the tombs. Ancients sometimes buried their dead with a favorite book or scroll, a prized possession of the deceased. But three weeks of prospecting in the ancient cemetery turned up nothing. Perhaps their hopes had been misplaced in Oxyrhynchus.

Finally, at the suggestion of local villagers, they turned their attention to the low mounds that lay on the outskirts of the ancient city. Villagers had reported seeing there papers fluttering in the wind and blowing off into the desert. Could these be the remains of discarded papers, letters, and books from Roman Oxyrhynchus? So, on a bright early January morning in 1897, Grenfell and Hunt set out to excavate these mounds. It turned out to be one of the most remarkable days in archaeological history. Bernard Grenfell related its unfolding later that year in an article for *McClure's Magazine:*

On January 11th we sallied forth at sunrise with some seventy workmen and boys, and set them to dig trenches through a mound near a large space covered with piles of limestone chips, which probably denotes the site of an ancient temple, though its walls have been all but entirely dug out for the sake of the stone. The choice proved a very fortunate one, for papyrus scraps began to come to light in considerable quantities, varied by occasional complete or nearly complete private and official documents containing letters, contracts, accounts, and so on; and there were also a number of fragments written in uncials, or rounded capital letters, the form of writing used in copying classical or theological manuscripts. Later in the week Mr. Hunt, in sorting through the papyri found on the second day, noticed on a crumpled uncial fragment written on both sides the Greek word KARFOS ("mote"), which at once suggested to him the verse in the Gospels concerning the mote and the beam. A further examination showed that the passage in the papyrus really was the conclusion of the verse, "Thou hypocrite, cast out first the beam out of thine own eye, and then shalt thou see clearly to pull out the mote that is in thy brother's eye;" but the rest of the papyrus differed considerably from the Gospels, and was, in fact, a leaf of a book containing a collection of sayings of Christ, some of which, apparently, were new. More than that could not be determined until we came back to England.

The leaf they had unearthed that day was Papyrus Oxyrhynchus 1. It was their first excavation. For weeks, nothing. And then, in an ancient rubbish heap, they hit the archaeological lottery: papyrus containing a series of heretofore unknown sayings of Jesus. Unbelievable. On one side they could read the following:

> " . . . and then you will see clearly to cast the splinter from your
>   brother's eye."
> Jesus says, "If you do not fast to the world, you will not find the
>   empire of God. And if you do not observe the Sabbath as a
>   Sabbath, you will not see the Father."
> Jesus says, "I stood in the midst of the world and in flesh I ap-
>   peared to them, and I found all of them drunk; and none of
>   them did I find thirsty. And my soul suffers for the children
>   of humanity, for they are blind of heart and do . . . see . . ."

On the other side they saw this:

> . . . comes to dwell in this poverty.
> . . . "Where there are . . . they are without God. But where there
>   is . . . I say, I am with . . . Raise the stone and you will find me,
>   split the wood and I am there."
> Jesus says, "A prophet is not accepted in his homeland, nor
>   does a physician heal those who know him."
> Jesus says, "A city built upon a high mountain and fortified
>   cannot fall, nor can it be hidden."

During their first remarkable season at Oxyrhynchus, Grenfell and Hunt unearthed hundreds of papyri. Many of the best manuscripts they turned over to Egyptian authorities. The rest, filling some 280 cartons, were shipped back to Oxford. Over the course of five seasons they filled 700 cartons with an estimated 500,000 papyri, enough to keep them and three generations of papyrologists busy deciphering and discerning their meaning. Among them they found two more fragments of the mysterious collection of Jesus's sayings, POxy 654 and POxy 655. There were also fragments of other unknown gospels—POxy 210, POxy 840, and POxy 1224—as well as many fragments of known New Testament texts and early Christian writings. But none was more exciting than POxy 1. Reports of its discovery in the London *Times* and around the world made Grenfell and Hunt instant celebrities. When, after their return to London, they published POxy 1 in pamphlet form, it sold over 30,000 copies. The sayings of Jesus also made them rich.

Grenfell and Hunt called their new gospel *Logia Jesou*—"Sayings of Jesus"—a title chosen with a good deal of thought. The designation of Jesus's words as *logia* had an ancient pedigree. In the fourth century, Eusebius, the famous bishop of Caesarea, was writing the first-ever chronicle of Christian history, when he paused to include a few words about one of the immediate successors to the apostles, a certain Papias. Papias, it seems, had written a five-volume collection (now lost) called *The Interpretation of the Oracles of the Lord*. Papias, he said, had collected these *logia*—"oracles"—over the course of many years listening to the apostles themselves (*Ecclesiastical History* 3.39). Could Grenfell and Hunt's remarkable discovery have been a fragment of Papias's lost book of Jesus's *logia*? But Papias had more to say, according to Eusebius. Papias, he claims, knew all the first-generation "elders," including the authors of Mark and Matthew. Of Matthew he says this: "Matthew collected the oracles (*logia*) [of Jesus] in the Hebrew language, and each interpreted them as best he could" (*Ecclesiastical History* 3.39). Had Grenfell and Hunt miraculously stumbled upon this lost source?

It turns out that Grenfell and Hunt had not discovered the Aramaic *logia* Papias says Matthew used—their papyrus fragment had, after all, been composed in Greek, not Aramaic. But there were Greek collections of Jesus sayings in the ancient world as well. Like the gospel whose scattered litter had turned up at Oxyrhynchus, these collections too had all disappeared into the mists of antiquity. All of them, that is, except one: a mysterious gospel scholars refer to as "Q."

THE DISCOVERY OF Q

One of the oddest things you will come across in most standard treatments of the New Testament and its history is a thing known simply as Q. "Q" is actually an abbreviation of a German word *Quelle,* which means "source." Q is a source of many sayings and anecdotes found in the gospels of Matthew and Luke. That scholars call it "Q," or the "source," rather than by its rightful name, is a consequence of the peculiar circumstances of its discovery. You see, Q has never really been found. That is why we don't know its actual name. On the other hand, Q was never really lost. For centuries it was hiding in plain sight. This deserves an explanation.

The story of Q's discovery begins not in the dry sands of Egypt or the dusty shelves of a museum storage chamber. It starts, rather, in a German scholar's study. His name was Christian Hermann Weisse. Weisse was born in 1801, at the dawn of a new century in which the European Enlightenment, the Age of Reason, would take hold and flower in every arena of human intellectual activity, including religion. Like many of his day, Weisse believed that Christianity was due for a new reformation, one in which old dogmas would be reexamined in the light of reason and rational thought. So when he began to hear about a new book by a young theologian that was shaking the foundations, he must have been excited.

That earthshaking book was the two-volume study of the Christian gospels published in 1835–36 by David Friedrich Strauss. It was called *The Life of Jesus Critically Examined*. This title must have sounded promising to scholars like Weisse, who hoped to ground a modern Christianity in the unadulterated life and teachings of Jesus. But Strauss surprised them. His massive study turned out to be more about the gospels than Jesus. In it he argued that the gospels, Matthew, Mark, Luke, and John, were not history but myth. By "myth" he did not mean something like a "fairy story" or "tall tale." By "myth" Strauss meant a deeply structured narrative by which a deeper religious truth comes to expression. This is what the gospels are, he argued. It was no use, he insisted, trying to wring even a limited amount of history from the gospels. They held none. Their sole purpose was to convey a singular, deep eternal truth: that God is incarnate in humanity. Students of philosophy will recognize immediately the intellectual pedigree of the young Strauss. This was the deep truth that Georg Wilhelm Friedrich Hegel had discovered just a few years before. Strauss was a Hegelian.

Strauss's book set off a firestorm in German theology. It became a bestseller overnight as classrooms and pubs boiled over with the "*Life of Jesus* controversy." The young and promising scholar soon found himself under attack. The tenured professorship that had been offered him at Zürich was withdrawn under a hail of criticism. Strauss's opponents would eventually succeed in having him banned from academic life, even while his book went through multiple printings and revisions. Eventually he left theology, married a famous opera singer, tried and failed at politics, and in time found success as a popular biographer. But throughout the nineteenth century his *Life of Jesus* continued to stoke the fires of controversy.

Not all of Strauss's opponents were conservatives. There were liberals too who found Strauss too radical. These were scholars like Weisse, who had hoped to recover through a historical and critical analysis of the gospels at least a remnant of the original teachings of Jesus. For them, Strauss had gone too far. In dismissing the gospels completely from historical consideration, he had not accounted for the fact that the gospels themselves are not all alike. Some had been written earlier, some later, some with greater degrees of theological interpretation, some with less. What if one could use literary and historical analysis to recover the earliest gospel or perhaps even its sources? Would one then not stand close enough to the original words of Jesus himself to permit at least a glimpse of the historical reality behind the texts? Soon critical scholars were poring over the gospels in search of a historical answer to Strauss's skepticism. They were looking for Jesus. What they found was something else.

By the nineteenth century scholars already knew quite a lot about the history of the New Testament gospels. They had already noticed that Matthew, Mark, and Luke share much in common, and that this distinguishes them generally from John. In the eighteenth century scholars generally accounted for these similarities in the gospels in the way Augustine had accounted for them fourteen hundred years earlier, by saying that Matthew, the apostle, had written first; then Mark wrote, making use of Matthew as a source; then Luke, using both Matthew and Mark; and finally John, whose author made use of all three of the other gospels. In other words, the order in which the gospels appear in the Bible represents the order in which the gospels were originally written.

Then in 1776, Johann Griesbach, a professor of New Testament in the old German town of Jena, published a new tool by which the relationships between the gospels could be studied more carefully. He called it a gospel *synopsis*. In Griesbach's clever book, the gospels that share the most in common—Matthew, Mark, and Luke—were laid out side by side in parallel columns, so that one could see exactly what they shared and how they differed. Griesbach immediately saw that, when compared closely, John's narrative really had little to do with the other three. So he left it out of his *synopsis* altogether. But the remaining three, Matthew, Mark, and Luke, were obviously closely related. They share a common story line, or plot, and dozens of individual stories, sayings, parables, and the like, many of which agree almost verbatim from gospel to gospel. These three, Matthew, Mark, and Luke, became known as the *synoptic gospels,* and accounting for their close and complex relationship became known as the *synoptic problem.*

Using his *synopsis* to study the synoptic gospels, Griesbach soon discovered that he could not solve the synoptic problem with Augustine's simple theory that the gospels were composed in canonical order, first Matthew, then Mark, and then Luke. He could see, for example, that Mark lacked about half of Matthew. Why would Mark's author have left out so much? And why had Luke's author apparently followed Mark some of the time, but followed Matthew at other times? In a detailed study of the precise wording of the resurrection stories laid side by side in his *synopsis,* Griesbach finally concluded that another order would better account for what he was seeing. Matthew had indeed written first, but Luke, not Mark, must have been second. Mark, he argued, must have come last. Mark makes sense only on the supposition that its author knew both Matthew and Luke and attempted to create a harmony of them, including only those things that Matthew and Luke shared in common. So Matthew came first, then Luke, and finally Mark, which combines their agreements. This became known as the Griesbach Hypothesis, and it was the first modern solution to the synoptic problem. It still has a small number of champions today.

Now, Strauss favored the Griesbach Hypothesis as a critical alternative to the traditional, orthodox account. So the enemies of Strauss soon became the enemies of Griesbach as well. If one could undo Griesbach, one could undermine Strauss. So the critics went to work. Using Griesbach's own synopsis, they began to make their own comparisons of the order and language of the gospels. One thing they noticed was that, in a word-for-word comparison, Mark's Greek is clearly the least polished of the three. Time and again they found themselves facing the question: Why would Mark wantonly ruin the perfectly good prose of Matthew and Luke? Wouldn't it make more sense if it were the other way around—that Luke and Matthew each in their turn had corrected and improved Mark's poor first attempt? They also noticed that Matthew and Luke seldom agree with one another against Mark in the order and wording of their shared passages. This too could be explained if Mark had been written first and the authors of Matthew and Luke had used it freely, each making his own alterations as he saw fit.

With such arguments, scholars began chipping away at Griesbach's theory. Gradually a handful of them became convinced of another solution to the synoptic problem: Mark, not Matthew, was the first gospel, and the authors of Matthew and Luke, working independently of one another, made use of Mark as a source. This is called the Hypothesis of Markan Priority, and over time most scholars have become convinced that it is a much better explanatory model by which to account for the details of the synoptic problem. Today it forms the basis of nearly all modern scholarship on the synoptic gospels. We shall return to this key point of biblical scholarship in the next chapter, but for now our attention can settle on just one thing about it: it has one very large loose end.

When Griesbach's critics noticed that Matthew and Luke tend not to agree with each other against Mark, they were thinking of Mark's narrative order. Matthew adds episodes and otherwise alters Mark's original story, but when he does, Luke never follows. Likewise, Luke's author makes his own alterations to Mark's story—most notably in the long travel narrative in Luke 9–19. But there is no trace of these changes in Matthew. This indeed suggests very strongly that Mark was the source for both Matthew and Luke, but that their authors edited the Markan story for their own purposes independently of one another.

However, Matthew and Luke do *share* a good deal of material *that is not found in Mark*. This material comprises mostly sayings and parables, which Matthew and Luke tend to use differently in their respective gospels. But there it is: Matthew and Luke do contain material not found in Mark. If their treatment of Mark's story seems to indicate that Matthew's and Luke's authors worked independently of one another, how is it that they *both* happen to come by this other material? Oral tradition?

No. When one examines this other shared material, one quickly finds that the Matthean and Lukan versions of it often agree with one another verbatim—never exactly 100 percent verbatim, but sometimes pretty close. The familiar passage on anxieties is a good example of the problem (see Fig. 1, On Being Anxious). This much verbatim agreement cannot be accounted for by appealing to oral tradition. Originally Jesus and all of his followers spoke Aramaic. If the contents of this speech were first uttered in Aramaic (very likely), how shall we imagine an oral process involving hundreds of retellings first in Aramaic, then eventually in myriad different Greek versions as bilingual storytellers made on-the-fly translations, in which at long last two separate, but virtually identical Greek oral renderings of this long passage somehow made their way independently into Matthew and Luke? Impossible. This was the large loose end that critical scholars like Christian Hermann Weisse saw. To tie it up, there could be only one solution. If Mark was one source for Matthew and Luke, there had to be another written source as well. But what?

Like many critical theologians of his day, Weisse was devoted to the ideas of the theologian Friedrich Schleiermacher. When Weisse was a student at Leipzig in the early 1820s, Schleiermacher published his magnum opus, *The Christian Faith*. This was the book in which Schleiermacher spoke of the feeling of "absolute dependence" on God, which could be seen in the life and teachings of Jesus. For young liberals like Weisse, Schleiermacher offered a thoughtful, critical alternative to the rigid dogmatism of the church, on the one hand, and the cold rationalism of the secular Enlightenment, on the other. As a young student, Weisse found in Schleiermacher a way of retaining his

---

FIGURE 1. ON BEING ANXIOUS

LUKE 12:22–31

Therefore I tell you, do not be anxious about your life, what you shall eat, nor about your body, what you shall put on. For *life is more than food and the body more than clothing.* Consider the ravens: *they neither sow nor reap,* they have neither storehouse or *barn, and yet* God *feeds them.* Of how much *more value are you than* birds. *And which of you by being anxious can add a cubit to his span of life?* If then you are not able to do as small a thing as that, *why are you anxious about* the rest? Consider *the lilies, how they grow; they neither toil nor spin; yet I tell you even Solomon in all his glory was not arrayed like one of these. But if* God *so clothes the grass which is alive in the field today and tomorrow is thrown into the oven, how much more will he clothe you, O you of little faith?*

And do not seek *what* you are to *eat* and *what* you are to *drink,* nor be anxious of mind. *For all the nations of* the world *seek these things; and your Father knows that you need them. But seek his kingdom and these things will be yours as well.*

MATTHEW 6:25–33

Therefore I tell you, do not be anxious about your life, what you shall eat or what you shall drink, *nor about your body, what you shall put on.* Is not *life more than food, and the body more than clothing?* Look at the birds of the air: *they neither sow nor reap* nor gather into *barns, and yet* your heavenly Father *feeds them.* Are *you* not *more valuable than* they. *And which of you by being anxious can add one cubit to his span of life?*

And *why are you anxious about* clothing? Consider *the lilies* of the field, *how they grow; they neither toil nor spin; yet I tell you, even Solomon in all his glory was not arrayed like one of these. But if God so clothes the grass* of the field, *which today is alive and tomorrow is thrown into the oven, will he not much more clothe you, O you of little faith?* Therefore, do not be anxious, saying, *'What* shall we *eat?'* or *'What* shall we *drink?'* or 'What shall we wear?' *For the nations seek* all *these things; and your Heavenly Father knows that you need them* all. *But seek* first *his kingdom* and his righteousness, *and* all *these things will be yours as well.*

Christian faith with a sense of intellectual integrity. He remained a lifelong devotee.

When Strauss published his *Life of Jesus* in 1835, one of his targets was Schleiermacher, whose views on Jesus he regarded as naive and historically indefensible. So when Weisse took up the challenge of refuting Strauss, he quite naturally returned to the ideas of his great teacher. In 1832 Schleiermacher had published an essay in which he argued that the author of Matthew must have incorporated a source of Jesus's sayings, or *logia*. When Weisse read this, he had an insight. What if the author of Luke had known this *logia* source as well? This would in fact solve the loose end left by Markan Priority. That is what Weisse argued. In 1838 Weisse published his two-volume study entitled *The History of the Gospels Critically and Philosophically Considered*. In it he articulated for the first time the modern solution to the synoptic problem. Matthew and Luke, it turns out, shared not one but two sources: Mark and a second source comprising mostly sayings of Jesus. Weisse had uncovered Q—the lost collection of sayings that lay behind Matthew and Luke. He called it "Λ" (the Greek letter lambda), short for the Greek word *logia*, "sayings."

But was "Λ" real, or just a mirage? A lost gospel? A hypothetical source consisting only of Jesus's sayings? Nothing about his birth, death, or resurrection? Who would care about such a gospel? Would one even call it a gospel? It is unclear who, if any, actually noticed Weisse's discovery. If they did, they shrugged and moved on. In the coming years, Weisse's second source played little role in the discussion of gospel origins, save as a necessary corollary to Markan Priority. Mark was the earliest gospel, and it was a real, surviving text. As for the second source, no one really knew what to do with it. The idea of a lost gospel, especially a gospel comprising only sayings of Jesus, was a little too theoretical for scholars to take seriously.

That all changed in 1897, when Grenfell and Hunt stumbled upon their mysterious collection of Jesus's sayings at Oxyrhynchus. Suddenly the sayings gospel was no longer simply a theoretical possibility. It was real. And just to make it all the more real, Grenfell and Hunt called their mysterious gospel *Logia Jesou*. The study of Q now took flight. Scholars went to work reconstructing Q and theorizing about its theology. In 1907 Adolf von Harnack, Europe's most influential Protestant theologian, published a book entitled *The Sayings of*

Jesus. The lost gospel was no longer the theoretical hypothesis of a few hard-core specialists. Q was real, and it was important.

But was it real—really? Q, after all, did not survive on its own. No one could actually lay hands on a copy of Q. And the Oxyrhynchus papyri were only scraps, fragments of ancient books whose full contents we could never know. Doubts about Q persisted. Catholic theologians could not even study Q without risking reprimand. If Q was real, why had no actual sayings gospel survived antiquity?

ANOTHER DISCOVERY, ANOTHER GOSPEL

In the fall of 1946 an Egyptian schoolteacher was settling down for the evening in the home of his sister and her husband, a Coptic priest in the village of al-Qsar, just across the Nile from the more substantial town of Nag Hammadi in Upper Egypt. Raghib Andrawus was an itinerant teacher who came to al-Qsar once a week to offer instruction in the parochial school attached to the Coptic Church there. While in al-Qsar, he always stayed with his sister and her husband. On this evening, as James M. Robinson relates the story, his brother-in-law was unusually glad to see him. Soon Raghib would understand why. The priest, it seems, had something to show him. What he saw that evening in al-Qsar must have indeed astonished him. There in the dusk of the early evening, the priest laid before him an ancient book. It was large and wrapped in a finely tooled leather binding. When he opened it, he could see that its brittle pages were inscribed in Coptic, not Arabic. But this was a dialect that was unfamiliar to the priest. This was ancient Coptic, the language of the pharaohs written in the script of the ancient Greeks. Where on earth had he found such a book? A neighbor had given it to him.

The neighbor was Muhammad Ali al-Samman—a man wanted for murder. Only a month before, he and his brothers had fallen upon a villager from the neighboring town of Hamra Dum and hacked him to death with their mattocks. This was an act of revenge. The victim had murdered their own father in a revenge killing just a few months earlier. Now they had struck back in a feud whose history extended back far earlier than these latest grisly episodes. Their victim this time, however, was the son of the local sheriff, who was not about to let the boys from al-Qsar get away with murder. Muhammad knew that soon the sheriff would put two and two together and come to search his house for evidence of his son's killing. He would find none, but Muhammad feared what he would find—the book.

Muhammad had found it in the winter of 1945 while digging with his brother, Khalifah Ali, in the talus that lies at the base of the cliffs that line the Nile near al-Qsar. He was digging for fertilizer. What he found, half exposed by the shifting of rocks and sand in the desert winds, was a large clay jar. When he broke it open, out tumbled a cache of books. That evening he and his brother took them back to the family compound. What did they want with these old books, crumbling and falling to pieces? In Robinson's account, Muhammad's mother used one of them to kindle the family fires that evening.

The next day they decided to get what they could for them. They set the price at 1 Egyptian pound each, but at that price they found no takers. So they bartered and traded most of them away to neighbors. One of them, a Coptic Christian, recognized their unusual script and told Muhammad that they were Christian books. Now he began to worry. Where would he say he had gotten the books? Would the authorities think he had stolen them? Were they grave goods, taken illegally from a tomb? The books might just be the excuse the sheriff would need to run them in for questioning. So they decided to give the one remaining book to the local Coptic priest, Raghib's brother-in-law, for safekeeping. No one would question such a book in the hands of a priest.

Raghib had seen such things before. He knew that the book could be quite valuable. So he agreed to take it to Cairo, where an acquaintance who knew something about ancient manuscripts might look it over and offer an opinion. A few weeks later Raghib showed it to the acquaintance, George Sobhi, a Cairo physician with an interest in antiquities. He also had an interest in the law about antiquities and knew that Raghib could not have come into possession of this ancient book legally. So he called the authorities. By the end of the afternoon, the book was in the custody of the Egyptian Department of Antiquities and Raghib Andrawus was bargaining for his own freedom. At last they let him go. Eventually they even agreed to pay him for his find—about 300 Egyptian pounds, a small fortune to a schoolteacher from Upper Egypt.

Soon the news of Raghib Andrawus's good fortune—and near disaster—reached the village. The books were worth something after all, but to possess them could be dangerous. What to do? One villager partnered with a merchant friend from Nag Hammadi and sold his book to an antiquities dealer in Cairo. Another set out for Cairo on his own to find a buyer for his. Now word began to spread through the antiquities market in Cairo that a cache of manuscripts had been discovered near al-Qsar. Phokion Tano, a Cypriot ex-patriot living in Cairo, specialized in such things. He quickly dispatched his business partner in Upper Egypt, Zaki Basta, to confirm. Basta enlisted an acquaintance from al-Qsar to assist in the negotiations, a certain Bahij Ali, a figure notorious in al-Qsar as a strongman and outlaw. Together, the smooth-talking Basta and the one-eyed Bahij Ali must have presented a picture right out of central casting. That day they managed to find just two of the books, which they spirited off to Cairo for a clandestine meeting with Tano.

Tano arranged for these shadowy figures to bring the manuscripts to the antiquities shop of M. A. Mansoor in the historic old Shepherd Hotel in Cairo. One of the books presented for sale that day was the manuscript later to be designated Codex II of the Nag Hammadi find. So it was that, in the winter of 1946, Charles Kuentz, director of the Institut français d'archéologique orientale, and a young graduate student, Jacques Schwartz—later professor at the Institut de papyrologie in Strasbourg—became the first scholars to lay eyes on the Coptic *Gospel of Thomas*. They passed. Perhaps they did not recognize what they were looking at. Perhaps they knew the manuscripts were illegally obtained and could not be possessed legally. Perhaps they caught sight of a menacing one-eyed bandit watching them clandestinely from the back of the store. Whatever the reason, Mansoor could not sell them the manuscripts. Phokion Tano, however, seemed to know their value. He bought them himself and sent Bahij Ali back to al-Qsar to find the rest. Before long he had returned with most of the remaining books. The resulting windfall meant that Bahij Ali's ruffian days were over. He settled down on the modest farm he was able to buy with the proceeds.

But Phokion Tano's luck was about to run out. He now possessed most of the volumes Muhammad and Khalifah Ali had discovered six months before in al-Qsar. But he would not be able to sell them. When he tried, word quickly passed to the Egyptian Department of Antiquities about the whereabouts of manuscripts matching the description of the book they had confiscated from Raghib Andrawus a few months before. Soon Tano would be forced to turn over his entire treasure to the authorities. The books were placed for safekeeping in the Coptic Museum in Cairo, where they remain today. Of the thirteen books discovered by Muhammad and Khalifah Ali in December of 1945, eleven were now in safe hands. Only one, Codex I, had been smuggled out of the country. It was purchased in 1952 by the Jung Institute in Zürich for a price of $8,000 (it was finally returned to Egypt in 1975). Another, Codex XII—of which only a few pages remain—had been used by Muhammad's mother to bake bread on a cool December night in the village of al-Qsar.

On January 11, 1948, a story appeared in the Egyptian daily *Le progress égyptien* describing a remarkable new discovery from the area around Nag Hammadi. Accompanying the story was a photograph of Togo Mina and Jean Doresse seated before a page of the Nag Hammadi volume now known as Codex III. Doresse sits primly to the left.

Mina hunches over a papyrus leaf encased in glass panes, cigarette dangling from his lips as he appears lost in translation. Mina was the then Director of the Coptic Museum in Cairo. Doresse was a young French scholar who had come to Egypt to study early Christian monasteries. The two likely met through Doresse's wife, whom Mina had known as a student in Paris. When the new manuscripts began showing up on the antiquities market, Mina invited Doresse to come along and help assess their value. It was a heady time for both young men.

When the whole collection came under Mina's control in 1947, it was Mina and Doresse who initially began making their way through the codices looking for titles and other indications of the contents of these remarkable ancient books. About two-thirds of the way down page 51 of Codex II they would have encountered these words: PEU-ANGELION PKATA THOMAS ("The Gospel According to Thomas"). The title, which comes at the end of the work, would have sent them backward, scanning the previous pages for content. They would have noticed immediately that this was not a gospel like those with which they were familiar. Every few lines they would have encountered a simple PEJE IESOUS ("Jesus said"), followed by a brief saying or anecdote. There was no narrative. No stories of Jesus's birth, life, or death. It was simply a list of Jesus's teachings. Some were familiar, others not. Finally they would have reached the beginning of the gospel on page 32, noticed more easily by the title of the previous work forming a clean break before the opening lines of "The Gospel According to Thomas." There they would have read: "These are the secret sayings that the living Jesus spoke and Didymos Judas Thomas wrote them down." Amazing! They had found the lost *Gospel of Thomas*.

Before Doresse and Mina found it in Codex II of the Nag Hammadi Library, scholars had known of the existence of a "Gospel According to Thomas," if only through tantalizing references to it in the writings of early Christians. Only once is it actually quoted by name, however. In the early third century, Hippolytus of Rome (170–235 CE) wrote a book that aimed to refute the ideas of all the teachers in Rome whom he considered to be mistaken—*Refutatio omnium haeresium* (*Refutation of All Heresies*) he called it. One of his targets was a group known as the Naasenes, who claimed that their tradition had descended from the teachings of James the Just. This James was the brother of Jesus himself and the leader of the Jerusalem church in the years immediately following Jesus's death. About them Hippolytus writes:

> [The Naasenes] transmit a tradition concerning this in the gospel entitled According to Thomas, which states expressly, "The one who seeks me will find me in children from seven years of age and onwards. For there, hiding in the fourteenth aeon, I am revealed." (5.7.20)

That is close enough to saying 4 in the newly discovered extant *Gospel of Thomas* to have caught the attention of experts. It reads:

> Jesus said, "The man old in his days will not hesitate to ask a child of seven days about the place of life, and he shall live. For there are many who are first who will become last, and they will become a single one."

But Doresse and Mina were young and not especially versed in the obscure doctrines of ancient Christian sects or their texts. It is doubtful that they would have marked this striking confirmation of the fact that this really was the long-lost "Gospel of Thomas," embraced by unorthodox Christians and later the Manicheans. Doresse, however, did what every young academic does with his or her latest exciting discovery: he told his mentor and doctoral adviser, Henri-Charles Puech. Puech must have come to Cairo *tout suite* to see the remarkable new texts (later in 1948 he and Doresse published a report of the discovery in the official publication of the French Academy of Science). When he read the opening lines of the "Gospel of Thomas," he would have known right away that he was indeed looking at the

"Gospel of Thomas" that Hippolytus had tainted with Naasene associations and Eusebius later threw into the dust bin of "apocryphal" gospels to be avoided by pious and discerning believers.

He would also have noticed something else. The first seven sayings in this gospel were a pretty close match to the seven sayings found in POxy 654—one of the unknown gospel texts discovered by Grenfell and Hunt fifty years earlier at Oxyrhynchus. Two of the other unknown gospel texts also contained sayings found now in this new gospel: POxy 655 had parts of the sayings we conventionally number now as sayings 36–39, and most astonishingly sayings 26–33 of the new gospel are the sayings—in order—that are found on the front and back of Grenfell and Hunt's famous POxy 1. Puech connected the dots. Grenfell and Hunt had actually discovered the "Gospel of Thomas" in 1897. They just did not know it. It turns out that their gospel fragments were the extant remains of a sayings gospel. Now, at last, that lost arc of gospel theory could be read, studied, and held in the hand.

The discoveries at Nag Hammadi gave us a complete text of the *Gospel of Thomas*. It is not in its original language—Greek—but ancient Coptic, the language used in Christian churches in the second, third, and fourth centuries in Egypt. There were Greek-speaking Christians also in Egypt at the time, but the *Gospel of Thomas* they could read survives only in the spare fragments discovered by Grenfell and Hunt at Oxyrhynchus. The first critical edition of the Coptic text from Hag Hammadi was published in 1959, simultaneously with translations into English, French, German, and Dutch. Since then, scholars throughout the world have pored over this text trying to learn more of its secrets.

And what about Q? The lost gospel is still lost. The *Gospel of Thomas* and Q must have shared much in common—about half their sayings overlap. But they are not the same gospel. Q was something else, another early sayings gospel. But even though it remains lost, scholars have not neglected it. To earlier reconstructions made in the early twentieth century, a thorough critical edition of Q was added in 2000, the product of more than a decade of research by an international team of scholars lead by James M. Robinson, Paul Hoffmann, and John Kloppenborg. But this reconstruction of Q, based solely on Matthew's and Luke's apparent use of it, is no substitute for the real thing. Perhaps even now a copy of this most ancient of Christian gospels lies buried beneath the sands of the Egyptian desert. Or there could be a copy of it hiding undetected in the museums and libraries of the West, which hold thousands of uncatalogued and untranslated manuscripts left over from the days when Americans and Europeans pillaged Egypt and the Middle East for their ancient literary treasures. Until 1945 the *Gospel of Thomas* was a mere echo in the minds of a few specialists in the arcane history of Christian heresy. Is Q still out there?

For Further Study

The story of **Grenfell and Hunt** and their discoveries at **Oxyrhynchus** is told especially well by Peter Parsons in *The City of the Sharp-Nosed Fish: Greek Lives in Roman Egypt* (London: Phoenix, 2007). Grenfell's firsthand account appeared in *McClure's Magazine* (October 1897) under the title "The Oldest Record of Christ's Life: The First Complete Account of the Recent Finding of the 'Sayings of Our Lord.'" The quote is from p. 1027.

The **Oxyrhynchus fragments of the *Gospel of Thomas*** were published by Grenfell and Hunt in the following publications: *LOGIA IHSOU: Sayings of Our Lord* (London: Henry Frowde [for the Egypt Exploration Fund], 1897); *New Sayings of Jesus and Fragment of a Lost Gospel from Oxyrhynchus* (London: Henry Frowde; New York: Oxford Univ. Press [for the Egypt Exploration Fund], 1904); and *The Oxyrhynchus Papyri*, vol. 1 (London: Henry Frowde [for the Egypt Exploration Fund], 1904). They are available now in a modern critical edition by Harold Attridge in Bentley Layton, ed., *Nag Hammadi Codex II,2–7 Together with XIII,2*, Brit. Lib. Or. 4926(1), and P. Oxy. 1, 654, 655*, vol. 1, Nag Hammadi Studies 20, Coptic Gnostic Library (Leiden: Brill, 1989), 113–25.

On **Papias and his lost "Oracles of the Lord,"** see Hans von Campenhausen, *The Formation of the Christian Bible* (Philadelphia: Fortress, 1972), 129–35.

A fine account of **the history of the Q Hypothesis** is to be found in John Kloppenborg, *Excavating Q: The History and Setting of the Sayings Gospel* (Minneapolis: Fortress, 2000), chap. 6, "The Jesus of History and the History of Dogma: Theological Currents in the Synoptic Problem." (Chaps. 7–9 of this work are also very useful in understanding the Q Hypothesis in the context of modern theology.)

David Friedrich Strauss's historic book is available in English in various editions, which can prove confusing. His original *Das Leben Jesu, kritisch bearbeitet* ("The Life of Jesus, Critically Examined") was published in 1835–36. A second edition appeared in 1837, a third in 1838–39, and a fourth in 1840. The third edition is much different from the first, second, and fourth. It is less combative, less a direct challenge to traditional Christian faith. It was translated into English in the 1840s under the title *The Life of Jesus, or, A Critical Examination of His History* (London: Henry Hetherington, 1841–45), but is rarely seen today. The fourth edition of 1840, however, was more or less the same book that appeared originally in 1835–36. It is the basis for the English translation by Mary Ann Evans (better known by her nom de plume, George Eliot), which goes by the English title *The Life of Jesus Critically Examined*. It was published originally in England in 1846 (London: Chapman) and later in America (New York: Calvin Blanchard, 1855). In 1972 Fortress Press published this translation again in a single-volume paperback edition, edited with an introduction by Peter Hodgson. This is the edition that students should consult. Hodgson offers, among other things, an extensive bibliography. The first edition of Strauss's *Leben Jesu* was never translated. Later in life, in 1864, Strauss wrote another book called *Das Leben Jesu für das deutsche Volk bearbeitet,* which also became very popular and was translated into English under the title *Strauss' New Life of Jesus* (London: Williams and Norgate, 1879). But one should remember that this is another book, different from the original *Leben Jesu,* which created such a stir in 1835. For an excellent study of Strauss in his times, see Marilyn Chapin Massey, *Christ Unmasked: The Meaning of* The Life of Jesus *in German Politics* (Chapel Hill: Univ. of North Carolina Press, 1983).

Johann Jakob Griesbach remains a figure obscure to all but a few specialists, though his ideas appear in most accounts of the history of the synoptic problem. His synopsis, which scholars used to crack the problem, was published in 1774 as part of his critical edition of the Greek New Testament (*Libri N. T. historici* [Halle, 1774]). It appeared separately in various editions later on. Griesbach explained his theory of synoptic gospel relationships in *Commentatio qua Marci Evangelium totum e Matthaei et Lucae Commentariis Decerptum esse monstratur* (Jena: Goepferdt, 1789–90). An English translation of this work may be found in Bernard Orchard and Thomas Longstaff, eds., *J. J. Griesbach, Synoptic and Text Critical Studies, 1776–1976,* SNTSMS 34 (Cambridge: Cambridge Univ. Press, 1978), 103–35.

Friedrich Schleiermacher's *The Christian Faith* was originally published as *Christliche Glaube nach den Grundsätzen der evangelischen Kirche im Zusammenhang dargestellt* (Berlin, 1821–22). It is available in English as *The Christian Faith* (Edinburgh: Clark, 1976). His essay on the *logia* was entitled "Über die Zeugnisse des Papias von unsern beiden ersten Evangelien" (*Theologische Studien und Kritiken* 5 [1832]: 735–68).

Christian Hermann Weisse's much ignored discovery was published in his book *Die evangelische Geschichte: Kritisch und philosophisch bearbeitet* (Leipzig: Breitkopf und Härtel, 1838). It has never been translated into English.

Adolf von Harnack's book was originally titled *Sprüche und Reden Jesu: Die Zweite Quelle des Matthäus und Lukas* (Leipzig: Hinrichs, 1907). The English translation appeared one year later as *The Sayings of Jesus: The Second Source of St. Matthew and St. Luke* (London: Williams and Norgate; New York: Putnam, 1908).

The story of **the discovery of the Nag Hammadi Library** is told by James M. Robinson in Stephen J. Patterson, James M. Robinson, and Hans-Gebhard Bethge, *The Fifth Gospel: The Gospel of Thomas Comes of Age,* rev. ed. (London: Clark, 2011), chap. 3, "The Story of the Nag Hammadi Library."

3

THE GALILEAN GOSPEL

Q is the most important historical document for our understanding of Jesus and the religious movement he helped to create—or it *would* be, if it had survived. It is, quite simply, the first written gospel we know about. It would have predated the Gospel of Mark by at least a decade, and Matthew and Luke by twenty, thirty, or forty years or more. It was the first attempt to codify and shape the message of Jesus among the people who had known him most intimately—his followers in the Galilee, Jesus's homeland. And yet hardly anyone today who otherwise shares an intense interest in Jesus knows about this mysterious document. We must begin, then, with the basics.

WHAT IS Q?

So what is Q, exactly? The best definition of Q is this: the material that is shared by the gospels Matthew and Luke, but not found in the Gospel of Mark. But why should the different contents of these gospels imply another, lost gospel? The answer is straightforward, but it requires a little patience to rehearse the evidence and the logic that have led scholars to posit the existence of Q since the first half of the nineteenth century. So bear with me a little.

As we saw in the last chapter, scholars have long noticed that three of the biblical gospels—Matthew, Mark, and Luke—share much in common. They have a shared story line, or plot, and they share many individual stories, sayings, and parables. Since these gospels were all created in a world where texts were rare, we might on first glance ascribe these similarities to a shared oral tradition. One might suppose, for example, that all three writers knew a common set of stories about Jesus and used them variously to tell the story of his life. Simple— but not very likely. The problems begin with the language of these gospels: Greek.

Matthew, Mark, and Luke were all written in Greek. But Jesus probably did not speak Greek. He was a Jewish peasant. He might have known a little Greek, but his normal tongue would have been the Semitic dialect commonly spoken by the peasants of Palestine in the first century CE, Aramaic. The original oral tradition associated with Jesus would have been communicated among the peasants of Galilee also in Aramaic. Now, here is the problem. When we compare the same stories in Matthew, Mark, and Luke, they agree not just in general or in gist, but often word for word, *verbatim*. Not 100 percent verbatim, but often as much as 80 percent, and sometimes even more. How shall we explain this?

Does a theory of oral transmission work? Say a set of stories circulated orally in Aramaic; they were told and retold in great variety. They usually communicated the gist but were never word for word the same. Then, gradually, bilingual listeners began to repeat the stories, now sometimes in Aramaic, sometimes in Greek. Greek versions began to circulate orally, told and retold in great variety, usually communicating the gist but never being told word for word the same. Imagine the various ways in which any particular story might have been told, in two different languages, by dozens of different people, in myriad different contexts. Now imagine a story from this oral tradition beginning with Jesus, spreading around in Aramaic, then trickling over into Greek, and spreading around again in the new language; finally one particular version falls on the ears of, say, the author of Matthew, who includes it in his gospel. Now imagine that a different author, say, the author of Luke, hears the same story, but a version of it that has taken a different route through that complex process of being passed on, and he also decides to include it in his gospel. What are the chances that these two versions of the story will agree with one another, *in Greek*, nearly *verbatim*? A clever mathematician could perhaps compute the odds. Let us just say, they would be astronomical.

But that's not all. Jesus was an aphorist and a storyteller. How many times would he have told one of his parables, a good one like the Sower? Dozens of times? Probably. But when a gospel writer includes a parable in his narrative, he can only really use it once. If he were to repeat it as Jesus actually had done, over and over again, that would be tedious. He has to choose one place to put it and one way to tell it. Now, when the authors of Matthew and Mark include the Parable of the Sower in their gospels, they both just happen to portray Jesus telling it right after a scene in which Jesus is accused of having a demon, Beelzebul, so that his family must come to try and take him away. And that story, in both gospels, follows close after a story in which Jesus is healing and exorcizing multitudes. And that story, in both gospels, follows one in which Jesus heals a man with a withered hand. And before that, in both gospels, there is a story about Jesus and his disciples passing through the grain fields of Galilee, feeding themselves from the gleanings. It is not just that Matthew, Mark, and Luke share a large number of stories, sayings, and parables, or that these common traditions often agree almost verbatim from gospel to gospel. They also present these things in the same order. Could oral tradition account for all of that? Never.

This is the problem. Matthew, Mark, and Luke share a large amount of material that is often in near verbatim agreement and often in the same order. As we have seen, we call them the *synoptic* gospels because they have all this in common. The problem posed by their apparently close relationship is called the *synoptic problem*. The Gospel of John is not included in the synoptic problem. It has different content and a different order. Neither is the *Gospel of Thomas* included in it. Different content; different order. For centuries scholars have noticed the synoptic problem and realized that it requires a literary solution. Oral tradition cannot account for it. Matthew, Mark, and Luke are somehow connected intertextually.

Over time and through careful study, scholars have discovered certain patterns in the synoptic agreements. One is that Matthew and Luke often agree with one another and with Mark, but they seldom agree with one another *against* Mark. This is true for the general story, or plot, followed by each gospel as well as the wording of individual stories that all three share. Now, Matthew has several episodes that are not found in Mark, but Luke does not share them. Luke also has many episodes not found in Mark, but Matthew does not share them. Put otherwise, in terms of plot and story, Luke and Matthew agree with each other only when they also agree with Mark. When one drills down into particular stories shared by all three gospels, the same patterns exist. Figure 2 shows three versions of the same story, the story of Jesus healing the unnamed mother-in-law of Peter, as found in Matthew, Mark, and Luke.

They all agree that the healing took place in the house of Peter's mother-in-law, she was sick, she had a fever, the fever left her, and afterward she set about serving those present. In Mark's version she serves "them," namely, all those gathered in the house to see this event. But in Matthew she serves "him," namely, Jesus. What about in Luke? Luke agrees with Mark—she serves "them." In Mark Jesus heals the woman simply by taking her by the hand. But in Luke he "rebukes" the fever to drive it away. In Matthew? Matthew agrees with Mark: he takes her "by the hand." And whose mother-in-law is it? In Mark it is "Simon's" mother-in-law. In Matthew this disciple is called "Peter." What about in Luke? You guessed it: he is called "Simon," as in Mark.

FIGURE 2. HEALING PETER'S MOTHER-IN-LAW

MATTHEW 8:14–15	MARK 1:29–31	LUKE 4:38–39
And when Jesus entered Peter's house,	And immediately he left the synagogue, and entered the house of Simon and Andrew, with James and John. Now	And he arose and left the synagogue, and entered Simon's house.
he saw his mother-in-law lying sick with a fever;	Simon's mother-in-law lay sick with a fever, and immediately they told him of her. And he came and took her by the hand and lifted her up,	Now Simon's mother-in-law was ill with a high fever, and they besought him for her. And he stood over her and rebuked the fever,
he touched her hand, and the fever left her, and she rose and served him.	and the fever left her; and she served them.	and it left her; and immediately she rose and served them.

In stories that occur in all three synoptic gospels, Matthew and Luke seldom agree against Mark. Scholars refer to this pattern as the *medial position* of Mark.

The simplest and most commonly accepted explanation for the medial position of Mark is, as mentioned in the previous chapter, the Hypothesis of Markan Priority. This hypothesis states simply that the Gospel of Mark was written first. The authors of Matthew and Luke wrote later, each independently of the other, making use of Mark as a source. Each takes his own liberties with Mark, altering this, adding that. But when Matthew changed something, Luke's author would not have known about this and so did not imitate what Matthew had done. Likewise, Matthew's author would not have been aware of the changes Luke's author made to Mark. So these do not show up in Matthew. Each used Mark, but independently of the other. This is clear enough. But where does Q come in?

The Hypothesis of Markan Priority is the best explanation for what scholars call the *triple tradition*, that is, stories, sayings, and parables that occur in *all three* synoptic gospels. But there is also a *double tradition,* that is, material that occurs only in Matthew and Luke, *not* Mark. This material includes a few stories, but it comprises mostly sayings and parables. Now, this material too has its own peculiar patterns not immediately apparent in a cursory reading of Matthew and Luke. One is this: although the authors of Matthew and Luke inserted these stories, sayings, and parables into the basic narrative they inherited from Mark, they seldom insert the same thing in the same place. The Parable of the Great Feast is a good example. Luke's author includes it midway through Mark's narrative, in chapter 14 (see Luke 14:15–24), while Matthew's author uses it in chapter 22 (see Matt. 22:1–14), near the end. Looking at this parable in Matthew and Luke, one might well suppose that this double tradition is simply the remnant of the continuing oral tradition picked up by chance by Matthew and Luke and used to supplement Mark. But some of it, like with the triple tradition, shows a high degree of verbatim agreement *in Greek.* As with the triple tradition, this could not happen unless the double tradition also is the result of some kind of literary relationship.

Now, here is a peculiar thing scholars have noticed. Although Matthew and Luke tend to insert these sayings and parables into the Markan story differently, when lifted out of their narrative contexts and laid side by side, one can see that the sayings and parables of the double tradition also tend to occur in the same order in Matthew and Luke. It is as though the authors of Matthew and Luke shared a list of sayings they could draw from to supplement the basic story they had from Mark, and each worked his way through this list peeling off snippets and inserting them into Mark as he saw fit. But the fact that they never manage to insert the same snippet in the same place means that they must have done this independently of one another. This hypothetical list is the basis of the Q Hypothesis. Verbatim agreement and a shared order—the same things that suggest Matthew and Luke used Mark for the triple tradition—suggest that they also used a second source for the double tradition. This second source is Q.

The Q Hypothesis is a necessary corollary of the Hypothesis of

Markan Priority. The authors of Matthew and Luke used Mark as a source, but they also must have had a second source from which they drew the material not found in Mark. This is the basis of the *Two-Source Hypothesis*, a combination of the Hypothesis of Markan Priority and the Q Hypothesis (see Fig. 3). It states that Matthew and Luke incorporate two common sources: Mark and a second, lost gospel, known as Q. This is the most widely accepted solution to the synoptic problem today.

FIGURE 3. THE TWO-SOURCE HYPOTHESIS

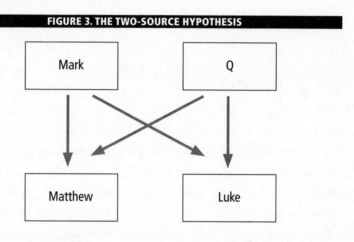

Other Explanations?

Are there other ways to solve the synoptic problem? Yes, but they are not nearly as persuasive as the Two-Source Hypothesis. One is called (confusingly) the Two-Gospel Hypothesis. This is actually close enough to what Johann Griesbach proposed in the eighteenth century to be known more clearly as the *Griesbach Hypothesis.* That is the term I will use. As we saw in the last chapter, the Griesbach Hypothesis holds that Matthew was written first, then Luke, making use of Matthew as a source. Finally, Mark came last. Mark's author, in this theory, worked carefully to combine the places where Matthew and Luke agree, but to omit their disagreements (see Fig. 4).

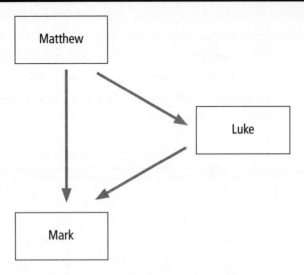

FIGURE 4. THE GRIESBACH HYPOTHESIS

The problem with the Griesbach Hypothesis is that it assigns to Mark's author some fairly inexplicable omissions. For example, according to Griesbach, Mark's author would have passed over the stories of Jesus's birth in Matthew and Luke and the Sermon on the Mount/Plain, again in both Matthew and Luke. Worst of all, even though Mark depicts Jesus as instructing the disciples to go to Galilee, where he will meet them after his resurrection from the dead, Mark ends, notoriously, with the empty tomb and no appearance stories, in Galilee or anywhere else (see 16:8, the original ending to the Gospel of Mark). But Matthew has just such an appearance story, set in Galilee (28:16–20), and Luke has the famous story of Jesus appearing to certain disciples on the road to Emmaus (24:13–35). According to Griesbach, Mark's author would need to have omitted appearance stories, even though Matthew and Luke each have one.

The impression left by the original ending of Mark is so jarring that later scribes created stories modeled on those in Matthew and Luke to complete the gospel in a way they thought more proper. In modern Bibles these stories are usually included as supplementary material at the end of Mark and noted as the "Shorter Ending" and the "Longer Ending" to Mark. But scholars are in unanimous agreement that Mark originally ended at 16:8. According to the Hypothesis of Markan Priority, the authors of Matthew and Luke felt the inadequacy of Mark's ending and supplemented it with appearance stories known to them. This is far more likely than the reverse, that Mark's author omitted these stories from Matthew and Luke because they did not completely agree with one another. Because of this and much more, similar counterevidence, the Griesbach Hypothesis has few adherents today.

Another alternative to the Two-Source Hypothesis is known as the *Hypothesis of Markan Priority Without Q* (see Fig. 5). Its advocates argue as it suggests, that Markan priority can be used to account for the triple tradition, but Q is unnecessary to account for the double tradition (the material found only in Matthew and Luke). One need only suppose that in addition to Mark, Matthew's author also knew the prior work of Luke or, as more commonly proposed, Luke's author also knew the prior work of Matthew. In other words, Matthew used Mark and added to it several sayings and parables. Later Luke wrote using both Mark and Matthew, thus accounting for both the triple tradition (things found in all three gospels) and the double tradition (things found only in Matthew and Luke). At first, this theory seems attractive, for it eliminates the need to posit a hypothetical, lost gospel, Q, to account for the double tradition. It seems simpler, but the devil is in the details.

Remember that little oddity of the double tradition—that Matthew and Luke each fold sayings and parables of the double tradition (i.e., Q) into the Markan narrative, but *never in the same place.* How would that little oddity be explained using the Hypothesis of Markan Priority Without Q? It would go something like this. Matthew's author used Mark but supplemented it with other sayings and parables. The author of Luke studied both Mark and Matthew. For the story line, he decided to use Mark, ignoring Matthew's deviations. But he

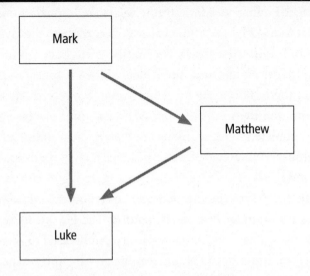

FIGURE 5. THE HYPOTHESIS OF MARKAN PRIORITY WITHOUT Q

liked many (though not all) of the sayings and parables that Matthew added to Mark and so included some of them. But almost every time he encountered one of these additions, he, for some reason, decided to sever it from the Markan context in which Matthew originally embedded it and move it to a new location. Not every time—there are just three exceptions out of the dozens of sayings involved—but almost. That is not impossible, but as an editorial policy it is fairly inexplicable. This is just too eccentric for most scholars studying this problem to accept. Possible, but very improbable.

So the Two-Source Hypothesis is still the most commonly used theory for solving the synoptic problem today. But does it have problems? Indeed, it does. The most obvious is that although Matthew and Luke *tend* not to agree against Mark, occasionally they *do*. Go back to the story of how Jesus healed Peter's mother-in-law (see Fig. 1). We noted earlier how each time Matthew diverges from Mark, Luke agrees with Mark, not Matthew, and when Luke diverges from Mark, Matthew follows Mark, not Luke—so that Matthew and Luke seldom agree *against* Mark. *Seldom,* but not *never.* Look in the last line of that story. Mark says that when Peter's mother-in-law was healed, "she served them." But Matthew and Luke say "she *rose and* served them/ him." This is a minor thing, but it poses a problem for the Two-Source Hypothesis. If Matthew's author did not know Luke, and Luke's author did not know Matthew, how could it happen that both, somehow, simultaneously altered Mark in just the same way?

These Matthew-Luke agreements against Mark are called *minor agreements*. Sometimes the minor agreements can be accounted for by simple coincidence. The authors of Matthew and Luke each saw in Mark an awkward turn of phrase, a poorly chosen word, or a mistake and simply corrected it. Occasionally they correct the mistake in the same way. Simple coincidence. This, or something like it, is probably what is going on in the story of Peter's mother-in-law. But this is not always the case. Sometimes the minor agreements in a synoptic story stack up to the point where they constitute a "major agreement." Then something else must be going on.

A good illustration of this problem is to be found in the three versions of the Parable of the Mustard (see Fig. 6). Notice how both Matthew and Luke speak of a man actually sowing the mustard seed in a garden (Luke) or field (Matthew). Mark simply says "when it is sown," without specifying where or by whom. This is odd, for one does not normally sow mustard in a field or garden. The rabbis advise against this, for mustard is a weed, an unclean plant that must not be mixed with other plants. Would Matthew and Luke simultaneously, independently, have "corrected" Mark in just this way?

Or notice this. Mark speaks of the mustard as the largest of shrubs, which provides shade in which birds might nest. This is accurate. Mustard *is* a shrub. A bird could nest in its shade. But both Matthew and Luke refer to the mustard as a "tree." That is a rather preposterous thing to call the small, weedlike mustard plant. It is not a tree by any reasonable measure. And both speak of its "branches," in which birds might build nests. But the spindly branches of the mustard bush could hardly support a bird, let alone the nest of a bird. Where would Matthew and Luke get the preposterous idea, independently of one

---

FIGURE 6. THE MUSTARD PARABLE

MATTHEW 13:31–32	MARK 4:30–32	LUKE 13:18–19
Another parable he put to them, saying, "The Empire of heaven is like a grain of mustard seed which a person took and sowed in his field. It is the smallest of all seeds,	And he said, "To what can we compare the Empire of God, or what parable shall we use for it? It is like a grain of mustard seed, which, when sown upon the ground, is the smallest of all the seeds on earth.	He said therefore, "What is the Empire of God like and to what shall I compare it? It is like a grain of mustard seed which a man took and sowed in his garden;
but when it has grown it is the greatest of all shrubbery and it becomes a tree,	But when it is sown it grows up and becomes the greatest of all shrubbery, and puts forth large branches, so that the	and it grew and became a tree,
so that the birds of the air come and make nests in its branches."	birds of the air can make nests in its shade."	and the birds of the air made nests in its branches."

---

another, to change Mark's mustard bush into the botanical monstrosity of a mustard tree with nice strong branches? This cannot be simple coincidence. It is almost as if behind Matthew and Luke there stands another version of the story, one in which a man sows mustard in a field or garden and it grows up to become a gigantic, improbable mustard "tree."

Indeed, that is how most scholars account for this sort of "major" minor agreement. Matthew and Luke had another source besides Mark, namely Q. The Mustard Parable, it turns out, was a tradition known both to Mark's author and to Q's. These instances of a Mark and Q overlap are not numerous, but they do occur. Perhaps they are more numerous than we know, for they only show up where Matthew and Luke both happen to prefer the Q version of the story over Mark's. In instances where one prefers Mark and the other Q, the Q version remains hidden without the minor agreements in wording to reveal it. And of course, if there are instances where both Matthew and Luke happened to prefer Mark's version to Q's, the Q version is simply lost. So we do not really know the full extent to which the contents of Mark and Q overlap, but it could have been quite a lot. John and Mark have no clear literary relationship, and yet they share several stories in common. There is no direct literary relationship between the *Gospel of Thomas* and the synoptic gospels, and yet they share dozens of common sayings and parables. If these models indicate anything, it may well be that Mark and Q overlapped considerably. In any event, the minor agreements do not ultimately undermine the Two-Source Hypothesis. To the contrary, they confirm what we would expect if it were true: that the two sources sometimes overlap.

RECOVERING Q

So how do we know what was actually in Q? A general idea may be had from a simple tally of the texts that are found in Matthew and Luke, but not Mark. One might call this *minimal Q*. By that method one can identify roughly 235 verses that belong to Q. Most scholars add to this several passages that are found in Mark as well as Matthew and Luke for which there is evidence of Mark-Q overlap, as with the Parable of the Mustard, as we have just seen. Another kind of evidence for Mark-Q overlap is the phenomenon of doublets.

A doublet is a story for which there are two versions in a single gospel. A good example is a story known as the "Mission Discourse," in which Jesus sends out his followers to cast out demons and heal people. There is one version in Mark 6:7–13, in which Jesus sends out twelve disciples to cast out demons and heal diseases. If people don't respond to them, they are to "shake the dust from their feet" and move on. In Matthew 10:5–15 there is a similar story: twelve are sent out to heal and exorcise demons, and, as in Mark, they are to "shake off the dust" if it doesn't go well. In Luke 9:1–6 there is the same basic story: Jesus sends out the twelve to heal and perform exorcisms; they are to "shake off the dust" when not welcome. All of this is good evidence for Markan Priority: Mark had a story, which the authors of Matthew and Luke copied, making various changes when it suited their purposes. This is altogether common in the synoptic tradition.

But then in Luke something peculiar shows up. In chapter 10 there is a *second* Mission Discourse, only this time there are not twelve disciples, but seventy. They are to knock on doors, say "Peace" to whoever should answer, ask to be taken in, eat what is put before them, and care for the sick they might find there (10:1–16). Two Mission Discourses in one gospel? How does a doublet like this happen?

Here is a hint. Some of the language of Luke's second Mission Discourse shows up also in Matthew. Some of it comes just before his version of the Markan Mission Discourse, some of it just after. For example, Luke 10:13–15 includes the names of some of the places where the followers of Jesus were turned away: Chorazin, Bethsaida, and Capernaum. These details are not found in Mark. But they are included in Matthew 11:20–24, just after the Mission Discourse Matthew copied from Mark. It looks, then, as if Matthew's author also knew Luke's second discourse and just could not resist taking a poke at those enemy towns it names. But how could he have known of Luke's second discourse? The solution to this puzzle is Mark-Q overlap. Luke contains two stories because its author read one version in Mark, which he used in chapter 9, and one in Q, which he used in chapter 10. Matthew's author also saw both stories but decided that one was enough. He preferred Mark's twelve-disciple version, and this is what he includes in his chapter 10. But he apparently liked some of the details of Q's Mission Discourse and so used them in the narrative surrounding his single, Markan discourse. Doublets like this often indicate Mark-Q overlap. In this instance it is almost certain that Q had a version of the Mission Discourse in which seventy rather than twelve disciples are sent out. This material, then, is also added to the contents of Q, even though it does not meet the basic definition of Q (the material found in Matthew and Luke, but not in Mark).

What about verses that are found in just one of the gospels, say Matthew or Luke? We call this Matthean Special Material when it occurs only in Matthew, and Lukan Special Material when it occurs only in Luke. Could some of this special material also have come from Q? Theoretically, yes. In fact, it is quite likely that on occasion one of the these authors would have read something in Q that did not fit his narrative or grand purpose, so he left it out, leaving just a single witness to Q. The trouble is, without a second witness, it is very difficult to identify these singly attested Q verses.

A good illustration is Luke 17:20–21:

> Once Jesus was asked by the Pharisees when the kingdom of God was coming, and he answered, "The kingdom of God is not coming with things that can be observed; nor will they say, 'Look, here it is!' or 'There it is!' For, in fact, the kingdom of God is among you."

These verses are not in Mark, but neither are they in Matthew—though Matthew 24:23 may contain remnants of them. They are usually considered Lukan Special Material. Could they have come from Q? Their location in Luke raises the question. They occur just before Luke launches into an apocalyptic speech that indeed came from Q (Luke 17:22–37). But 17:20–21 appear to be *anti*-apocalyptic. Would Luke have added these verses to his narrative, only then to include Q's apocalyptic speech in 17:22–37? This makes little sense. How, then, did 17:20–21 happen to land in the Gospel of Luke? Perhaps the verses were already in Q, in which material had been gathered up with less attention to internal tensions and contradictions. Luke included them because they were in Q, but Matthew omitted them because he could not abide the tension they created with his own apocalyptic view. In Q, or not in Q? Some scholars include these verses; others do not. The evidence is just too ambiguous to permit certainty one way or the other.

Finally, how certain can we be that the double tradition in Matthew and Luke, together with the clearer cases of Mark-Q overlap, give us a good idea of what was actually in Q? Could there have been material in Q that both Matthew and Luke omitted? Certainly. But caution is in order. Speculation about what ought to be there but isn't will likely reflect the prejudices and presuppositions of the scholar. Some, for example, speculate that Q must have included stories about Jesus's death and resurrection. After all, all of the canonical gospels have this kind of passion narrative ending. Perhaps Matthew and Luke simply did not use Q's passion narrative because they preferred Mark's. Q's passion narrative is "hiding" behind Mark in this case. But not all gospels do have a passion narrative. We have one other gospel made up primarily of sayings—the *Gospel of Thomas,* of course. It makes no mention of Jesus's death and resurrection. If the formal similarity between Q and *Thomas* offers any guidance, we should not expect to find a passion narrative in Q at all.

Reconstructing Q

Scholars can, within limits, determine the contents of Q, more or less. But sometimes it would be helpful to know more precisely what Q actually said. Is it possible, using Matthew and Luke, to reconstruct the actual wording of the Q text that lay behind these two extant witnesses? Yes, but only with an attention to detail that can try the patience of even the most seasoned biblical scholar. A brief example will probably be enough to satisfy average curiosity. Below are the Matthean and Lukan versions of a collection of beatitudes, or blessings. Matthew's version comes from the Sermon on the Mount, Luke's from the Sermon on the Plain. Since these sermons have other things in common, they probably derive from a common sermon that each author found in Q. The beatitudes would have been the opening lines of that original Q version of the sermon. Figure 7 shows the beatitudes in parallel columns so that you can easily compare them.

FIGURE 7. THE BEATITUDES

LUKE 6:20–23	MATTHEW 5:3–12
20b"Blessed are you poor, for yours is the kingdom of God. 21a"Blessed are you who hunger now, for you shall be satisfied. 21b"Blessed are you who weep now, for you shall laugh.	3"Blessed are the poor in spirit, for theirs is the kingdom of heaven. 4"Blessed are those who mourn, for they shall be comforted. 5"Blessed are the meek, for they shall inherit the earth. 6"Blessed are those who hunger and thirst for righteousness, for they shall be satisfied. 7"Blessed are the merciful, for they shall obtain mercy. 8"Blessed are the pure in heart, for they shall see God. 9"Blessed are the peacemakers, for they shall be called sons of God. 10"Blessed are those who are persecuted for righteousness' sake, for theirs is the kingdom of heaven.
22"Blessed are you when men hate you, and when they exclude you and revile you, and cast out your name as evil, on account of the Son of man! 23Rejoice in that day, and leap for joy, for behold, your reward is great in heaven; for so their fathers did to the prophets."	11"Blessed are you when men revile you and persecute you and utter all kinds of evil against you falsely on my account. 12Rejoice and be glad, for your reward is great in heaven, for so men persecuted the prophets who were before you."

By comparing the two columns one can readily see the common elements of these texts, each a list of blessings, or beatitudes. Both lists begin with beatitudes about poverty (compare Luke 6:20 and Matt. 5:3). Luke's second beatitude (6:21) is about hunger. Matthew has a hunger beatitude too, but it is the fourth in his list (see 5:6). Luke's third beatitude is about weeping or crying (6:21). Matthew's second beatitude about mourning (5:4) might be comparable to this. Luke's last beatitude is a more complex statement about when people hate you (6:22–23), which finds a close parallel in Matthew's conclusion (5:11–12). These four beatitudes, then, would have been in Q's original sermon. But notice now that Matthew has several more beatitudes in his list: the meek (5:5), the merciful (5:7), the pure in heart (5:8), the peacemakers (5:9), and the persecuted (5:10).

When scholars of Q look at a tradition like this, they wish to know two things about it. First, where Matthew and Luke share a beatitude, which version lies closer to the Q original? And, second, Matthew's extra beatitudes—did Matthew's author add them, or were they in Q and Luke's author omitted them?

To answer these questions, one needs to know quite a lot about the two texts in question, Matthew and Luke. Let us begin with the hunger beatitude—Luke's second and Matthew's fourth. Luke's version simply blesses the hungry and promises a day when they will be satisfied. Matthew's version speaks instead of hungering and thirsting *for righteousness*. This is a less literal rendering of the blessing. Matthew does not have in mind actual hungry persons, but those who have pangs for righteousness. Scholars of Matthew will immediately recognize in this a common Matthean theme: righteousness. In fact, a major statement of it follows close after the Matthean beatitudes in 5:17–20, where Matthew's author says, "Unless your righteousness exceeds that of the scribes and the Pharisees, you will never enter the kingdom of heaven" (5:20). The rest of Matthew 5 consists of examples of this new, higher level of righteousness. So a good educated guess would be that Matthew has transformed the hunger beatitude from a statement about hungry people into a beatitude about people who hunger and thirst for righteousness. Q's beatitude originally read: "Blessed are you who hunger, for you will be satisfied."

This may help us with the first beatitude. Luke's version is about poor people—people in a state of need—as with the hunger beatitude. Matthew's version is about something else—people who are poor *in spirit*. Believe it or not, scholars have never reached a consensus about what that means exactly—"poor in spirit." But we can at least say that it doesn't mean simply "poor." So perhaps here too Matthew's author has transformed a Q beatitude about people in a state of need into one about people who cultivate this virtuous quality—whatever poor in spirit might mean. When we look at Matthew's other beatitudes that are not found in Luke, we find that this tendency continues. Matthew's list tends to lay blessings on people who pursue certain virtuous qualities: meekness (6:5), mercy (6:7), purity of heart (6:8), peacemaking (6:9), and suffering for the sake of righteousness (6:10). The more we look at it, the more it looks like a Matthean list. When we consider that Matthew was written in the aftermath of the Jewish war, which ended in disaster and suffering for the Jews of the Roman East, Matthew's specific transformations also seem to make a lot of sense: those who mourn will be comforted (5:4), the meek will inherit the earth (5:5), the peacemakers will be called children of God (5:9). In this case, Luke will have preserved the original gist of Q's first beatitude: "Blessed are you poor, for yours is the kingdom of God."

The Q scholar will want to proceed from here to try to arrive at the original wording of each individual beatitude—whether it was "kingdom of God" or "kingdom of heaven"; whether "you shall be satisfied" or "they shall be satisfied"; and so on. Sometimes these questions can be answered with confidence, sometimes not; it depends on the particulars in each decision. Fortunately, that work has been done for us by a group of Q specialists working in concert for more than a decade in something called the Society of Biblical Literature International Q Project (IQP). The result was a massive 600-page document detailing every difference between Matthew and Luke in the double tradition and deciding which version, if either, can be ascribed to Q. By a system of *sigla* the IQP also indicates where the text of Q is more and less certain. The text of Q I have included in Chapter 4 of this volume is a simplified version of the IQP text. It may not be the original text of Q, but it is close enough to give us a pretty good idea of what was in this very ancient document of nascent Christianity. It was, arguably, the first written gospel.

When and Where Was Q Written?

Before reading Q, however, one may wish to know a little more about it. For example, when and where was it written?

All that we know for certain is that Q was written before Matthew (ca. 85 CE) and Luke (ca. 90–140 CE), because these gospels incorporate it. So how much earlier than these gospels was Q composed? If truth be told, no one really knows. But here is a hint, perhaps. The other gospels in the synoptic family all demonstrate knowledge of an event that transformed the lives of Jews living in the Roman East in the last decades of the first century: the Judean war. In the mid-60s CE Jews in the Jewish homeland broke into open rebellion against Roman rule. This war culminated in the sacking of Jerusalem in the year 70 CE. The Jewish temple was destroyed and the inhabitants of the city were either killed or sold into slavery. The author of the Gospel of Mark associated this event with the arrival of the apocalypse (Mark 13), so traumatic was it. The authors of Mark, Matthew, and Luke, each in their own way, were coming to grips with this tragic and jarring reality.

Q, however, bears no obvious mark of this event. If Q, like other gospels in the synoptic family, was written in the Roman East, it is hard to imagine this unless Q was written considerably earlier than the revolt. But how much earlier? There are many passages in Q that speak of the imminent judgment of "this generation." A few of these passages may reflect the time leading up to the war. Here is a good example. Jesus speaks:

> Ah, Jerusalem, Jerusalem, who kills the prophets and stones the messengers sent to her! How many times have I wanted to gather your children together, like a hen gathers her chicks beneath her wings, and you were unwilling! Look, your house is abandoned! (13:34–35)

With such passages, one could perhaps think of Q in the 60s, even during the war itself. But some of that judgment material in Q is directed to another, less momentous set of circumstances: the simple rejection of the Q people's message. If this is the origin of the judgment passages in Q, then a date even earlier is possible, perhaps in the 50s CE. The truth is, beyond the outer limit of the Judean war in the mid-60s, we do not really know when to date Q. Within it, however, are many very early traditions, some of which may even go back to the earliest days of the Jesus movement.

The question of *where* Q was written is a little easier to answer. This is because Q contains some place-names, some of them small, out-of-the-way places that would have been unknown outside the immediate environs of the region. They occur in the passage we spoke of above called the Mission Discourse. At the end of that list of instructions about how to travel, what to take along, what to say when you come to a place, and what to do if your message is rejected ("shake off the dust") are these words:

> Woe to you, Chorazin! Woe to you, Bethsaida! For if the miracles that happened in you had been done in Tyre and Sidon, they would have changed long ago, in sackcloth and ashes. . . . And you, Capernaum, will you be exalted unto heaven? You'll go straight to Hades! (10:13, 15)

This is a good example of the words of prophetic judgment scattered throughout this gospel. What shall we make of it?

Apparently, these were a few of the places where the community of itinerants who used Q had to "shake off the dust," and they were not happy about it. Capernaum was a small fishing village on the shore of the Sea of Galilee. In the first century it had around a thousand inhabitants. It was an unremarkable town, probably unknown to any, except of course those who lived there. And that is probably why it was well known to those who wrote Q. In the Gospel of Mark, Capernaum is mentioned as a place where Jesus once lived (2:1) and the home of the apostle Peter's mother-in-law (1:21–28). So it was the home turf, so to speak, for the Jesus movement. Bethsaida might have been a little bigger, but archaeologists have not yet discovered it. It was apparently also a fishing village located near where the Jordan River enters the Sea of Galilee, just a few miles from Capernaum. The Gospel of John (1:44) identifies it as the hometown of Peter and two other disciples, Philip and Andrew. Chorazin was also not far from Capernaum. Today it is a site in Israel's marvelous Archaeological Parks system. But in spite of extensive excavations, first-century Chorazin was so small that archaeologists have yet to find any evidence of its existence.

These small villages are not places of mythic importance, like Jerusalem or Sodom. Neither are they well-known cities in the Galilee, like Sepphoris, near Nazareth, or Scythopolis (Beth-She'an), to the south of the Sea of Galilee (see Fig. 8). Q never mentions these larger places. Instead, its rage is focused on these tiny villages. They appear in Q because their rejection of the Jesus movement was taken personally by the Q folk. This is where they lived.

Q IN THE GALILEE

What was going on in the Galilee in the middle of the first century CE? A picture of it as a bucolic backwater, an out-of-the-way place where nothing happened and no one cared, is entirely mistaken. A look at the Galilee today, say, using Google Earth, reveals something of enormous importance about it. In the vast dry spaces of the Levant, what once was the Roman East, there are two green spaces. One is in Egypt—the Nile Delta. The other is in the Galilee—in the rift valley that connects the springs feeding the Jordan at the base of Mt. Hermon with the Sea of Galilee and then runs farther south, through drier country, until it reaches the Dead Sea. There is water in the Galilee.

FIGURE 8. MAP OF GALILEE

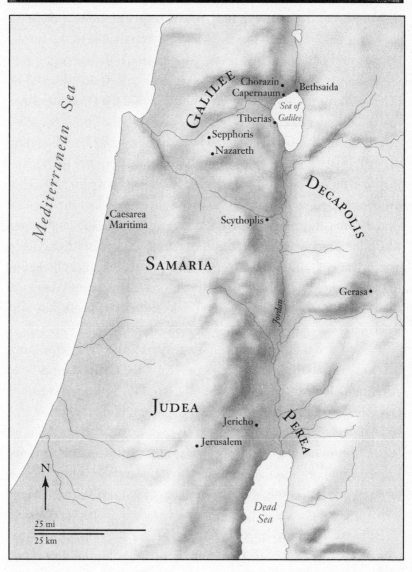

Water meant that you could grow things in the Galilee. The Roman Empire was an agrarian empire, in which agriculture was the basic economic engine. Places like the Galilee were valuable to the empire because of their agricultural potential. But the Galilee was important to the Roman Empire for another reason as well. It was situated on the eastern frontier of the empire. In this period the Euphrates River was the empire's easternmost boundary. Beyond the Euphrates was a desert neutral zone separating the Romans from their feared rivals to the east, the Parthians, who had the Tigris and Euphrates Rivers. The Parthian threat was real—or at least Romans believed it was. They feared that marauding armies from the ancient land of the Persians would come storming across the desert and retake the lands upon which the Roman people now grew wealthy—Egypt and Asia Minor. The careers of would-be emperors were made or lost campaigning in the east, holding at bay the Parthian threat. The natural resources of the Galilee meant that Rome could develop it as a staging ground, when necessary, for military operations in the East.

Rome ruled the Galilee through a Jewish client king, Herod Antipas. Antipas was the son of Herod the Great, the first and most powerful Roman vassal in the Roman East. Herod the Great had ruled the entire Jewish homeland; Antipas inherited from him only part of that larger kingdom—the Galilee and a few adjoining districts. Like his father, Herod Antipas was a builder. Herod the Great, eager to impress Rome with his loyalty, had in his day built Caesarea Maritima, a large artificial harbor on the Mediterranean coast parallel to the Galilean heartland. Built to serve the empire, he named it appropriately: *Caesarea*. It existed not to import cheap goods for the prosperous peasants of the Galilee, but to export the grain and olive oil that would be grown on the estates being developed in the Galilee by Roman colonists. Herod Antipas built cities as well. Sepphoris, which had been destroyed during the insurrection that marked the beginning of Antipas's rule, was rebuilt as his "jewel of the Galilee." Sepphoris was located just a short walk from Jesus's own native town, Naza-reth. Later Antipas built Tiberius on the southeastern shore of the Sea of Galilee, a more comfortable place for him to decamp during the hot months of the Galilean summer. With Caesarea Maritima on the coast, Caesarea Philippi, built by Antipas's brother, Philip, in the northern Galilee, and now Antipas's Sepphoris and Tiberius, the Gal-ilee was becoming urbanized.

These colonial cities were not like modern cities. They did not grow organically as populations shifted and gathered. They were built from the ground up in strategic places to serve the larger eco-nomic and political aims of the empire. They were expensive to build. Public buildings and markets were constructed of imported marble. Large-scale temples were technically difficult and required labor and money to construct and then to function. The Herods paid for these enormous building projects by extracting tribute from their Jewish subjects.

Ancient cities were parasitic. Each was assigned a *chora,* a large agricultural area surrounding it, upon which the city could draw for its basic food supply and income. These were the richest agricultural lands in the Galilee. The larger populations that came to occupy these colonial cities needed, in addition to food, water. The inhabi-tants of these cities were used to Roman-style baths, which required large amounts of water. In Sepphoris, well-off Jewish families had in their homes the customary *miqvaoth,* ritual baths. More basically, of course, these large cities needed lots of water for human consumption and agriculture. Then, as now, to control water was to control the means to life itself. Large aqueducts brought water from more remote springs to be stored in reservoirs and cisterns in or near these cities. Caesarea Philippi was constructed around the very springs that are the source of the Jordan River. These cities colonized and consumed the most precious resources in the Galilee—arable land and potable water. Peasants who had lived in the Galilee before colonization now found themselves struggling to compete for the things that had sustained them for generations. Cities brought change.

Wealthy entrepreneurs came to these cities to make money. They invested in land upon which to grow olives or wheat for export. These cities also housed bureaucrats and bankers, who managed the monetization of the economy, so that taxes and tribute could be exacted and debt tracked. It was through these cities that the Roman imperial system actually functioned in a province like Roman Palestine. The empire existed to extract wealth from its provincial districts. Cities were the means by which this was accomplished.

Urbanization, monetization, commercialization of agriculture—these were not positive developments for local peasants farming on ancestral lands in the Galilee. A monetized economy made it possible to levy taxes and tribute. The tribute exacted from small holders in an agrarian province of the empire was roughly half to two-thirds of the year's production—a heavy burden on peasants living at subsistence level. With heavy taxation comes debt. Debts must be settled by selling assets—first, perhaps, a child to work as a slave, but eventually the land upon which one's ancestors had subsisted for generations. In the Galilee of the Jesus movement, we should probably imagine the steady, debilitating transfer of lands from small peasant holdings to larger estates. The peasants who had worked these lands worked them still, only now as tenants or slaves. The larger estates would have produced luxury crops for export—wine, olive oil, and wheat—thus crowding out crops grown for local consumption. Food prices would have been on the rise. Small wonder that, by the middle of the first century, the Galilee was becoming a place of considerable unrest. By the 60s it had erupted into open rebellion. One of the first things to go up in flames when the war broke out was the debt archive in the city of Tiberius by the Sea of Galilee. This is the context in which our lost gospel, Q, came into existence.

WHAT DID Q ADVOCATE?

One of the best-known traditions that comes down to us from Q is
something that Christians still repeat in weekly worship all around
the globe. Today we call it the Lord's Prayer. There are various modern
versions of it—most Christians use the version found in the Gospel
of Matthew (6:9–13). Protestants usually add an additional phrase
found in only a few ancient manuscripts of Matthew, "For thine is the
kingdom and the power and the glory forever. Amen." But the Lord's
Prayer is found also in Luke (11:3–4), which means its pedigree goes
back to Q. By carefully comparing Matthew's version of the prayer
with Luke's, we can actually reconstruct its earliest-known form. This
is how the Lord's Prayer would have appeared in Q:

> Father—Holy be Your name!—may your empire come.
> Give us each day our daily bread;
> And forgive us our debts, for we also have forgiven our debtors.
> And lead us not into trial. (11:2–4)

When stripped down to these original bare bones, it is easy to see
that the Lord's Prayer has a context—Galilee in the middle of the first
century. Its concerns are the concerns of Galilean peasants trying to
survive Roman colonization: food, debt, and trial.

Food. Though the newly commercialized agriculture of the Galilee
probably produced more food in the first century than ever before, it
was not food meant for local consumption. Wheat, olives, and wine
could be grown and exported for sale elsewhere. Local peasants, who
once had been able to grow enough food to sustain themselves and
their families, now had to buy food or grow what they could on lesser
plots. Now, even daily bread is not guaranteed.

Debt. Here is the fear that haunts every small holder in the empire. Will I be able to pay the taxes and still hold on to my plot for
another year? The prayer appeals to God on the basis of the ancient

Jewish custom of the Sabbath Year—every seven years all debts were to be forgiven in Israel (Deut. 15:1–6). With the arrival of Roman rule, the Jewish custom of debt remission went by the wayside. Now debts were permanent, and debilitating. Debt was the first step toward destitution.

Trial. Debt usually led to a trial before a magistrate, who confiscated the peasant's holdings and sold them to the highest bidder to pay off the debt. In an agrarian empire, where agriculture forms the basis of the economy, to lose one's land was to lose one's life. Change "debts" to "sins" and "trial" to "temptation" and the concerns of the Q folk are transformed into common morality. But these early followers of Jesus were not concerned primarily with morality. Their concern was survival. Consider this very practical piece of advice, also found in Q:

> When you are on your way (to the authorities) with your accuser, make an effort to get away from him, lest he turn you over to the judge, and the judge to the assistant, and he will throw you into prison. I say to you, you'll never get out of there until you pay every last cent. (12:58–59)

So what was it that these early followers of Jesus turned to God for? Our gaze is directed to the first line of the prayer: "Father—Holy be your name!—may your empire come!" My translation probably sounds odd, if you are accustomed to saying the Lord's Prayer in church. We usually say something like "Thy kingdom come." But this fails to capture the sound of the phrase to ancient ears, in my view. The followers of Jesus in Galilee lived under Roman imperial rule. They knew the Roman Empire, perhaps not as a modern historian would know it—its politics, its inner workings, its grand scope—but as peasants would know it, as the "surround of force" that dominated every aspect of life. The empire meant the presence of cities. It meant taxation. It meant the presence of troops when a voice of protest was raised. When the Lord's Prayer speaks of the possibility of a *new* empire coming, *God's* empire, it is in the context of a present empire that is unbearable.

It is one thing to pray for a new empire and to hope for one, but did the Q folk have in mind something more concrete and real? Here is another very familiar-sounding Q text, one, however, that is very often misunderstood:

Do not worry about your life, what you will eat, nor about your body, what you will wear. Isn't life more than food and the body more than clothing? Think about the ravens: they neither sow nor reap nor gather into barns, and yet God feeds them. Aren't you more valuable than the birds? But who among you can add (even) a cubit to his height by worrying? And why do you worry about clothes? Study the lilies, how they grow: they do not work, nor do they spin. But I say to you, not even Solomon in all his glory was arrayed like one of these. But if God so clothes the grass in the field, which is here today and tomorrow thrown into the oven, how much more (will he clothe) you, you people of little faith! Therefore, do not worry, saying, "What will we eat?" or "What will we drink?" or "What will we wear?" For the Gentiles pursue all these things. Your Father knows that you need all these things. But seek his empire and all these things will be provided to you. (12:22b–31)

On first inspection one might entertain the thought that these Q sages had their heads in the clouds, that their confidence in God's providence gave rise to a pie-in-the-sky theology. But peasants living on the edge of subsistence cannot really afford pie-in-the-sky. Too many days of pie-in-the-sky could mean starvation on the ground. For this reason, the final line of this little sermon might be the most important: "Seek [God's] empire and all these things will be provided to you." Food, clothing, life itself—these things will come to you when you seek the empire of God. Now, one might well understand these things as a reward for seeking the empire. But it may be that food, clothing, shelter—these necessities of life—come from seeking the empire, because the empire of God is all about basic human needs. Recall the beatitudes in the Q sermon: "Blessed are you poor, for yours is the empire of God. Blessed are you who hunger, for you will be satisfied." To seek the empire of God might just mean seeking out that way of life by which all have access to the means to life, even the poor and the hungry.

There may be evidence for this understanding of the empire of God in another Q passage that speaks of its arrival. This text is the Q version of the Mission Discourse. It originally read something like this:

> [Jesus] says to his disciples, "The harvest is plentiful, but the workers are few. So ask the lord of the harvest to send out workers into his harvest. Go. Look, I am sending you out like sheep in the midst of wolves. Carry no bag, no pack, no shoes, no staff and greet no one on the road. As for any house that you might enter, first say 'Peace to this house!' And if a child of peace is there, let your peace come upon him. But if not, let your peace return to you. And stay at that house, eating and drinking whatever they offer, for the worker is worthy of his reward. (Do not move from house to house.) And whenever you enter a town and they take you in, eat what is set before you and care for the sick there and say to them, 'The empire of God has come to you.'" (10:2–9)

What does it actually mean for the empire of God to come? It begins with a knock at the door. On the stoop stand two itinerant beggars, with no purse, no knapsack, no shoes, no staff. They are so ill-equipped that they must cast their fate before the feet of a would-be host. This is a point often made by historical Jesus scholar John Dominic Crossan. These Q folk are sort of like ancient Cynics, but their goal is not the Cynic goal of self-sufficiency; these itinerants are set only for dependency. To survive they must reach out to other human beings. They offer them peace—this is how the empire arrives. And if their peace is accepted, they eat and drink—this is how the empire of God is consummated, in table fellowship. Then another tradition is tacked on, beginning with the words "Whenever you enter a town." This is perhaps the older part of the tradition, for this, and only this, also has a parallel in the *Gospel of Thomas* (14). There is also an echo of it in Paul's letter known as 1 Corinthians (10:27). Here, as in the first tradition, the itinerants are instructed, "Eat what is set before you." Again, the first move is to ask. The empire comes when someone receives food from another. But then something is offered in return: care for the sick. The empire of God here involves an exchange: food for care.

This warrants pause. Food for care. In the ancient world, those who lived on the margins of peasant life were never far from death's door. In the struggle to survive, food was their friend and sickness their enemy. Each day subsistence peasants earn enough to eat for a day. Each day they awaken with the question: Will I earn enough to eat today? This is quickly followed by a second: Will I get sick today? If I get sick, I won't eat, and if I don't eat, I'll get sicker. With each passing day the spiral of starvation and sickness becomes deeper and deeper and finally, deadly. Crossan has argued that this little snippet of ancient tradition is critical to understanding why the followers of Jesus and their empire of God were compelling to the marginalized peasants who were drawn to it. "Eat what is set before you and care for the sick." Here is the beginning of a program of shared resources of the most basic sort: food and care. It's an exchange. If some have food, all will eat; if any get sick, someone who eats will be there to care for them. The empire of God was a way to survive—which is to say, *salvation*.

As we explore this tradition further, though, we find some sobering caveats in Q:

And whenever you enter a town and they take you in, eat what is set before you and care for the sick there and say to them,

"The empire of God has come to you." As for any town (*polis*) you might enter that does not receive you, as you are leaving that town, shake the dust from your feet. I say to you, on that day Sodom will fare better than that town. (10:8–12)

Not every town will welcome them. They know this. But they also know that ancient traditions are with them. Sodom was notorious for its ill treatment of the stranger, for which it was destroyed. Eventually the Q folk in fact encountered harsh treatment. We know this because, remember, someone tacked these words onto the original discourse:

Woe to you, Chorazin! Woe to you, Bethsaida! For if the miracles that happened in you had been done in Tyre and Sidon, they would have changed long ago, in sackcloth and ashes. Indeed, Tyre and Sidon will fare better than you in the judgment. And you, Capernaum, will you be exalted unto heaven? You'll go straight to Hades! (10:13–15)

Now rejection is no longer hypothetical. It has actually happened at Chorazin, Bethsaida, and Capernaum. Here, for the first time, Q's Jesus speaks about judgment. Most scholars think that this probably refers to an imagined apocalyptic event expected soon to arrive, the details of which are discussed later in Q (in chapter 17). Perhaps, though, it is simply poetic venting. In any event, the Q folk pursued their new empire seriously enough to get thrown out of town occasionally, and when they did, they did not take it lying down.

But why were they rejected? Why was a little communal activity to ensure food for the hungry and care for the sick a threat to towns like Capernaum and Bethsaida? The answer lies in the teaching they promulgated in the name of their teacher and hero, Jesus. Here is just a sampling from Q of what they conveyed:

Love your enemies and pray for those who persecute you. (6:27–28)

Whoever strikes you on the cheek, turn to him the other as well. And to anyone who wants to take you to court to get your shirt, give him your coat as well. Give to anyone who asks of you and do not ask for your things back from anyone who borrows from you. (6:29–30)

Follow me, and leave the dead to bury their own dead. (9:60)

The last will be first, and the first last. (13:30)

Anyone who does not hate father and mother cannot be my disciple; and anyone who does not hate son or daughter cannot be my disciple. (14:26)

Anyone who does not take up his cross and follow me cannot be my disciple. (14:27)

These are all challenging words, even threatening. "The last shall be first, and the first last" might sound good to the marginal and "last," but to the "first" it would sound like nothing less than a revolution. The Jesus followers who created Q clearly embraced an ethos that demanded much from those who would join them, even abandoning their families and villages. Not everything one reads in Q is this provocative. But some things that sound innocent to modern ears may not have sounded so to ancient ones.

Consider, for example, these two parables of Jesus, which were apparently treasured by the Q folk:

What is the empire of God like and to what shall I compare it? It is like a mustard seed, which a person took and threw into his garden. And it grew and became a tree, and the birds of the sky nested in its branches.

And again, to what shall I compare the empire of God? It is like yeast, which a woman took and hid in three measures of flour until the whole batch was leavened. (13:18–21)

Mustard and leaven—both sound benign enough to modern ears. But in Jewish Galilee mustard was not just a harmless plant. It was a weed. It is a plant that proliferates so fast, that once it gets started, it is almost impossible to get rid of. Throwing mustard in a garden is like sowing dandelions in your suburban yard. And what about those birds? Does anyone want birds in their freshly sown garden? Or consider the leaven. In Jewish and pagan culture alike, leaven was a symbol of spoilage and putrefaction; the word would have sounded more like "mold" sounds to our ears than, say, "yeast." Sneaking mold into a storage jar full of flour is a kind of sabotage. And what a surprise when the unsuspecting cook tries to use it! Leavened flour behaves much differently than unleavened. Both of these parables about the new empire convey, with a wry sense of humor and a heavy dose of irony, that when the empire of God comes, it might not be what you were expecting—or wanting.

Sometimes in Q one reads words that pass from the mildly threatening to outright condemnation and judgment of the surrounding world. Here are some examples:

This generation is an evil generation. It seeks a sign, and no sign will be shown it, except the sign of Jonah. For just as Jonah became a sign to the Ninevites, so will the Son of Man be to this generation. (11:29–30)

Do you think that I have come to sow peace upon the earth? I have not come to sow peace, but a sword! For I have come to divide son against father, and daughter against her mother, and daughter-in-law against her mother-in-law. (12:49, 51, 53)

Ah, Jerusalem, Jerusalem, who kills the prophets and stones the messengers sent to her! How many times have I wanted to gather your children together, like a hen gathers her chicks beneath her wings, and you were unwilling! Look, your house is abandoned! I say to you, you will not see me again until (the time) comes that you say, "Blessed is the one who comes in the name of the Lord." (13:34–35)

Most scholars of Q assume that these words refer to a day of reckoning, an apocalypse in which God will intervene in the course of human events to set things aright on behalf of the righteous. In chapter 17 of Q one finds a clustering of material that seems to refer explicitly to a coming apocalypse, in which the "Son of Man" will play a role:

If they should say to you, "Look, he is in the desert," do not go out (there). (Or) "Look, (he is) in the back room," don't follow. For as lightning comes out of the east and flashes to the west, so will the Son of Man be on his day. (17:23–24)

Like it happened in the days of Noah, so will it be on the day of the Son of Man. For, just like in those days, they were eating and drinking, marrying and giving in marriage, until the day when Noah entered the ark and the flood came and took everyone. Even so will it be on the day when the Son of Man is revealed. (17:26–27, 30)

These passages reveal another side to Q. The Q folk took care of one another and conveyed a radical ethic of shared resources and selfless giving. But they also proved divisive. They sought a radical social reversal. "The first shall be last, and the last first." And when others did not share that vision, they turned on them. They railed against their fellow Galileans, even their own families. They spoke a word of judgment and imagined an apocalyptic reckoning when the Son of Man, Jesus, would return like lightning to do what God once did with the flood. Some have wondered if the same Q folk who created those communities of radical care through sharing would also have called down fire and brimstone on their enemies. Well, why not? Utopian visionaries can certainly be both caring and vindictive.

But literary studies of Q have suggested that the Q folk were not initially given to such apocalyptic thoughts. At the heart of Q are a series of speeches—like the inaugural sermon that begins with the beatitudes in Q 6:20–49, the Mission Discourse in Q 10:2–12, and the speech on cares in Q 12:22–31—speeches that comprise, more or less, a series of wisdom teachings and advice on how to live in the new empire of God. The sayings of judgment often appear to be tacked onto these speeches—as with the curses against Chorazin, Bethsaida, and Capernaum appended to the end of the Mission Discourse. New Testament scholar John Kloppenborg has argued that Q likely began as a series of these speeches, the collected wisdom of the Q folk, so to speak. But as they began to experience rejection and persecution, they turned to the Jewish prophetic and apocalyptic tradition to give expression to their frustrations and hope for eventual vindication. This resulted in a second edition of Q, one in which sayings of judgment added a new, apocalyptic dimension to the collection. Others have argued that the original author of Q knew these speeches as stand-alone compositions and gathered them up into a new document (Q), now framed with elements of apocalyptic judgment.

However one imagines the literary history of Q, it is important to recognize that those who created and used this document were sectarians. Their message was not an easy one to accept, and they had little tolerance for those who did not receive it approvingly. Their radical ethos drove a wedge between them and the villages and families from which they came. They demanded loyalty. "Whoever is not with me is against me, and whoever isn't gathering with me is scattering" (11:23). The Q folk were radicals. They came not to "sow peace upon the earth . . . , but a sword" (12:49, 51). We should not imagine that they attracted a large following.

WHAT HAPPENED TO Q?

The people who composed and used Q do not appear as a distinct community in the annals of early Christianity. Q itself survived into the later years of the first century, when the authors of Matthew and Luke made use of it, but then we lose track of it. No one seems to have used it after Luke, no one mentions it, and, so far as we know, it did not survive intact as a document in its own right. So what happened to Q and those who created and used it?

We don't know. But there are theories. One is that when the Jews rebelled against Roman rule in the 60s CE, the Q folk, alongside many Jews living in the Galilee, were simply killed in the course of the war. Only their book, it seems, survived to be used by Matthew's and Luke's authors. Another theory is that sayings collections fell out of favor in early Christianity, because of their tendency to drift in unorthodox directions. This theory relies on the other text we shall introduce in this volume (Chapter 6), the *Gospel of Thomas*, and the perception that this sayings gospel has a Gnostic orientation. But regardless of how one appraises the *Gospel of Thomas*, it must be realized that sayings collections were very common in the philosophical world of antiquity and were used to express every conceivable religious and philosophical belief. Sayings collections were not necessarily unorthodox, heretical, or esoteric. More recently, James M. Robinson has made the commonsense suggestion that the Q folk were Jews who never came to understand themselves as a distinct, new religious movement. Their radical ethos was difficult to sustain and so, with the passage of time, they simply dissolved back into the Galilean social landscape with nothing to distinguish them from other Jews.

Although the Q folk did not survive as a distinct community or church, their text did. Thanks to an uncreative streak in the authors of Matthew and Luke, Q managed to survive submerged in the text of those gospels. Based on their use of Q, we believe that we can get a fairly clear idea of what was in this early sayings gospel. In recent years, scholars have labored to draw this text forth from the shadowy recesses of the gospels in which it was embedded, so that this once lost chapter of nascent Christianity can be studied and appreciated once again.

FOR FURTHER STUDY

For more on why it is **necessary to posit Q** to solve **the synoptic problem,** see John S. Kloppenborg, *Excavating Q: The History and Setting of the Sayings Gospel* (Minneapolis: Fortress, 2000), chap. 1, "Q and the Synoptic Problem"; and Christopher Tuckett, *Q and the History of Early Christianity* (London: Clark, 1996), chap. 1, "Introduction: The Existence of Q."

For **an argument against the necessity of Q**, one might consult Mark Goodacre, *The Case Against Q: Studies in Markan Priority and the Synoptic Problem* (Harrisburg, PA: Trinity, 2002).

On **the language that Jesus spoke** amid the other languages spoken in the first century in the Galilee, see John Meier, *A Marginal Jew: Rethinking the Historical Jesus,* vol. 1, *The Roots of the Problem and the Person* (New York: Doubleday, 1991), 255–68.

For more about the **Griesbach Hypothesis,** see the best known of the relatively few modern-day supporters, William R. Farmer, *The Synoptic Problem: A Critical Analysis* (New York: Macmillan, 1964).

For more about the **Markan Priority Without Q** theory, see Goodacre, *The Case Against Q.*

The process of recovering Q from the extant texts in Matthew and Luke is discussed in Kloppenborg, *Excavating Q,* chap. 2, "The Character and Reconstruction of Q."

The date of Q is a difficult question, and scholars vary widely in their estimates. Dale Allison argues that the earliest materials in Q date very soon after the death of Jesus (*The Jesus Tradition in Q* [Valley Forge, PA: Trinity International, 1997], 49–54). Paul Hoffmann, on the other hand, suggests a date near the end of the Judean revolt in about 70 CE ("The Redaction of Q and the Son of Man: A Preliminary Sketch," in Ronald Piper, ed., *The Gospel Behind the Gospels: Current Studies on Q* [Leiden: Brill, 1995], 159–98). For a discussion of the options and opinions, see Kloppenborg, *Excavating Q,* 80–87.

The **location of Q in the Galilee** is a common opinion among scholars. New weight was given to this theory by Jonathan Reed's studies on the geography reflected in Q. See, for example, "The Social Map of Q," in John Kloppenborg, ed., *Conflict and Intervention: Literary, Rhetorical, and Social Studies on the Sayings Gospel Q* (Valley Forge, PA: Trinity International, 1995), 17–36. See also Kloppenborg's discussion in *Excavating Q,* 171–75. Kloppenborg is also helpful in **reading Q in the Galilee**; see *Excavating Q,* 214–61. For general conditions in the Galilee during the first century, see Jonathan Reed, *Archaeology and the Galilean Jesus: A Reexamination of the Evidence* (London: Bloomsbury/Clark, 2002).

John Dominic Crossan's analysis of Q's Mission Discourse is found in *The Historical Jesus: The Life of a Mediterranean Jewish Peasant* (San Francisco: HarperSanFrancisco, 1991), 341–44.

The theory that **Q's judgment passages represent a relatively late stage** in Q's development is embraced variously among Q scholars. Dieter Lührmann thinks that an editor (or several) gathered up disparate wisdom sayings and apocalyptic pronouncements and created from them a document stressing the coming judgment against those who rejected Q's message; see *Die Redaktion der Logienquelle,* WMANT 33 (Neukirchen-Vluyn: Neukirchener Verlag, 1969). An excerpt of this work in English is "Q in the History of Early Christianity," in John Kloppenborg , ed., *The Shape of Q* (Minneapolis: Fortress, 1994), 59–74. Kloppenborg's own theory is more complex: Q unfolded in a series of editions, beginning with a collection of wisdom speeches (he calls this Q¹), which was later revised with the addition of apocalyptic materials announcing impending judgment (Q²); see *The Formation of Q: Trajectories in Ancient Wisdom Collections* (Philadelphia: Fortress, 1987). I find Kloppenborg's case to be compelling, though many scholars remain skeptical of such theories.

James M. Robinson's theory about the disappearance of the Q folk is in his essay, "First Century Christianities: Galilee," which is soon to be published in the journal *Forum.*

4

Q RECONSTRUCTED

The following reconstruction of Q is based on the parts of Matthew and Luke scholars believe were taken from Q. It was arrived at by the International Q Project (IQP) by comparing the Matthean and Lukan versions of these common texts and, on the basis of known patterns and habits found within them, surmising what their common Q source must have been. (For more on how scholars go about reconstructing Q texts, see the discussion in Chapter 3.) The IQP, comprising more than two dozen scholars, including myself, working as a team, has reconstructed the original Greek text of Q; I have created the following translation based upon it. The work of the IQP is readily available in James M. Robinson, Paul Hoffmann, and John S. Kloppenborg, eds., *The Sayings Gospel Q in Greek and English, with Parallels from the Gospels of Mark and Thomas* (Minneapolis: Fortress, 2002).

Because we don't have the original text of Q, and because we can well assume that Matthew and Luke did not in fact include every last word of Q, the reconstructed text is fragmentary. For this reason, I have labeled each discrete unit of the text as "Fragment 1," "Fragment 2," and so on. Sometimes the IQP has reconstructed the original Q text of a fragment with relative confidence; sometimes, however, portions of the original text were simply missing and had to be guessed at. Also, it sometimes happens that Q overlaps with Mark, making it difficult to know what comes from Q and what from Mark. In these cases of relative uncertainty I have set the text in *italics* to indicate a certain threshold of guesswork. Also, sometimes the Greek remnants of a Q text obviously need one or two additional words to make sense. These are supplied in parentheses to ease the experience of reading Q.

The order in which the extant fragments of Q originally stood in Q is somewhat uncertain. This is because the author of Matthew seems to have moved his Q material around to create a series of five lengthy speeches (like the Sermon on the Mount) to serve as the literary backbone of his story. Q scholars therefore generally refer to Q texts by their chapter and verse notation in Luke (thus, Q 3:2–3 = Luke 3:2–3; Matt. 3:1, 5). The IQP also generally followed the order of the fragments as they come up in Luke in establishing their text of Q. Occasionally, however, there are good reasons to suppose that in a particular case Matthew, rather than Luke, has preserved the original position of a fragment. This produces a few oddities like the fact that 17:33 precedes 14:34–35 and 15:4–5a follows 17:1–2. That is all to say, the convention of following the Lukan chapter and verse notation to refer to Q texts creates a useful system that looks like, but does not always act like, a conventional biblical chapter and verse notation system.

The Text of Q

Incipit [lost]
The Words of Jesus

Fragment 1
²John was *baptizing in the wilderness* ³*and people* from the whole region of the Jordan *came to him.*

Q 3:2–3 (Matt. 3:1, 5; Luke 3:2b–3a)

Fragment 2

⁷He said to the crowds that came to be baptized, "You brood of vipers! Who told you to run from the impending wrath? ⁸Therefore, bear fruit that is fitting of repentance and do not think you can say to yourselves, 'We have Abraham as our father.' For I say to you, God can raise up children of Abraham from out of these rocks! ⁹But already the ax lies at the root of the trees. Therefore, every tree that does not bear good fruit is to be chopped down and thrown into the fire."

Q 3:7–9 (Matt. 3:7–10; Luke 3:7–9)

Fragment 3

¹⁶"I baptize you in water, but the one who comes after me, whose sandals I am not fit to remove, is stronger than I. He will baptize you in a holy spirit and fire. ¹⁷His pitchfork is in his hand and he will clear his threshing floor and gather the wheat into his granary, but the chaff he will burn in an unquenchable fire."

Q 3:16–17 (Matt. 3:11–12; Luke 3:16–17)

Fragment 4

²¹*Now, when everyone was being baptized,* Jesus too came and was baptized. *And the* sky *opened* ²²and *the Holy Spirit descended* upon him *in the form of a dove. And a voice from the sky said, "This is my* son, *in whom I am delighted."*

Q 3:21–22 (Matt. 3:16–17; Luke 3:21–22)

Fragment 5

¹And Jesus was led into the wilderness by the Spirit ²to be tested by the devil. And *he ate nothing* for forty days, *after which* he was hungry. ³And the devil said to him "If you are a son of God, speak that these stones might become bread." ⁴And Jesus answered: "It is written that a person shall not live by bread alone."

⁹So the devil took him to Jerusalem and stood him on the pinnacle of the temple and said to him, "If you are a son of God, throw yourself down, ¹⁰for it is written that he will command his angels to surround you ¹¹and they will bear you upon their hands, lest you strike your foot against a stone." ¹²And Jesus said to him, "It is written, 'You shall not test the Lord your God.'"

⁵And the devil took him to a very high mountain and showed him all the empires of the world in all their glory ⁶and said to him, "All these things I will give to you if you will worship me." And Jesus said to him, "It is written, 'You shall worship the Lord your God and serve only him.'"

¹³Then the devil left him.

Q 4:1–4, 9–12, 5–8, 13 (Matt. 4:1–11; Luke 4:1–13)

Fragment 6

¹⁶*And Jesus returned to the region of* Nazareth, *his hometown, and there began to gather disciples.*

Q 4:16 (Matt. 4:13; Luke 4:16)

Fragment 7

²⁰And he opened his mouth and taught them, saying:

"Blessed are you beggars, for yours is the empire of God.

²¹"Blessed are you who hunger, for you shall be filled.

"Blessed are you who mourn, for you shall be comforted."

Q 6:20–21 (Matt. 5:1–4, 6; Luke 6:20–21)

Fragment 8

²²"Blessed are you when they insult and persecute you and utter every sort of evil against you because of the Son of Man. ²³Be glad and rejoice, for so they persecuted the prophets who came before you."

Q 6:22–23 (Matt. 5:11–12; Luke 6:22–23)

Fragment 9

[27]"Love your enemies [28]and pray for those who persecute you, [35]so that you may become sons of your Father, for he raises his sun on both the bad and the good and makes it rain on both the just and the unjust."

Q 6:27–28, 35 (Matt. 5:44–45; Luke 6:27–28, 35)

Fragment 10

[29]"Whoever strikes you on the cheek, turn to him the other as well. And to anyone who wants to take you to court to get your shirt, give him your coat as well. [30]Give to anyone who asks of you and do not ask for your things back from anyone who borrows from you."

Q 6:29–30 (Matt. 5:39–42; Luke 6:29–30)

Fragment 11

[31]"And just as you want people to treat you, treat them likewise."

Q 6:31 (Matt. 7:12; Luke 6:31)

Fragment 12

[32]"If you love those who love you, what reward do you have? Don't the tax collectors do the same thing? [34]And if you lend to those from whom you hope to receive, what reward do you have? Don't even the Gentiles do the same thing?"

Q 6:32, 34 (Matt. 5:46–47; Luke 6:32, 34)

Fragment 13

[36]"Be merciful, just as your Father is merciful."

Q 6:36 (Matt. 5:48; Luke 6:36)

Fragment 14

[37]"Do not judge, lest you be judged. For with the judgment you

give out, you will be judged. [38]And with the measure you give out, it will be measured out to you."

Q 6:37–38 (Matt. 7:1–2; Luke 6:37–38)

Fragment 15

[39]"Can the blind lead the blind? Won't they both fall into a pit?"

Q 6:39 (Matt. 15:14; Luke 6:39)

Fragment 16

[40]"The disciple is not above the teacher. It is enough for the disciple to become like his teacher."

Q 6:40 (Matt. 10:24–25; Luke 6:40)

Fragment 17

[41]"And why do you see the speck in your brother's eye, but fail to notice the beam that is in your own eye? [42]How do you say to your brother, 'Let me remove the speck from your eye,' and look, there is the beam in your own eye? Hypocrite, first take the beam out of your own eye, and then you will see clearly so as to remove the speck from your brother's eye."

Q 6:41–42 (Matt. 7:3–5; Luke 6:41–42)

Fragment 18

[43]"No good tree bears rotten fruit; neither does a rotten tree bear good fruit. [44]For the tree shall be known by its fruit. Are figs gathered from thorns or grapes from brambles? [45]The good person brings out good things from his good treasure, and the evil person evil things from his evil treasure. For the mouth speaks from the overflow of the heart."

Q 6:43–45 (Matt. 7:16, 18; 12:33–35; Luke 6:43–45)

Fragment 19

⁴⁶"Why do you call me 'Lord! Lord! and do not do what I say?"

Q 6:46 (Matt. 7:21; Luke 6:46)

Fragment 20

⁴⁷"Everyone who hears my sayings and does them ⁴⁸is like the person who built his house upon the rock. And the rain came down and the rivers rose and the winds blew and beat against that house, and it did not fall, for it was founded upon the rock. ⁴⁹And everyone who hears my sayings and does not do them is like a person who built his house upon the sand. And the rain came down and the rivers rose and the wind beat against that house, and immediately it collapsed, and its collapse was great."

Q 6:47–49 (Matt. 7:24–27; Luke 6:47–49)

Fragment 21

¹And it happened that when he had finished these sayings, he entered into Capernaum. ³A centurion came to him and begged him, saying, "My child is sick." And he says to him, "Shall *I* come and heal him?" ⁶And the centurion answered and said, "Lord, I am not worthy for you to come under my roof, ⁷but speak a word and let my child be healed. ⁸For I too am a person under authority, with soldiers under me, and I say to this one 'Go' and he goes and to another 'Come' and he comes, and to my slave, 'Do this' and he does it." ⁹And when Jesus heard this he was amazed and said to those who were following, "I say to you, Not even in Israel have I found such faith." ¹⁰*And when the centurion returned home he found the boy well.*

Q 7:1, 3, 6–10 (Matt. 7:28, 8:5–10, 13; Luke 7:1, 3, 6–10)

Fragment 22

¹⁸When John heard all these things he sent word to him through

his disciples [19]and said to him, "Are you the one who is to come, or shall we look forward to someone else?" [22]He replied and said to them, "Go and report to John the things you are hearing and seeing: blind people see again and lame people walk, leapers are cleansed and deaf people hear, and dead people are raised and poor people hear good news. [23]And blessed is the one who is not offended my me."

Q 7:18–19, 22–23 (Matt. 11:2–6; Luke 7:18–19, 22–23)

Fragment 23

[24]After these emissaries had gone, he began to talk to the crowds about John. "What did you go out into the wilderness to see? A reed shaken by the wind? [25]What then did you go out to see? A person all dressed up in fancy clothing? Look, those who dress in fancy clothing live in palaces. [26]What then did you go out to see? A prophet? Yes, I say to you, and even more than a prophet. [27]This is the one about whom it is written, 'Behold, I am sending a messenger ahead of you, who will prepare the way before you.' [28]I say to you, among those born of women, none has arisen who is greater than John. But the least person in the empire of God is greater than him."

Q 7:24–28 (Matt. 11:7–11; Luke 7:24–28)

Fragment 24

[29]*When the* tax collectors *and sinners who had been baptized by* John *heard this, they justified God,* [30]*but the Pharisees and the lawyers, who had not been baptized, rejected God's plan.*

Q 7:29–30 (Matt. 21:32; Luke 7:29–30)

Fragment 25

[31]*Jesus said to them,* "To what shall I compare this generation? What is it like? [32]It is like children sitting in the marketplaces calling to others, saying, 'We piped for you but you would not

dance, we wailed but you would not cry.' ³³For John came neither eating nor drinking, and you say he has a demon. ³⁴The Son of Man came eating and drinking and you say, look, a glutton and a drunkard, a friend of tax collectors and sinners. ³⁵Even so, Wisdom (Sophia) is justified by all her children."

Q 7:31–35 (Matt. 11:16–19; Luke 7:31–35)

Fragment 26

⁵⁷And a certain person said to him, "I will follow you wherever you go." ⁵⁸So Jesus said to him, "Foxes have dens and birds of the sky have nests, but a person has nowhere to lay his head." ⁵⁹But another said to him, "Lord, let me first go and bury my father." ⁶⁰And Jesus said to him, "Follow me, and leave the dead to bury their own dead."

Q 9:57–60 (Matt. 8:19–22; Luke 9:57–60)

Fragment 27

²He says to his disciples, "The harvest is plentiful, but the workers are few. So ask the lord of the harvest to send out workers into his harvest."

Q 10:2 (Matt. 9:37–38; Luke 10:2)

Fragment 28

³"Go. Look, I am sending you out like sheep in the midst of wolves."

Q 10:3 (Matt. 10:16; Luke 10:3)

Fragment 29

⁴"Carry no bag, no pack, no shoes, no staff and greet no one on the road."

Q 10:4 (Matt. 10:9–10; Luke 10:4)

Fragment 30

⁵"As for any house you might enter, first say 'Peace to this house!' ⁶And if a child of peace is there, let your peace come upon him. But if not, let your peace return to you. ⁷And stay at that house, eating and drinking whatever they offer, for the worker is worthy of his reward. (Do not move from house to house.) ⁸And whenever you enter a town and they take you in, eat what is set before you ⁹and care for the sick there and say to them, 'The empire of God has come to you.'"

Q 10:5–9 (Matt. 10:7–8, 10–13; Luke 10:5–9)

Fragment 31

¹⁰"As for any town you might enter that does not receive you, as you are leaving that town, ¹¹shake the dust from your feet. ¹²I say to you, on that day Sodom will fare better than that town."

Q 10:10–12 (Matt. 10:14–15; Luke 10:10–12)

Fragment 32

¹³Woe to you, Chorazin! Woe to you, Bethsaida! For if the miracles that happened in you had been done in Tyre and Sidon, they would have changed long ago, in sackcloth and ashes. ¹⁴Indeed, Tyre and Sidon will fare better than you in the judgment. ¹⁵And you, Capernaum, will you be exalted unto heaven? You'll go straight to Hades!"

Q 10:13–15 (Matt. 11:21–24; Luke 10:13–15)

Fragment 33

¹⁶"Whoever accepts you accepts me, and whoever accepts me accepts the one who sent me."

Q 10:16 (Matt. 10:40; Luke 10:16)

Fragment 34

²¹Then he said, "I bless you, Father, Lord of heaven and earth,

for you have hidden these things from sages and scholars and revealed them to babes. Yes, Father, for this is what seemed right to you."

Q 10:21 (Matt. 11:25–26; Luke 10:21)

Fragment 35

[22]"All things have been entrusted me by my Father. And no one knows the son except the Father, and none the Father except the son, and anyone to whom the son wishes to reveal (him)."

Q 10:22 (Matt. 11:27; Luke 10:22)

Fragment 36

[23]"Blessed are the eyes that see what you see. [24]For I say to you, many prophets and kings have wanted to see what you see, but never saw (them), and to hear what you hear and never heard (them)."

Q 10:23–24 (Matt. 13:16–17; Luke 10:23–24)

Fragment 37 (The Lord's Prayer)

[2]"Father—Holy be Your name!—may your empire come.
[3]Give us each day our daily bread;
[4]And forgive us our debts, for we also have forgiven our debtors.
And lead us not into trial."

Q 11:2–4 (Matt. 6:9–13; Luke 11:2–4)

Fragment 38

[9]"I say to you: Ask and it shall be given to you, seek and you shall find, knock and it shall be opened to you. [10]For everyone who asks receives, and anyone who searches finds, and to the one who knocks it shall be opened. [11]What person is there among you who would offer a stone when his child asks for bread? [12]Or offer him a snake when he asks for a fish? [13]There-

fore, if you who are evil know how to give good gifts to your children, how much more will your Father in heaven give good things to those who ask him?"

Q 11:9–13 (Matt. 7:7–11; Luke 11:9–13)

Fragment 39

¹⁴And he exorcized a "mute" demon. And when the demon had been exorcized, the mute person spoke. And the crowds were amazed. ¹⁵But someone said, "He exorcizes demons in (the name of) Beelzebul, the ruler of the demons." ¹⁷But he knew what they were thinking and said to them, "Every empire that is divided against itself is laid waste, and every household that is divided against itself will not stand. ¹⁸And if Satan is divided against himself, how shall his empire stand? ¹⁹And if I exorcize demons in (the name of) Beelzebul, in (whose name) do your sons exorcize? For this reason they shall be your judges. ²⁰But if it is by the finger of God that I exorcize demons, then the empire of God has come upon you."

Q 11:14–15, 17–20 (Matt. 9:32–34; 12:25–28; Luke 11:14–15, 17–20)

Fragment 40

²¹*"A strong person's house cannot be looted. ²²But if someone stronger overpowers him, then he does get looted."*

Q 11:21–22 (Matt. 12:29; Luke 11:21–22)

Fragment 41

²³"Whoever is not with me is against me, and whoever isn't gathering with me is scattering."

Q 11:23 (Matt. 12:30; Luke 11:23)

Fragment 42

²⁴"When an unclean spirit has left a person, it wanders through arid places looking for a place to rest and it finds none. Then

it says, 'I will return to my home, where I came from.' ²⁵And it goes and finds it. When it has swept and cleaned up, ²⁶it then goes and invites seven other spirits more evil than itself, who enter and settle in there (too). So in the end things are worse for that person than they were before."

Q 11:24–26 (Matt. 12:43–45; Luke 11:24–26)

Fragment 43

²⁷*And it happened that a woman in the crowd raised her voice and said to him, "Blessed is the womb that bore you and the breasts that you suckled!"* ²⁸*But he said to her, "No, blessed are those who hear the word of God and keep it."*

Q 11:27–28 (Luke 11:27–28)

Fragment 44

¹⁶And some people sought a sign from him, ²⁹but he said, "This generation is an evil generation. It seeks a sign, and no sign will be shown it, except the sign of Jonah. ³⁰For just as Jonah became a sign to the Ninevites, so will the Son of Man be to this generation."

Q 11:16, 29–30 (Matt. 12:38–40; Luke 11:16, 29–30)

Fragment 45

³¹"The Queen of the South will be raised in the judgment with this generation and condemn it, for she came from the ends of the earth to listen to the wisdom of Solomon, and look, something better than Solomon is here! ³²Ninevite men will arise in the judgment with this generation and condemn it, for they changed at the preaching of Jonah, and look, something better than Jonah is here!"

Q 11:31–32 (Matt. 12:41–42; Luke 11:31–32)

Fragment 46

[33]"No one lights a lamp and puts it in a hidden place, but on a lamp stand, and it provides light to everyone in the house."

Q 11:33 (Matt. 5:15; Luke 11:33)

Fragment 47

[34]"The eye is the lamp of the body. If your eye is generous, your whole body is luminous; but if your eye is evil, your whole body is dark. [35]Therefore, if the light that is in you is dark, how great is the darkness!"

Q 11:34–35 (Matt. 6:22–23; Luke 11:34–35)

Fragment 48

[39a]*And Jesus said to the Pharisees,* [42]"Woe to you, Pharisees, for you tithe mint and dill and cumin and have given up on judgment, mercy, and faithfulness. But it was necessary to do these former things without giving up on the latter.

[39b]"Woe to you, Pharisees, for you cleanse the outside of the cup and dish, but inside they are full from plunder and spoil. [41]Cleanse the inside of the cup and its exterior will be clean (enough).

[43]"Woe to you, Pharisees, for you love the first couch at banquets and the first seat in the synagogue and greetings in the marketplace.

[44]"Woe to you, Pharisees, for you are like forgotten tombs, and people who walk on them don't know it."

Q 11:39a, 42, 39b, 41, 43–44
(Matt. 23:1–2a, 6–7, 23, 25, 26b–27; Luke 11:39, 41–44)

Fragment 49

[46b]"And woe to you interpreters of the Law, for you bind burdens and load them onto peoples' backs, but you yourselves would not lift a finger to move them.

[52]"Woe to you interpreters of the Law, for you close (the doors) of the empire of God in peoples' faces; you did not enter, nor would you allow those who would enter to do so.

[47]"Woe to you, for you build the tombs of the prophets, but your forebears killed them.

[48]"You bear witness that you are (indeed) your forebears' descendants."

> Q 11:46b, 52, 47–48 (Matt. 23:4, 13, 29–32; Luke 11:46b–48, 52)

Fragment 50

[49]Because of this Wisdom also said, "I will send them prophets and sages, and some of them they will kill and persecute, [50]so that the blood of all the prophets that has been spilled from the foundation of the world (until now) will be required from this generation— [51]from the blood of Abel to the blood of Zechariah, murdered between the altar and the temple—yes, I say to you, it will be required from this generation!"

> Q 11:49–51 (Matt. 23:34–36; Luke 11:49–51)

Fragment 51

[2]"Nothing is covered up that will not be revealed, or hidden that will be not be made known. [3]That which I say to you in the dark, speak it in the light, and that which you hear with your ear, preach it on the housetops."

> Q 12:2–3 (Matt. 10:26–27; Luke 12:2–3)

Fragment 52

[4]"And do not fear those who kill the body, but cannot kill the soul. [5]Rather, fear the one who can destroy both the body and the soul in Gehenna!"

> Q 12:4–5 (Matt. 10:28; Luke 12:4–5)

Fragment 53

⁶"Aren't five sparrows sold for two pennies? And not one of them will fall to the ground without your Father's consent. ⁷As for you, every single hair on your head has been numbered. Fear not—you are worth more than many sparrows."

Q 12:6–7 (Matt. 10:29–31; Luke 12:6–7)

Fragment 54

⁸"Anyone who speaks up for me before people, ⁹the Son of Man will also speak for him before the angels."

Q 12:8–9 (Matt. 10:32–33; Luke 12:8–9)

Fragment 55

¹⁰"Whoever speaks a word against the Son of Man, it will be forgiven him; but whoever speaks against the Holy Spirit, it will not be forgiven him."

Q 12:10 (Matt. 12:32a–b; Luke 12:10)

Fragment 56

¹¹"When they haul you before the synagogues, don't worry about how or what to say. ¹²For the Holy Spirit will give you something to say when the time comes."

Q 12:11–12 (Matt. 10:19; Luke 12:11–12)

Fragment 57

³³"Do not store up for yourselves treasures on earth, where moth and consumption destroy and thieves break in and steal. But store up for yourselves treasures in heaven, where neither moth nor consumption destroys and thieves do not break in and steal. ³⁴For where your treasure is, there will your heart be also."

Q 12:33–34 (Mat 6:19–21; Luke 12:33–34)

Fragment 58

²²ᵇTherefore I say to you, "Do not worry about your life, what
you will eat, nor about your body, what you will wear. ²³Isn't
life more than food and the body more than clothing? ²⁴Think
about the ravens: they neither sow nor reap nor gather into
barns, and yet God feeds them. Aren't you more valuable than
the birds? ²⁵But who among you can add (even) a cubit to his
height by worrying? ²⁶And why do you worry about clothes?
²⁷Study the lilies, how they grow: they do not work, nor do they
spin. But I say to you, not even Solomon in all his glory was
arrayed like one of these. ²⁸But if God so clothes the grass in
the field, which is here today and tomorrow thrown into the
oven, how much more (will he clothe) you, you people of little
faith! ²⁹Therefore, do not worry, saying, 'What will we eat?' or
'What will we drink?' or 'What will we wear?' ³⁰For the Gentiles
pursue all these things. Your Father knows that you need all
these things. ³¹But seek his empire and all these things will be
provided to you."

Q 12:22b–31 (Matt. 6:25–33; Luke 12:22b–31)

Fragment 59

³⁹"But know this: If the householder had known in which hour
of the night the thief was coming, he would not have allowed
his house to be broken into. ⁴⁰You too get ready, because the
Son of Man is coming at a time you don't expect."

Q 12:39–40 (Matt. 24:43–44; Luke 12:39–40)

Fragment 60

⁴²"Who, then, is the trustworthy and wise slave, whom the master
sets over his household to distribute the food at the appointed
time? ⁴³Blessed is that slave whom the master finds doing this
when he comes. ⁴⁴Truly I say to you, he will set him over his
whole estate. ⁴⁵But if that slave should say to himself, 'My mas-

ter is delayed' and begin to beat his fellow slaves, (and) eat and drink with the drunkards, [46]the master of that slave will come on a day he does not expect and at a time he does not know, and he will cut him down and give him his due with the unfaithful."

Q 12:42–46 (Matt. 24:45–51; Luke 12:42–46)

Fragment 61

[49]*"I have come to sow fire upon the earth, and how I wish that it were already ablaze! Do you think that I have come to sow peace upon the earth?* [51]I have not come to sow peace, but a sword! [53]For I have come to divide son against father, and daughter against her mother, and daughter-in-law against her mother-in-law."

Q 12:49, 51, 53 (Matt. 10:34–35; Luke 12:49, 51, 53)

Fragment 62

[54]*He said to them,* "When evening has come you say, 'This bodes well, for the sky is red!' [55]And in the morning (you say), 'Today will be cold, for the glowering sky is red!' [56]You know how to read the sky, but you cannot read the times."

Q 12:54–56 (Matt. 16:2–3; Luke 12:54–56)

Fragment 63

[58]"When you are on your way (to the authorities) with your accuser, make an effort to get away from him, lest he turn you over to the judge, and the judge to the assistant, and he will throw you into prison. [59]I say to you, you'll never get out of there until you pay every last cent."

Q 12:58–59 (Matt. 5:25–26; Luke 12:58–59)

Fragment 64

[18]"What is the empire of God like and to what shall I compare it? [19]It is like a mustard seed, which a person took and threw

into his garden. And it grew and became a tree, and the birds of the sky nested in its branches."

Q 13:18–19 (Matt. 13:31–32; Luke 13:18–19)

Fragment 65

[20]"And again, to what shall I compare the empire of God? [21]It is like yeast, which a woman took and hid in three measures of flour until the whole batch was leavened."

Q 13:20–21 (Matt. 13:33; Luke 13:20–21)

Fragment 66

[24]"Enter through the narrow door, for many will try to enter but those who (actually) go in by this way are few in number. [25]When the householder has gotten up and barred the door, and you stand outside and start to knock, saying, 'Master, open up for us,' and he will answer you by saying, 'I don't know you!' [26]then you will start to say, 'We ate and drank in your company and you taught in our streets!' [27]And he will speak to you saying, 'I don't know you! Leave me alone, you criminals!'"

Q 13:24–27 (Matt. 7:13–14, 22–23; 25:10–12; Luke 13:24–27)

Fragment 67

[28]"Many will come from the east and the west and dine [29]with Abraham and Isaac and Jacob in the empire of God, but you will be cast out into the outer darkness, where there will be wailing and gnashing of teeth."

Q 13:28, 29 (Matt. 8:11–12; Luke 13:28–29)

Fragment 68

[30]"The last will be first, and the first last."

Q 13:30 (Matt. 20:16; Luke 13:30)

Fragment 69

³⁴"Ah, Jerusalem, Jerusalem, who kills the prophets and stones the messengers sent to her! How many times have I wanted to gather your children together, like a hen gathers her chicks beneath her wings, and you were unwilling! ³⁵Look, your house is abandoned! I say to you, you will not see me again until (the time) comes that you say, 'Blessed is the one who comes in the name of the Lord.'"

Q 13:34–35 (Matt. 23:37–39; Luke 13:34–35)

Fragment 70

¹¹"Anyone who promotes himself will be humbled, and anyone who humbles himself will be promoted."

Q 14:11 (Matt. 23:12; Luke 14:11)

Fragment 71

¹⁶"A certain person prepared a great banquet and invited many (guests). ¹⁷And at the appointed time for the banquet he sent his slave to say to the invited guests, 'Come, for it is already prepared!' ¹⁸*But one declined in order to tend to his farm.* ¹⁹*And another declined in order to tend to his business.* ²⁰*And another declined because he was newly married.* ²¹So the slave *reported* these things to his master. Then the householder became angry and said to the slave, ²³'Go out on the roads and invite whomever you find, so that my house might be filled!'"

Q 14:16–21, 23 (Matt. 22:2–10; Luke 14:16–21, 23)

Fragment 72

²⁶"Anyone who does not hate father and mother cannot be my disciple; and anyone who does not hate son and daughter cannot be my disciple."

Q 14:26 (Matt. 10:37; Luke 14:26)

Fragment 73

[27]"Anyone who does not take up his cross and follow me cannot be my disciple."

Q 14:27 (Matt. 10:38; Luke 14:27)

Fragment 74

[33]"Whoever finds his life will lose it, and whoever loses his life for my sake will find it."

Q 17:33 (Matt. 10:39; Luke 17:33)

Fragment 75

[34]"Salt is good, but if salt is made to lose its flavor, how will it be seasoned? [35]It is fit neither for the earth nor the manure pile, (so) they throw it out."

Q 14:34–35 (Matt. 5:13; Luke 14:34–35)

Fragment 76

[13]"No one can serve two masters, for he will hate the one and love the other or attend the one and disregard the other. You cannot serve both God and riches."

Q 16:13 (Matt. 6:24; Luke 16:13)

Fragment 77

[16]"The Law and the Prophets lasted until John. Since then the empire of God has been under attack and the attackers are plundering it."

Q 16:16 (Matt. 11:12–13; Luke 16:16)

Fragment 78

[17]"But it is easier for heaven and earth to pass away than for one iota or one serif of the Law to fall."

Q 16:17 (Matt. 5:18; Luke 16:17)

Fragment 79

[18]"Everyone who divorces his wife and (re)marries commits adultery, and whoever marries a woman who is divorced commits adultery."

Q 16:18 (Matt. 5:32; Luke 16:18)

Fragment 80

[1]"Traps will inevitably come along, but woe to the one through whom they come. [2]It will be better for him if a millstone is put around his neck and he is thrown into the sea than that he should set a trap for one of these little ones."

Q 17:1–2 (Matt. 18:7, 6; Luke 17:1–2)

Fragment 81

[4]"What man among you, if he had a hundred sheep and lost one of them, would not leave the ninety-nine in the mountains and go and look for the one that is lost. [5a]And if he should happen to find it, [7]I say to you, he celebrates more over it than the ninety-nine that had not wandered off."

Q 15:4–5, 7 (Matt. 18:12–13; Luke 15:4–5, 7)

Fragment 82

[8]"Or, what woman who has ten drachmas, if she should lose one drachma, does not light a lamp, sweep the house, and search until she finds (it)? [9]And when she finds (it), she summons her friends and neighbors, saying, 'Celebrate with me, because I have found the drachma that I lost!' [10]Just so, I say to you, there is joy before the angels over one sinner who repents."

Q 15:8–10 (Luke 15:8–10)

Fragment 83

[3]"If your brother wrongs you, scold him; and if he apologizes,

forgive him. [4]Even if he wrongs you seven times in a day, you shall forgive him seven times."

Q 17:3–4 (Matt. 18:15, 21; Luke 17:3–4)

Fragment 84

[6]"If you had faith like a mustard seed, you would say to this mulberry bush, 'Be uprooted and replanted in the sea!' and it would obey you."

Q 17:6 (Matt. 17:20b; Luke 17:6)

Fragment 85

[20]*But when he was asked when the empire of God is coming, he answered them and said, "The empire of God is not coming with signs. [21]Nor will anyone say, 'Look, here!' or 'There!' For, look! The empire of God is in the midst of you!"*

Q 17:20–21 (Matt. 24:23; Luke 17:20–21)

Fragment 86

[23]"If they should say to you, 'Look, he is in the desert,' do not go out (there). (Or) 'Look, (he is) in the back room,' don't follow. [24]For as lightning comes out of the east and flashes to the west, so will the Son of Man be on his day."

Q 17:23–24 (Matt. 24:26–27; Luke 17:23–24)

Fragment 87

[34]"Where the corpse (is), there the eagles will gather."

Q 17:37 (Matt. 24:28; Luke 17:37)

Fragment 88

[26]"As it happened in the days of Noah, so will it be on the day of the Son of Man. [27]For, just as in those days, they were eating and drinking, marrying and giving in marriage, until the day

when Noah entered the ark and the flood came and took everyone. [30]Even so will it be on the day when the Son of Man is revealed."

Q 17:26–27 (28–29?), 30 (Matt. 24:37–39; Luke 17:26–30)

Fragment 89

[34]"I say to you, there will be two (men) in the field, one is taken and one is left. [35]Two (women) will be grinding at the mill, one is taken and one is left."

Q 17:34–35 (Matt. 24:40–41; Luke 17:34–35)

Fragment 90

[12]"A certain person, when he was about to take a trip, [13]called ten of his own slaves, gave them ten minas, and told them, 'Make yourselves useful until I come (back).' [15]After a long while the master of those slaves comes (back) and settles up with them. [16]The first came and said, 'Master, your mina has earned ten more minas.' [17]And he said to him, 'Excellent, good slave! (Since) you have been trustworthy over a little, I will put you in charge of much.' [18]And the second came and said, 'Master, your mina has earned five more minas.' [19]He said to him, 'Excellent, good slave! (Since) you have been trustworthy over a little, I will put you in charge of much.' [20]And the other one came and said, [21]'Master, since I knew that you are a hard man, reaping what you did not sow and gathering where you did not winnow, I was afraid and went away and buried your mina in the ground. Here, you have what is yours.' [22]He says to him, 'You evil slave! You knew that I reap what I did not sow and gather where I did not winnow! [23]So you should have invested my money with the moneylenders, so that when I came (back) I would have received back what is mine with interest. [24]Therefore, take the mina from him and give it to

the one who has ten minas.' ²⁶For to all who have, it will be given, and from he who does not have, even that which he has will be taken from him."

Q 19:12–13, 15–24, 26

(Matt. 25:14–15b, 19–29; Luke 19:12–13, 15–24, 26)

Fragment 91

²⁸"You who have followed me ³⁰will sit upon thrones judging the twelve tribes of Israel."

Q 22:28, 30 (Matt. 19:28; Luke 22:28, 30)

FOR FURTHER STUDY

Since there is not yet a standard translation of Q, comparing different efforts to render Q into English is often helpful. The following reflect reliable scholarly efforts.

Burton L. Mack, *The Lost Gospel: The Book of Q and Christian Origins* (San Francisco: HarperSanFrancisco, 1993), 71–102. Mack created this translation before the IQP critical text was available. He used his own reconstruction based on John Kloppenborg, *Q Parallels* (Sonoma, CA: Polebridge, 1987). He actually produces two versions of Q here, "The Original Book of Q" and "The Complete Book of Q," the former reflecting Kloppenborg's theory about an early edition of Q lacking the materials announcing apocalyptic judgment (see Chapter 2, For Further Study).

James M. Robinson, Paul Hoffmann, and John S. Kloppenborg, eds., *The Sayings Gospel Q in Greek and English, with Parallels from the Gospels of Mark and Thomas* (Minneapolis: Fortress, 2002). This is the source of the Greek text I used in this translation. The IQP offers its own translation in this volume.

Richard Valantasis, *The New Q: A Fresh Translation with Commentary* (London: Clark, 2005). Valantasis also used the Greek text of the IQP to create this lively colloquial translation.

Robert J. Miller, ed., *The Complete Gospels,* 4th rev. ed. (Salem, OR: Polebridge, 2010), 257–83. This translation was prepared for the Scholars Version Project sponsored by the Westar Institute and Polebridge Press. It is also based on the IQP text. Earlier editions of *The Complete Gospels* present Q texts from Matthew and Luke in parallel columns; this edition offers a single translation. It was prepared by Arland Jacobson, a noted Q scholar.

5

PLATO'S GOSPEL

When the *Gospel of Thomas* was rediscovered fifty years ago, it was as though a ghost had returned from the grave. What secrets of the past might it reveal to the living? Might it hold the real truth about what happened in the misty beginnings of Christianity? One could hardly blame a young scholar like Jean Doresse if his heart began to race just a little as he sat down in a small room in the Coptic Museum in Cairo in 1948 to read, perhaps for the first time in more than a thousand years, the arresting opening lines of this long-lost text:

> These are the secret sayings that the living Jesus spoke and Didymos Judas Thomas wrote them down.

The *Gospel of Thomas* begins with these enigmatic words. We call this the text's *incipit,* which means simply the "beginning." But ancient authors poured much into their opening lines. In antiquity a text was often known simply by its *incipit.* This text would perhaps have been known originally as "The Secret Sayings of the Living Jesus." If scholars were ever to learn what the *Gospel of Thomas* had to teach us about Jesus and the origins of Christianity, they would have to understand what its author might have meant by these mysterious opening words.

SECRET SAYINGS

To find a collection of *sayings* would not have been surprising in the ancient world. As we have already seen, it was common for students to collect the notable sayings of great teachers and sages and to arrange them into a list. This is what the *Gospel of Thomas* is, a list of sayings of the great teacher Jesus. According to the current conventional division and enumeration of the sayings, there are 114 of them. Their arrangement is uncomplicated. Sometimes clusters of sayings elaborate upon a theme. But usually one saying follows after another based upon a simple catchword association—a word in saying A calls to mind a similar word in saying B; a word in saying B to a similar word in saying C; and so forth. It is a very simple form, rooted in the predominantly oral culture from which the *Gospel of Thomas* comes. Lists like this would have been used by students to learn by rote the teachings of their master. Historically this form, or genre, is associated especially with ancient Near Eastern wisdom theology, as seen for example in the biblical book of Proverbs. Greek and Roman philosophical schools also collected sayings and anecdotes of their great teachers, like Epictetus, Epicurus, or Diogenes. Whoever created this collection would have revered Jesus as just such a great teacher.

Our *incipit* calls these sayings the "secret" sayings of Jesus. As hard as it may be to imagine, scholars don't really know yet what to make of this. Early Christians were no strangers to the idea of secret teachings. In the letter known as 1 Corinthians, the apostle Paul writes of wisdom teaching that is "secret and hidden, which God decreed before the ages for our glory" (2:6–7). This secret teaching is intended, he says, only for the "mature" and "spiritual"; it is not for ordinary

FIGURE 9. THE ROMAN EAST

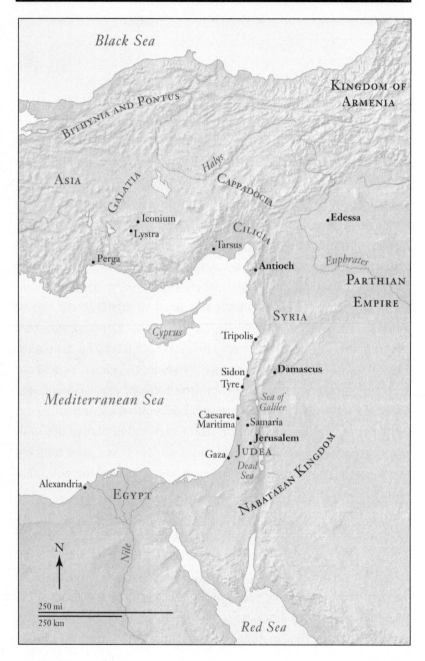

Black Sea

KINGDOM OF
ARMENIA

BITHYNIA AND PONTUS

ASIA

GALATIA

Halys

CAPPADOCIA

•Iconium
•Lystra

CILICIA

•Tarsus

•Perga

•**Edessa**

•**Antioch**

Euphrates

PARTHIAN
EMPIRE

SYRIA

Cyprus

Tripolis•

Mediterranean Sea

Sidon•
Tyre•

•**Damascus**

*Sea of
Galilee*

Caesarea
Maritima

•Samaria

•**Jerusalem**

Gaza• JUDEA

*Dead
Sea*

NABATAEAN KINGDOM

Alexandria•

EGYPT

N

Nile

250 mi

250 km

Red Sea

believers. And in the Gospel of Mark Jesus is given to say that the parables were intended only for the inner circle of Jesus's followers, lest outsiders hear them, turn, and be forgiven (4:12).

Later we encounter entire tracts bearing titles like the *Apocryphon of James* and the *Apocryphon of John*—*apocryphon* means "secret teaching." We can only surmise that in calling these sayings "secret" our author intended only to add mystery and value to his collection and to raise the expectations of readers. He might have thought of them as advanced teachings, intended—as Paul said of his secret wisdom—only for the spiritually mature. And if people should read and understand these secret sayings? Saying 1 promises that they "will not taste death."

DIDYMOS JUDAS THOMAS

Who was the author? We don't really know, but this is not unusual. Most early Christian texts were written anonymously or pseudonymously. This is probably the case with the *Gospel of Thomas* as well. Still, sometimes the pseudonyms attached to texts can tell us much about them. Today we commonly call this text the *Gospel According to Thomas*. That is because a title placed at the end of the text in the Nag Hammadi Library says this. But this title was added late, and it does not exactly square with the *incipit* of the gospel. The *incipit* identifies the author as Didymos Judas Thomas. In the Greek fragments from Oxyrhynchus there is a simpler version of this name: Judas Thomas. Who was Didymos Judas Thomas or Judas Thomas, as he was called at Oxyrhynchus?

There was, of course, a very famous apostle named Judas—Judas Iscariot, who betrayed Jesus. Surprisingly, scholars have recently identified another early gospel attributed to this infamous Judas, but this is not the Judas of our *incipit*. There is also a famous apostle named Thomas, sometimes known as the "doubting Thomas." This is the apostle who refused to believe that Jesus had been raised from the dead until he could see for himself and "place [his] finger in the mark of the nails in his hands" (John 20:25). Many scholars think that this is indeed the supposed author of our gospel. But they are wrong.

Judas Thomas was neither Judas Iscariot nor "doubting Thomas." He was the patron apostle of Edessa, an ancient city that lay east of the Euphrates River in eastern Syria. Today it is the modern city of Urfa in far eastern Turkey. The name Judas Thomas appears in several texts associated with this region, including the *Acts of Thomas* and the *Book of Thomas*. He is also central to the legend of how Christianity came to Edessa in the first place. According to the ancient church historian Eusebius, King Abgar of Edessa once wrote to Jesus asking him to come to his kingdom to bring healing to the sick among his people. Jesus replied—by a letter Eusebius claims to have seen in the archives of Edessa—that he could not come, but that he would send a disciple. After Jesus's death, Eusebius says that Judas Thomas made good on this promise by sending the apostle Thaddaeus, who healed the sick of Edessa and evangelized the city (*Ecclesiastical History* 1.13.1–22). But the Edessenes knew another version of this story. In the fourth century a Gallic pilgrim named Egeria traveled to Edessa and found there the tomb of Judas Thomas, who, according to the Edessenes, had himself been sent to them by the Lord after his ascension (*The Travels of Egeria* 17.1). This must be why Judas Thomas is so closely associated with texts from this region: he was its patron saint and his bones were venerated there for generations.

So who did the Christians of Edessa think Judas Thomas was? In addition to Judas Iscariot, who betrayed Jesus, there was apparently another apostle named Judas. In John 14:22 he is referred to as "Judas, not Iscariot," to distinguish him from the infamous apostle with whom he shared a name. The author of Luke also knew of this other Judas. He refers to him as "Judas of James" (Luke 6:16; Acts 1:13), again, to distinguish him from Judas Iscariot, who betrayed Jesus. The Letter of Jude is also attributed to this apostle—there he is identified as the brother of James (1:1), which is what Luke must have meant by calling him "Judas of James."

In any event, there were two apostles named Judas, Judas Iscariot and "Judas, not Iscariot." Now, in Syriac translations of John 14:22 "Judas, not Iscariot" is called "Judas Thomas." This is who Judas Thomas was to the Edessenes—the other Judas, "Judas, not Iscariot." Why is he called Judas *Thomas*? In the *Acts of Thomas* 31 and 39 he is called the "Twin of the Christ." And in the same work Jesus appears in the guise of Judas and says to his charges: "I am not Judas, but I am the brother of Judas" (*Acts of Thomas* 11). Among the Christians of eastern Syria Judas Thomas was apparently thought of as the twin brother of Jesus. This is why he is called Judas *Thomas*. *Thoma* is the Semitic word for "twin" in various dialects. *Didymos* is its Greek equivalent. The *Gospel of Thomas* ought rightly to be called the "Gospel of Judas the Twin."

But did Jesus have a twin brother named Judas? Historically this would be hard to say. But according to the Gospel of Mark he did indeed have a brother named Judas. In Mark 6:3 the people of Nazareth are said to have expressed great astonishment that Jesus, a local boy, could be stirring up so much dust: "Is this not the carpenter," they ask, "the son of Mary and the brother of James and Joses and *Judas* and Simon, and aren't his sisters here with us? And they were offended by him." So, according to this tradition, Jesus did indeed have a brother named Judas. He also had a brother named James. Later James became a prominent leader in the Jesus community in Jerusalem and acquired the nickname "James the Just." Now, it just so happens that this character also shows up in our gospel. Saying 12 of the *Gospel of Thomas* reads like this:

> The disciples said to Jesus, "We know that you will depart from us. Who is to become preeminent among us?"
> Jesus said to them, "Wherever you have come from, you are to go to *James the Just*, the one for whom heaven and earth came into being."

Somehow this gospel came to be associated with Judas Thomas and James the Just, both of whom were said to be brothers of Jesus. There is a story here, but no one yet knows exactly how to tell it. Was our *Gospel of Thomas* originally the gospel of Jesus's own family? Was there a post-Jesus "caliphate" that carried on the Jesus tradition in Jerusalem and later in Edessa? Perhaps. In any event, what we may gather from these names is that the so-called *Gospel of Thomas* was not originally attributed to the apostle Thomas, but to another apostle, Judas Thomas. This *other* Judas was thought to be the twin brother of Jesus. Since the name Judas Thomas was associated especially with Edessa, in eastern Syria, most scholars today assume that the "Gospel of Judas Thomas" was in its present form an Edessene gospel. At some point it may also have been associated with the Jesus followers in Jerusalem, where James the Just was a leader.

EDESSA

What do we know about Edessa? Not very much, it turns out. As noted already, Edessa was a city of eastern Syria, what is now far eastern Turkey. To get there travelers would have headed east out of Antioch, followed the old Silk Road across the Syrian desert, crossed the Euphrates River at the ancient city of Zeugma, and then continued east another day or so into Mesopotamia—"the land between the rivers"—at last to arrive at Edessa. Edessa was a caravan town, an oasis not only on the east–west route connecting the Mediterranean basin with India and China far to the east, but also on a north–south route connecting Armenia in the north with Egypt to the south. Jews had been living in Mesopotamia from the sixth century BCE, when Nebuchadnezzar II forced thousands of Jews to leave Jerusalem and go into exile in Babylon. By Roman times the Jewish communities in these desert cities would have been centuries old and well established. Adiabene, farther east, beyond the Tigris River, enjoyed a series of Jewish kings and queens at about this time. In Edessa, Jews seem to have blended into the multicultural cityscape to become part of the busy ebb and flow of life in this crossroads town.

What is perhaps most important about Edessa, however, is the fact that it lay outside the boundaries of the Roman Empire. In 214 CE the emperor Caracalla made Edessa a Roman colony. But before that the Euphrates River was the eastern frontier of the Roman Empire. Farther to the east was Parthia, Rome's imperial rival. Edessa lay in a broad, desolate buffer zone between these two great powers. Occasionally it was asked to take sides, but for most of its history, Edessa was allowed to carry on its life as a commercial crossroads without harassment. This, as we shall see, made quite a lot of difference to the Jesus followers who came to dwell there sometime in the latter half of the first century. Most other early centers of Christian activity were located in the Roman Empire. In that setting, the followers of the crucified messiah were necessarily dissidents, resisters against an empire that had executed their hero, Jesus. But in Edessa this was not the case. Here the followers of Jesus were, like other Jews, simply part of the crowd. For them, Jesus's death was a tragedy, but not the defining issue of their lives. They were interested in the sayings of the "living Jesus."

THE LIVING JESUS

What, then, shall we make of the unusual title given to Jesus in our text's *incipit*? Who is the "living Jesus"? Many scholars have assumed that this must be a reference to Jesus's resurrection. Jesus died but was raised from the dead to live again. These are the sayings that he spoke to Judas Thomas after his resurrection from the dead. Indeed, there are several early Christian gospels that involve just such a fiction. During his lifetime Jesus spoke openly, publicly. But after his death he appeared to the elect few to communicate the more important "secret" or "hidden" sayings. This is the scenario presupposed by the opening lines of the *Apocryphon of James,* for example:

> Now the twelve disciples were sitting all together at the same time, and, remembering what the Savior had said to each one of them, whether secretly or openly, they were setting it down in books. And (as) I was writing what was in my book—lo, the Savior appeared, after he had departed from us while we gazed at him. (trans. Cameron, *The Other Gospels*)

Thereupon follows the extensive novel teaching that Jesus is said to have revealed to James and Peter "550 days after he rose from the dead."

Does the *Gospel of Thomas* presuppose a similar scenario? It is unlikely. In the *Gospel of Thomas* there is no mention of Jesus's death or resurrection. And many of the sayings in the *Gospel of Thomas* are well known from Matthew, Mark, and Luke—gospels that purport to recount the words and deeds of Jesus during his lifetime. Formally, most of these sayings appear in *Thomas* as part of a short vignette, or *chreia,* that depicts a brief scene in the life of Jesus. These all would have been known as sayings Jesus uttered in his lifetime, not in post-resurrection secret sessions with his disciples. But if the "living Jesus" does not refer to the risen Jesus, to what does it refer?

The concept of resurrection in Jewish myth and lore is associated with *eschatology,* that is, ideas about what will happen at the end of time. But not all ancient Jews were interested in what will happen at the *end* of time. They saw more theological potency in speculation about what happened at the *beginning.* After all, the Torah says nothing about what happens at the end. But it devotes an entire book to what happened "in the beginning"—Genesis. Saying 18 of the *Gospel of Thomas* says this:

> The disciples said to Jesus, "Tell us how our end will be."
> Jesus said, "Have you discovered the beginning, then, that

you now seek the end? For where the beginning is, there the end will be. Blessed is are those who will stand at the beginning, and they will come to know the end and not taste death."

The quest for life and immortality in this gospel is focused not on eschatology, but *protology*—speculation about what happened at the *beginning*.

So what happened at the beginning? Jewish theologians from this period took a special interest in the first three chapters of Genesis. In the first chapter we read of how God created the world in seven days—light and darkness, the dry land and the gathered seas, the dome of heaven above with its tiny lights and the two great lights, the sun and the moon, living creatures of every kind, and finally humankind:

So God created humankind in his image,
in the image of God he created them;
male and female he created them. (1:27)

Now, careful readers will notice that in Genesis there are actually two creation stories. After the familiar seven-day account in Genesis 1, there is another account, quite different, that begins in Genesis 2:4. This is the story—also familiar—of how God creates the first human by molding him from the dust of the earth and breathing into him the "breath of life" (2:7). This is how, says Genesis, "the man became a living being." When this ancient and hoary text of Genesis was written, Jews did not generally believe in immortality. This first man, Adam, was not immortal. Neither was the first woman, created from Adam's rib. According to the myth they *might* have become immortal if they had dared to eat from the Tree of Life (3:22). But they did not. They ate from the Tree of the Knowledge of Good and Evil. So God became fearful and drove them from the garden, lest they should now also eat from the Tree of Life and "live forever."

In the period of Christian origins, though, many Jews and Christians did believe in immortality. They were influenced, like other intellectuals of their day, by Plato, who argued that in addition to a mortal body, human beings were also endowed with an immortal soul, or "mind" (*nous*). So they returned to Genesis, only now with Plato whispering in their ear. They no longer read Genesis as their ancestors had, as the story of our mortality, but as the story of our immortality. The two different versions of the creation story abetted their efforts. When a philosophically minded Jewish theologian like Philo, the famous sage of Alexandria, came to Genesis 1:27 and read that God created the human being in his own image, he reasoned, this could not be the human being in its entirety—the walking, talking, eating, mortal-flesh human being.

In his work *On the Creation of the World*, Philo explains that Moses was not so crude as to imagine God as a mere human being. Rather, "it is in respect of the mind (*nous*), the sovereign element of the soul, that the word 'image' is used" (*On the Creation* 69). Only the immortal mind was created in the image of God. The rest of the human being—the walking, talking, eating, mortal-flesh part—was created later. This is where Genesis 2:7 comes in. Here is where Genesis speaks of molding the human one out of dust. According to Philo, this second episode is where the mortal part of the human being was created:

> For man as formed now [in Gen. 2:7] is perceptible to the external senses, partaking of qualities, consisting of body and soul, man or woman, by nature mortal. But man, made according to the image of God [in Gen. 1:27], was an idea, or a genus, or a seal, perceptible only by the intellect (*nous*), incorporeal, neither male nor female, imperishable by nature. (*On the Creation* 134)

By reading Genesis 1 and 2 episodically, Philo found a way to read

Plato into the biblical narrative. The human being consists of a mortal part and an immortal part. The immortal part was created first, in the image of God (1:27); the mortal part second, from the dust of the earth (2:7). When Genesis says that God "breathed the breath of life" into the human one, Philo believed that he was reading about the origins of the immortal soul. It is God's divine breath that renders the soul, or *mind,* immortal and thus makes us into the Platonic human beings we are, part mortal and part immortal.

That is what happened at the beginning—at least by the reckoning of many philosophically inclined Jews and Christians intent on reading Genesis with the generous help of Plato. And this, more or less, is the world of thought in which the *Gospel of Thomas* is at home. In the *Gospel of Thomas* God is the Living One (37; 111) or the Living Father (3; 50). As in Genesis, it is God who gives life. The *Gospel of Thomas* teaches that "whoever is living from the Living One will not see death" (111). Jesus is a "son of the Living One" (37), as are all of the elect (50:2). That is why Jesus too is called the "living one" in this gospel (52:2; 59). The Living Jesus in the *Gospel of Thomas* is not the risen Jesus, but the immortal Jesus, whose wise sayings promise to guide others to discover the source of their own immortality (1). There will be much more to say about this as we explore more of what it is that the Living Jesus teaches.

WHAT DOES THE *Gospel of Thomas* TEACH?

What, then, does the Living Jesus teach? How does one discover the divine image within? One begins by searching:

> Jesus said, "Let all who seek seek until they find, and when they find, they will be disturbed, and when they are disturbed, they will marvel, and they will rule over the universe." (2)

The *long search* is the concept that lies at the heart of the ancient wisdom tradition. In the Jewish book of Proverbs the personified voice of Wisdom promises, "Those who earnestly seek me will find me" (8:17). It is an optimistic idea—that revelation lies close at hand. And it belonged not just to Jews, but also to Greeks and others who sought to become wise and thereby draw closer to God. "Seek and you will find, for nature has given you resources to find the truth," says the famous Cynic philosopher Epictetus (*Discourses* 4.1.51).

In many ways the *Gospel of Thomas* is indeed a wisdom book, the collected wisdom of the sage Jesus. As such, it contains many well-known proverbs and aphorisms of Jesus, like these:

> Jesus said, "No prophet is accepted in his (own) village. A physician never heals those who know him."
>
> Jesus said, "A city built upon a high mountain (and) fortified cannot fall, nor can it be hidden."
>
> Jesus said, "That which you hear in your ear, preach from your housetops. For no one lights a lamp and puts it under a bushel, nor do they put it in a hidden place. Rather, they set it on a lamp stand, so that everyone who comes in and goes out will see its light."
>
> Jesus said, "If a blind person leads a blind person, both will fall into a pit."
>
> Jesus said, "It is not possible for someone to enter a strong man's house and take it by force unless he (first) binds his hands. Then he will loot his house."
>
> Jesus said, "Do not worry from morning to evening and from evening to morning about what you will wear." (31–36)

It also includes many of the most treasured parables of Jesus: the Mustard Seed, the Leaven, the Great Feast, the Rebellious Tenants, the Wheat and the Weeds, and this, the Parable of the Rich Fool:

Jesus said, "There was a rich man who had much money. He said, 'I will invest my money so that I may sow, reap, plant, and fill my storehouses with produce so that I might lack nothing. These were the things he was thinking in his heart, but that very night he died. Whoever has ears should listen." (63)

There are also many other traditional forms from the repertoire of Jesus, such as blessings and woes—some of them also familiar:

Jesus said, "Blessed are the destitute, for the empire of heaven is yours." (54)

Jesus said, "Blessed is the one who has struggled and found life." (58)

Jesus said, "Blessed are you whenever you are hated (and) persecuted. (68:1)

Jesus said, "Blessed are those who have been persecuted in their hearts. They are the ones who have truly come to know the Father. Blessed are those who go hungry, so that the belly of the needy will be satisfied." (69)

Many of the same sharply countercultural sayings from Q show up here as well:

Jesus said, "Those who do not hate their father and mother cannot become my disciples. And those who do not hate their brothers and sisters and take up their crosses in my way will not be worthy of me." (55)

[Jesus said,] "If you have money, do not lend (it) at interest. Rather, give [it] to someone from whom you will not get it back." (95)

Jesus said, "[Foxes have] their dens and birds have their nest. But a human being has no place to lay his head down (and) rest." (86)

These are all very old sayings from the earliest days of the Jesus movement, when the followers of Jesus still took to heart his advice to leave home and village and embrace a more detached, mendicant life. They belong to the legacy of countercultural wisdom that made up the earliest common stock of the Jesus tradition. Like Q, the *Gospel of Thomas* is a wisdom gospel containing much from the distinctive countercultural wisdom of Jesus of Nazareth. Those who used and treasured this gospel must have still embraced this radically countercultural lifestyle and perspective.

Indeed, the kind of Christianity that would eventually grow up and thrive east of the Euphrates valorized the ideal of the wandering ascetical apostle, aloof from the world and spreading the word that the world is a mere temporal phenomenon, a corrupt and corrupting place unworthy of our devotion and effort. Consider these *Thomas* statements:

If you do not fast from the world, you will not find the empire. (27:1)

Jesus said, "Whoever has come to know the world has found a corpse, and whoever has found a corpse, of them the world is not worthy." (56)

Does not Jesus say, "Those who have found themselves, of them the world is not worthy"? (111:3)

Jesus said, "Become passersby." (42)

Thomas is first of all a wisdom gospel espousing the countercultural wisdom of Jesus.

More Than Wisdom, Enlightenment

But there is more to the *Gospel of Thomas* than the straightforward wisdom of the early Jesus tradition. Like the better-known biblical gospels Matthew, Mark, Luke, and John, *Thomas* too bears its own distinctive theological stamp. As we have already seen, those who created and used this tradition were particularly interested in Plato as he was read and interpreted in the period of Christian origins. This was the era of Middle Platonism, when, after a long hiatus, intellectuals and others began to read anew the more speculative dialogues of Plato, like the *Timaeus, Alcibiades, Sophist,* and others, in which the big questions of life are posed: What is a human being, where do we come from, where are we going, and how can anyone know about such things? These are the questions and this is the tradition that animates the more speculative and mysterious sayings of the *Gospel of Thomas.*

To see this we might begin at the beginning of *Thomas*'s search for wisdom. Consider saying 3 of the gospel:

Jesus said, "If those who lead you say to you, 'Behold, the empire is in the sky,' the birds of the sky will precede you.' If they say to you, 'It is in the sea,' then the fish will precede you. Rather, the empire is inside you and outside you. When you come to know yourselves, you will be known and you will realize that you are sons of the Living Father. But if it happens that you never come to know yourselves, then you exist in poverty, and you are the poverty."

The search for real insight begins in the *Gospel of Thomas* with knowledge of the self. "Know thyself," the ancient Delphic maxim of Thales, was the watchword and mantra of the Middle Platonists. Originally it meant something like, "Know thyself, that you are merely human," but in the hands of the Middle Platonists it became an affirmation of the divine element dwelling within each human being: "Know thyself, that you are divine." The Roman politician Cicero was influenced by this way of self-understanding:

> For he who knows himself will realize, in the first place, that he has a divine element within him, and will think of his own inner nature as a kind of consecrated image of God, and so he will always act and think in a way worthy of so great a gift of the gods, and, when he has examined and thoroughly tested himself, he will understand how nobly equipped by nature he entered life, and what manifold means he possesses for the attainment and acquisition of wisdom. (*On the Laws* 1.22.59)

The search for true wisdom begins with the quest to know the true self. When those who used our gospel came to that familiar saying of Jesus, "Behold, the kingdom of God is within you," they did not first think of a social reality unfolding among the followers of Jesus. They thought of the Platonic claim that within them there is something that relates them intimately to God. To know yourself truly is to realize that you are "children (sons) of the Living Father."

The Platonists liked to speak of this divine element dwelling within as the "image of God"—as Cicero says, "a kind of consecrated image of God." Seneca, who was also profoundly influenced by this tradition, called it "a god dwelling as a guest in a human body," "an image in the likeness of God" (*Epistles* 31.11). This way of speaking offered a ready point of entry for Jews interested in this tradition. As we have seen, Genesis, after all, made a similar claim that in the beginning God had created Adam "in the image and likeness of God" (1:27). Recall how Philo had read this passage: the image of God, he says, does not refer to the whole flesh-and-blood human being. This comes later—in Genesis 2:7—where God creates Adam from the dust of the earth. No, Genesis 1:27 refers only to the immortal part of the human being—what Plato called the "mind," "incorporeal, neither male nor female, imperishable by nature" (Philo, *On the Creation* 134). In other words, Philo believed that Genesis taught what Plato (later) taught, that each person bears within him- or herself the image of God. This part of the human being was created first and later implanted in the flesh-and-blood human being created from the dust of the earth, so that each person has both a mortal and an immortal part.

These are the ideas that render some of *Thomas*'s most difficult and mysterious sayings intelligible. Consider saying 84:

Jesus said, "When you see your likenesses you are full of joy. But when you (pl.) see your (pl.) images which came into existence before you—they neither die nor become manifest—how much will you bear?"

This saying plays with what must have been the novel and exciting experience of seeing oneself in a mirror: "when you see your likenesses." But if this is exciting, imagine how much more exciting, even overwhelming, it will be to discover one's "image"—the immortal self, created "before you," at the beginning of time—in the image of God. When you discover this image of God dwelling within, "How much will you bear?"

How, then, will the seeker find this true self dwelling within? Another of *Thomas*'s more mysterious sayings offers a clue:

Jesus said to [his disciples], "When you make the two one and when you make the inside like the outside and the outside like the inside and the above like the below—that is, in order to make the male and the female into a single one, so that the male will not be male and the female will not be female—when you make eyes in place of an eye and a hand in place of a hand and a foot in place of a foot, an image in place of an image, then you will enter the empire." (22:4–7)

This is an odd saying, to be sure, a riddle to be pondered. But its basic solution lies once again in those opening chapters of Genesis. Recall that in Genesis Adam is originally alone, a solitary human being living in paradise. But God sees that it is not good for him to be alone and so decides to create a second person to be his companion. Placing Adam in a deep sleep, God takes a rib from Adam's side and from it creates Eve. Where once there was one, now there were two. Where once there was a genderless, undifferentiated human being, now there stood a man and a woman, male and female. From here the story begins to spiral down. Adam and Eve defy God, discover their nakedness, and fall from grace. Paradise is lost.

This tale offered early Judaism the basic framework for a rich elaboration on the nature of gender, sin, and redemption. For paradise to be regained, the only way forward was to go back—back before the single one became two, back before the genderless one became male and female, back before the image of God was clothed beneath garments of skin (Gen. 3:21). This is the key to this saying. *Thomas* 22 counsels seekers to strive for paradise regained: when the two will become one, the male and female will become a single one, and the image of fallen humanity will be replaced, part by body part, until the image of God is restored.

The Platonic notion of the divine spark within comes to expression in the *Gospel of Thomas* in many different ways. In 24:3 the true, divine self appears very simply as a "light":

There is a light within people of light, and they shed light on the whole world. If they do not shine, there is darkness.

In saying 29 it is called the "spirit":

Jesus said, "If the flesh came into being because of the spirit, it is a marvel; but if the spirit (came into being) because of the body, it is a marvel of marvels. But I marvel at how this great wealth has come to dwell in this poverty."

This juxtaposition of spirit and body (or flesh) leads of course to the deprecation of the latter. In 37:2 Jesus advises:

When you undress without being ashamed and take your clothes (and) put them under your feet like little children and trample them, then [you] will see the son of the Living One, and you will not be afraid.

This saying likely draws on the common notion in both Platonism and early Judaism that the body is like a suit of clothes. Genesis says that God gave Adam and Eve "garments of skin"—a reference, these Jewish philosophers believed, to the body itself. Before the fall they did not need them, for though they were naked, they were not ashamed (2:25). The point of saying 37 comes from this idea: the body is but a suit of clothes to be shed in the end, so that the soul might stand naked and unashamed before the living God. This freedom from the body could be symbolized ritually in baptism, when initiates shed their clothes and descend into the water only to reemerge as new persons, spiritually transformed.

This, then, is the goal: to free the spirit (soul, mind, true self, the image of God) from its earthly chains to fly heavenward, back to the living God. The elect have come from God and to God they are destined to return. Two sayings offer a brief catechism for how this is to take place:

Jesus said, "Blessed are the solitary, the chosen ones, for you will find the empire. For you come from it and you will return to it. (49)
Jesus said, "If they say to you, 'Where do you come from?' say to them, 'We have come from the light, the place where the

light came into being by itself, established itself, and appeared in their image.' If they say to you, 'Is it you?' say 'We are his children, the elect of the Living Father.' If they ask you, 'What is the sign of your Father within you?' say, 'It is movement and rest.'" (50)

Here is the Platonic idea of the soul's journey from heaven and its eventual return home. As the spirit is released from the body, it rises upward. As it travels up through the threefold heavenly structure, at each point it is met with a question from those who guard the path home: "Where do you come from?" ("The place of light!") "Is it you?" ("We are his children!") "What is the sign of your Father within you?" ("It is movement and rest.") This last response comes right out of Plato's *Timaeus,* in which the whole purpose of the well-led life is to bring the erratic motions of the embodied soul (or "mind") into alignment with the harmonious revolutions of the universe itself. If one can achieve such harmony, the soul is said to be both moving and at rest (*Timaeus* 90).

Some see sayings 49 and 50 as instructions for the final journey home; others see them as a dress rehearsal achieved in a trancelike state of mystical experience. Both are possible. And both require a clear head and a wakeful disposition. Jesus's stated purpose is to guide people out of their stupor into enlightened awareness of their true state. All come from God, and all will one day return:

Jesus said, "I stood in the midst of the world and in the flesh I appeared to them. I found all of them drunk; none of them did I find thirsty. And my soul ached for the human race, for they are blind of heart and cannot see. For they came into the world empty, and empty too they seek to leave the world. But now they are drunk. When they have shaken off their wine, then they will change their minds." (28)

The image of unenlightened humanity as "drunk" and the goal of life as enlightenment in preparation for the soul's journey home are ideas often associated with the ancient religious tradition known as Gnosticism. For this reason many scholars have regarded the *Gospel of Thomas* as a Gnostic gospel. But today scholars are more cautious in applying this label to *Thomas*. The term "Gnostic" itself has become so ill-defined and vague that many advocate its banishment from modern discussions. Those who would retain it demand greater precision with it.

Two things now are seen as critical for a text to be understood as truly Gnostic. First, the world must be seen as fundamentally evil, the result of the blind ambition of a rebellious creator god. Second, the fact that human beings dwell in this abortive universe is itself the result the pernicious activity of this rebellious creator. The *Gospel of Thomas* does not include these ideas. The world is dead, a corpse (56), but it is not necessarily evil. As in Platonism generally, it is an irrelevance to be overcome, material, like the body, and therefore nothing worthy of one's concern. In saying 80 Jesus says:

> Those who have come to know the world have discovered the body. But those who have discovered the body, of them the world is not worthy.

In saying 42 Jesus advises simply, "Become passersby." This is not Gnosticism; it is simply a Jewish take on Platonism.

THOMAS AND CHRISTIAN ORIGINS

In 1959 the public got its first look at the *Gospel of Thomas,* when the scholars originally charged with creating an international translation finally published their work. The news of a new gospel broke like a storm. For more than eighteen hundred years there had been only four gospels in the Christian canon. Most people did not even know that there had been other gospels. Now a lost gospel, recovered (literally) from the sands of time, was front-page news. Where had it come from? Was it real? What could it tell us that the other gospels could not? Had we at last discovered the source that would set the record straight on what Jesus really taught, or was it all a hoax, or something else, something less interrupting?

As scholars began to examine the new gospel, they were divided almost immediately into two camps. On one side were the enthusiasts, who regarded *Thomas* as a new and independent source for the original teachings of Jesus. On the other side were the disparagers, who argued that *Thomas* was late, heretical, and dependent upon the canonical gospels for its material. For them, *Thomas* was an interesting artifact of second-century Gnosticism, nothing more. Now, after more than fifty years of study, there is still no consensus about the *Gospel of Thomas*. Critical scholars still argue over a range of issues. Meanwhile, a new generation of evangelical scholars has entered the discussion with a single voice of condemnation. *Thomas* has become an ideological flashpoint in the search for Christian origins.

Some of the most critical issues with *Thomas* will perhaps never be settled. One is *Thomas*'s date. It is, after all, a sayings collection, little more than a simple list. Lists are malleable, easily expanded or contracted with each new iteration. Which version of the list shall we date? The earliest? The latest? And if a particular version could be identified and dated, what would that tell us about the rest of the collection? It is unlikely that scholars will ever agree on how or when to date this gospel.

More critical than the issue of dating, however, is the matter of literary dependence. Very simply, this is the question of whether and to what extent *Thomas*'s authors drew material from the canonical gospels—especially Matthew, Mark, and Luke. A quick survey of the contents of these gospels reveals that roughly 50 percent of *Thomas*'s sayings have a parallel in one or more of the synoptic gospels. The implications of this are very significant. If *Thomas* came by these sayings independently of the synoptic texts, then conceivably in *Thomas* we have a new vantage point from which to view the history of these sayings. By comparing them to *Thomas,* one might gain new insights about how one or another of the biblical authors adapted and changed the traditions they inherited. *Thomas,* in other words, could help us to "walk back" the tradition, before Mark, before Q, perhaps even to Jesus himself. On the other hand, if the author of the *Gospel of Thomas* pilfered these sayings from the synoptic gospels, then all it will yield is insight into a peculiar second-century heresy.

In my view there is little reason to doubt the basic independence of the *Gospel of Thomas.* In a world where books were rare and oral modes of communication predominated, one should not assume that different texts have a direct literary relationship unless there is compelling evidence to the contrary. Consider by contrast the case of the synoptic gospels, Matthew, Mark, and Luke. Most scholars agree that they share an intimate literary relationship. The evidence for this is not just the fact that they share a lot of material. They actually agree in the way this material is *worded* and in the *order* in which it is presented. Common wording and common order—the two facts that establish the literary relationship between Matthew, Mark, and Luke—are almost entirely lacking in the case of the *Gospel of Thomas.*

The *Thomas* versions of these commonly held sayings are differently worded, and they appear in an order that bears no discernible relationship to any one of the synoptic gospels. This means that *Thomas* is basically independent of the synoptic texts—my term is "autonomous"—allowing for late additions or scribal alterations that may have been influenced by the synoptic gospels or simply scraps of memory of the synoptic texts present in the oral tradition itself. Those who created and used this text assembled it from oral and written traditions that were distinct from the synoptic gospels and their sources. This means that *Thomas* offers scholars another view of how the Jesus tradition could and did develop from those early roots laid down by Jesus and his first followers. What will these developments tell us about those roots themselves?

THE *GOSPEL OF THOMAS* AND JESUS

Coaxing information about the historical Jesus from any of the extant Christian gospels is one of the most difficult challenges of biblical scholarship, whether we are speaking of the canonical gospels, found in the Bible, or noncanonical gospels, like *Thomas*. The biblical gospels all date from a time decades removed from the days when Jesus actually walked the earth. More important, they were all written under unique circumstances that have left an indelible imprint on the oral and written traditions they incorporate. And before gospels appeared, the oral tradition itself was constantly changing and adapting to new circumstances. There is little hope in this for finding a direct line back to Jesus. A few scholars initially thought that *Thomas* would change all of that. They argued that the dozens of close parallels between *Thomas* and the synoptic gospels proved that Matthew, Mark, and Luke had been remarkably accurate after all. But soon scholars began noticing the differences as well as the similarities and how fundamental the differences actually are.

Thomas and the synoptic gospels share many things. They share several parables. They share many proverbs and aphorisms. And they share many prophetic sayings, sayings of public and private critique. The thing about all these sayings, however, is that they are all very flexible—*polyvalent* is the physics term some scholars have borrowed to describe it. That is, they can combine with different literary frameworks to produce quite different meanings or interpretations.

In the synoptic tradition these sayings are all placed within an apocalyptic and martyrological framework. They are used to tell the story of Jesus's death and to comment on the coming judgment to which this was to have been the prelude. In the case of the parables, they are sometimes turned into allegories to serve as commentary on recent events. An example of this is the Parable of the Tenants, which in the Gospel of Mark (12:1–12) serves as an explanation for the destruction of Jerusalem at the end of the Judean revolt in 70 CE, an event that had recently rocked the world of Mark's author. The parable, now altered and treated as an allegory, suggests that because Jesus was martyred in Jerusalem, God allowed it to be destroyed by the Romans and given over to be ruled by Gentiles. The synoptic gospels are replete with this sort of adaptation.

In spite of the sometimes very obvious ways in which the synoptic authors adapted their sources, scholars have nonetheless tended to give them the benefit of the doubt on the big picture. That is, they've assumed that Mark and, following Mark, Matthew and Luke were essentially right. Jesus *was* a prophet of apocalyptic judgment. Over against this view stood the rare champion of the fourth gospel, John, which uses a much different framework. In the Gospel of John Jesus is not an apocalyptic prophet, but a wisdom figure, a descending and ascending messenger from God sent to awaken people to the truth: "You shall know the truth, and the truth will set you free" (8:32). But John's Jesus speaks so often in such downright bizarre ways that it was difficult not to prefer Mark's more down-to-earth Jesus.

Now, enter *Thomas*'s Jesus. Like John's Jesus, the *Thomas* version of Jesus is a wisdom figure, not an apocalyptic seer. But when he opens his mouth, out come the parables, aphorisms, and prophetic sayings of the synoptic Jesus. And here is the surprising thing: without the apocalyptic framework of the synoptic gospels, these sayings don't sound so apocalyptic anymore.

An example is in *Thomas* 61:1:

Jesus said, "Two will rest on a bed. The one will die and the other will live."

The same saying is found in Luke 17:34. Jesus says:

I tell you, in that night there will be two in one bed; one will be taken and the other left.

It is the same saying but worded differently—just as one would expect from two authors drawing from a common oral tradition. But when one reads each version in context, it is astonishing how differently the versions have been interpreted. In Luke the context is a speech warning of the coming apocalypse. When the Son of Man arrives, one person will survive, and another will not. In *Thomas,* the context is a dialogue about immortality. One who is enlightened will live on; the one who is not will die. So which is the original, Luke's apocalyptic interpretation or *Thomas*'s Platonic interpretation? Or is neither the original? Taken alone, the saying does carry its own aphoristic punch. Why does one person die and another live? Why, when death comes, is there often no explanation? The world of the ancient peasant was filled with death randomly dealt from disease, war, and natural disaster. These could strike at any time. One person lives, another dies. Why?

There are dozens of similar examples among the parallels between *Thomas* and the synoptics. So did the synoptic evangelists get Jesus right, or did *Thomas*? Or do both traditions derive ultimately from something else, a wisdom tradition malleable enough to accommodate the apocalyptic interpretation of the synoptics and the Platonic spin of *Thomas*? These are the questions that animate the new discussion of Christian origins sparked by the discovery of the *Gospel of Thomas*. *Thomas* is not a new, more authentic account of what Jesus taught. But by exposing the potential of the Jesus tradition to move in directions quite different from the synoptic gospels, it has forced the question of whether the synoptic Jesus is the historical Jesus after all. This is one of the reasons why controversy still swirls around the *Gospel of Thomas*.

One of the best-known and most effective attempts to integrate the *Gospel of Thomas* into the historical Jesus debate is that of John

Dominic Crossan. Crossan recognizes that if the *Gospel of Thomas* is an independent source for the sayings of Jesus, then one of its chief uses will be to establish the antiquity of many sayings that, before *Thomas,* attracted no particular attention. The principle behind his work is this. Since the gospel writers wrote relatively late and with a good deal of creativity, it is often difficult to know what material comes from earlier sources and what belongs simply to the creativity of the gospel writer himself. One way to identify earlier source material is by *independent multiple attestation.* When material occurs independently in two or more sources, then it is certain that it comes from an earlier oral or written source they shared.

Now, prior to the discovery of the *Gospel of Thomas,* independent multiple attestation was relatively rare. There were the occasional Mark-Q overlaps, a few more Mark-John overlaps, and a handful of others. But all told, there were not more than a dozen or so instances of this. But the advent of *Thomas* as an independent source of Jesus's sayings means that now we have dozens and dozens of sayings independently attested in *Thomas* and Q alone. Roughly half of *Thomas*'s 114 sayings have synoptic parallels. In Crossan's view, this changes everything. Before *Thomas,* what belonged to the earliest presynoptic layers of the Jesus tradition was decided without controls, sometimes arbitrarily. Now the historian has a way to identify a large number of sayings that in fact belong to the early, presynoptic layer of the tradition. Crossan argues that this is where one should begin.

This new beginning, it turns out, makes quite a difference. Crossan immediately noticed that when these early sayings are viewed apart from their synoptic context, on the one hand, and their *Thomas* context, on the other, they take on a much different character. Like the saying about the suddenness of death, they no longer supported the long-held synoptic view that Jesus was an apocalyptic preacher or for that matter the newer *Thomas* view that Jesus spoke of immortality and a future life in heaven. Jesus, who told parables, who coined the aphorisms and sayings of prophetic critique, was a wisdom teacher, of sorts. Crossan calls him a "peasant Jewish Cynic," that is, a Jewish version of the ancient street philosophers (Cynics) who needled their contemporaries with troubling observations about the absurdities of conventional life and advocated greater reliance on nature and the providence of God. But while Cynics counseled their followers to survive through greater "self-reliance," Jesus taught his followers to survive by relying more on one another.

One of the Q-*Thomas* overlaps is particularly critical to this view, the Mission Discourse, which we saw first in Q 10:1–12. The Matthean version of this discourse (10:5–15) combines Q with a version of the same discourse in Mark (see Mark 6:7–13), so we must rely mostly on Luke 10:1–12 for Q in this case. In the midst of the discourse we find these instructions:

> Whenever you enter a town and they take you in, eat what is set before you and care for the sick there and say to them, "The empire of God has come to you." (Q 10:8–9)

Crossan notices that this same saying, without the rest of the discourse, occurs in *Thomas* 14:4:

> And if you go into any land and walk about in the countryside and they take you in, eat what they set before you and care for the sick among them.

This, he suggests, is the oldest part of the tradition. This is confirmed by the apparent fact that the apostle Paul used a snippet of this saying in the context of his own mission work some years earlier:

> If an unbeliever invites you to dinner and you wish to go, *eat what is set before you* without consideration of conscience. (1 Cor. 10:27)

As we saw in our close reading of Q's Mission Discourse, this saying presupposes an activity of going from place to place *in order to* encounter strangers. The Jesus followers ask to be taken in. When they are, they are to eat whatever their hosts provide, and they, in turn, are to care for the sick they find there. Food is received; care is given. Crossan sees in this a myth of origins for the thing the Jesus movement actually did: it created new communities in which the basic needs of subsistence peasants were met in a very practical way. These are the stark realities to which every peasant awakens each morning: Will I work today and therefore eat; or will I get sick today, not work, and therefore not eat? One of the first glimpses we get of the empire of God in this tradition is of a chance gathering of peasants, initially strangers, who exchange food for care in a new strategy for coping with the vicissitudes of life.

Is Crossan right? Can *Thomas* be used to walk back the tradition to a time before the synoptic evangelists had placed their particular stamp on Jesus? Or are the biblical gospels still to be trusted with offering the most reliable picture of Jesus, a picture that *Thomas* merely obscures with an early form of Christian Platonism? The *Gospel of Thomas* has helped to spark one of the most interesting and important debates about the historical Jesus in the history of modern biblical scholarship.

JESUS HAD A BROTHER—JAMES

That the wisdom of Jesus should find its heart in the creation of communities in which the poor and the sick would care for and support one another is evident from another early Christian wisdom collection with close ties to the *Gospel of Thomas*. This is the New Testament book known as the Letter of James. Recall, for a moment, the fact that the *Gospel of Thomas* actually contains a kind of tribute to James. In saying 12 of *Thomas*, Jesus responds to a question about who will be his successor:

> Wherever you have come from, you are to go to James the Just,
> the one for whom heaven and earth came into being.

James the Just—this was James, the brother of Jesus, who is believed to have led the community of Jesus followers in Jerusalem in the years following Jesus's death. This saying creates a memory of how that happened. Jesus, according to saying 12, appointed him.

The Letter of James is ostensibly the work of this self-same James—James the brother of Jesus. Historically, this is improbable. James the Just came from the same family of peasant handworkers as Jesus. It is unlikely, therefore, that he could have written the fairly sophisticated Greek composition that is the Letter of James. James, then, is a kind of forgery but without malicious intent. Whoever wrote it wanted to indicate that his roots lay in the ideas and wisdom of James, even the brother of Jesus. These are roots he apparently shared with the Jesus followers behind the *Gospel of Thomas.*

Like *Thomas,* the Letter of James is actually a wisdom collection. It is presented as a letter: "James . . . to the twelve tribes of the dispersion" (1:1). But this is pure artifice. The recipients—the lost tribes of Israel—have no known address, and formally the "letter" is not really a letter. It is actually a collection of wisdom sayings comprising many proverbs, aphorisms, and much advice. In form, it is not terribly different from Q or *Thomas.* And it opens with this invitation:

> If anyone is lacking in wisdom, let them ask God, who gives to
> everyone generously and without reproach, and it will be given
> them. (1:5)

This might by now sound familiar. "Ask and it shall be given to you, seek and you shall find, knock and it shall be opened to you" (Q 11:9; cf. *Thomas* 92). James, like Q and *Thomas,* is a wisdom book.

For years the Letter of James has been an outlier of sorts. Scholars haven't always known what to do with it. The New Testament contains no other James books. And this book seems to contradict, even attack the apostle to whom over half of the New Testament is attributed: "What good does it do, brothers and sisters, if a person says he has faith, but not works? Can faith save him? . . . Show me your faith apart from works and I, by my works, will show you my faith" (James 2:14, 18). Through the centuries Christianity has much preferred the apostle Paul's idea that one cannot be justified by works, but only through faith (cf., e.g., Gal. 3:10–14). James just doesn't endorse this idea. Martin Luther even excluded James from his version of the New Testament—an "epistle of straw," he called it, too much at odds with Paul's doctrine of grace. All of that involved some rather serious mis-understandings of Paul. But for its part, James is easily understood: "faith without works is dead" (2:26). If much of the rest of the New Testament could be wrangled into line with Paul, James could not. So where had this odd book come from? And why was it attributed to Jesus's own brother, James?

Thomas 12 offers a hint about where a book like James could have come from. Here is another early wisdom text from people who culti-vated the idea that following Jesus meant tending the word that comes from God and living by it. What did that mean to the James people? It turns out that it meant something fairly close to what it meant to those who created the *Gospel of Thomas*. Here is James's summary claim:

> Religion that is pure and undefiled before our God and Father
> is this: to watch over the orphans and widows in their troubles,
> and to keep oneself unstained by the world. (1:27)

The James people thought that the poor and destitute were to be honored as "heirs to the kingdom" (2:1–7) and cared for (2:14–17). The rich were to be seen as fools, or worse (5:1–6). The James followers believed that they possessed a wisdom that had come "from above" (3:17), that all good gifts come from the "Father of Lights, before whom there is no variation or shadow of change" (1:17)—a remarkably Platonic theological statement. They believed that God had "chosen those who are poor in the world to be rich in faith" (2:5) and that "anyone who wants friendship with the world is an enemy of God" (4:4). Here is a text that is cut from the same cloth as *Thomas* (and Q).

Remarkably, it is a wisdom book in the tradition of Jesus of Nazareth ("James, servant of God and Lord Jesus Christ," 1:1), but, unlike Q and *Thomas*, its wisdom is *not* attributed to Jesus. This is the wisdom of James. Jesus appears only in the introduction (1:1) and then again in 2:1. Otherwise, the wisdom sayings and advice in this book all come from "James." But who authorized James to carry on so, to teach wisdom as though he had been the chosen one? Remember *Thomas* 12: "Wherever you have come from, you are to go to James the Just, the one for whom heaven and earth came into being." That is an extraordinary statement. The Letter of James is evidence that someone somewhere actually took this passing of the torch seriously.

If James offers another glimpse of this early, socially radical wisdom tradition, it also gives us clues about how difficult it would have been for those who embraced this unusual way of life to survive from generation to generation. The main body of James opens with a hypothetical scene of gathering (2:1–7). The faithful are assembled together at what looks like a banquet, perhaps a communal meal like those common among the earliest followers of Jesus. In walk a rich man and a poor man, and the text describes the response: "You fawn over the one who wears fine clothing and say, 'Sit here, if you like,' and you say to the poor man, 'Stand over there,' or 'Sit at my feet'" (2:3). The author of the text is furious. "You have dishonored the poor! Is it not the rich who oppress you, and they who drag you into court?" (2:6). What has happened in the communities under the watchful eye of this sage?

Consider: it is possible to imagine a generation of socially radical mendicants going from place to place, penniless, eating what was placed before them, and caring for the sick. But that is a level of commitment that few would actually have embraced. The new relationships of care and support that would have grown from this activity would have been seated in local communities from which the mendicants would have come and gone. What would have happened as those local communities grew and developed their own structure and habits? When they gathered together, who would have provided the space? The food? The money to support those widows and orphans? The scene in James 2:1–7 supposes a situation where one of those little communities of care attracted the attention of a patron, someone with money who, for whatever idealistic reasons, decided to buy into its cause. This eventually happened all across the Jesus movement, or else we would not have Q, *Thomas*, Mark, or any of the writings we are discussing—texts did cost money in the ancient world.

But the advent of rich patrons would have altered the structure of those early communities considerably, and exactly as the author of James imagines it. With money comes power, with power authority and honor, and before you know it, the "poor of the world" are standing off to the side or sitting at your feet, where they belong, while the rich guy who just paid for the meal holds forth on some matter of importance to him (ah, the next chapter of James is all about what authorizes a real teacher of wisdom). If the *Gospel of Thomas* is the product of a continuing robust mendicant life east of the Euphrates, James may represent the first signs of its faltering back in the Jewish homeland.

THE *GOSPEL OF THOMAS* AND PAUL

And what about that more famous apostle, Paul, with whom James appears to be so at odds? Can *Thomas* shed any light on the relationship between Paul and other followers of Jesus? This relationship poses some of the most vexing problems in the reconstruction of Christian origins. Paul's letters are the earliest writings of the New Testament, and yet when we encounter these earliest "Christian" writings, it is apparent that they come from someone who never actually knew Jesus. In fact, he was initially hostile to the Jesus movement (see Gal. 1:13, 23; Acts 8:3). But later he had a mystical religious experience in which Jesus was, in Paul's own words, "revealed in him" (Gal. 1:16). So his relationship to the historical Jesus was strictly through the later followers of Jesus—the Jesus movement. But here is a peculiar thing about Paul: through all of his correspondence with the Christ communities he founded, he makes reference to the teachings of Jesus less than a dozen times, and aside from his death by crucifixion, he never refers to episodes in Jesus's life. This is a long-standing puzzle in the story of Christian origins. One would think that Paul at least learned something about Jesus from the Jesus movement. Can *Thomas* shed any light on this mystery?

A little. *Thomas* does help us to see connections between Paul and the Jesus movement that were obscured before. Consider, for example, what we have just seen in Crossan's use of *Thomas* to reconstruct some of the most basic features of the Jesus movement—how it began when subsistence peasants formed communities in which they could share basic necessities and care for one another. This more or less describes Paul's project, carried on, though, in larger cities rather than the rural villages of the Galilee. He was himself a mendicant, without permanent home or family, who gave up everything to proclaim the kingdom of God. And much of the ink he spills in defense of his version of the gospel is devoted to keeping these communities true to their initial calling to care for one another. It is in the midst of such a defense that he makes use of the Jesus saying about eating what is set before you (1 Cor. 10:27; cf. *Thomas* 14:2; Q 10:8).

Now, the Jesus movement was committed to reaching across the social boundaries that kept people marginalized in the ancient world—poverty, disease, possession (mental illness). But it is not clear that it was willing to cross the ethnic boundary that separated Jew from Gentile. This was one of the distinctive things about Paul, though. The urban Christ communities he founded were not strictly

Jewish, but a mix of Jews and Gentiles. He believed that Gentiles should be able to join the Jesus movement even though they weren't Jewish and had no plan to become Jewish by going through the rite of circumcision. This became a bone of contention with other leaders in the Jesus movement, such as James and Peter (see esp. Gal. 2:11–14). In fact, until the discovery of the *Gospel of Thomas* one might have concluded that Paul stood virtually alone in his position. But now we have this saying from *Thomas:*

> His disciples said to him, "Is circumcision beneficial or not?"
> He said to them, "If it were beneficial, their father would beget
> them out of their mother already circumcised. But the true
> circumcision, in the spirit, brings profit in every way." (53)

This, surprisingly, is almost exactly the way Paul justifies his position to the Roman churches, writing to them in about 54 CE: "Real circumcision is a matter of the heart; it is spiritual, not literal" (Rom. 2:29).

Another thing that was distinctive about Paul's communities was a tendency to disregard the social distinctions that marked male and female in the ancient world. As with more progressive philosophical movements like the Epicureans, Paul recognized and encouraged women as leaders in these communities. This may come as a surprise, for several letters attributed to Paul have made the apostle appear patriarchal and misogynistic. But Paul did not actually write these letters (e.g., Ephesians or 1 Timothy). More indicative of the apostle's real attitude is Romans 16, a letter of recommendation for a woman named Phoebe, who was the leader of the community at Cenchreae, the port town of Corinth. This tradition of women apostles in the Pauline branch of the Jesus movement is captured in a later work called the *Acts of Paul and Thecla,* a collection of legends and traditions about Thecla, a woman who becomes Paul's follower and a preacher in her own right. But to do this she must adapt to the patriarchal world around her, which did not countenance women wandering from place to place on their own. So Thecla cuts her hair short in the fashion of a man and dons male clothing to pass as a man.

All of this puts one in mind of *Thomas* 114, which reads:

> Simon Peter said to them, "Let Mary leave us, for females are not worthy of life."
> Jesus said, "Look, I will guide her along so as to make her male, so that she too may become a living spirit similar to you males. For every woman who makes herself male will enter the empire of heaven."

The bitter opposition Peter voices against Mary (presumably Mary Magdalen) in this saying crops up also in other early Christian texts, like the *Gospel of Mary* and *Pistis Sophia*, where Peter, representing the patriarchal view, also stands in opposition to Mary, the first and most prominent of the women apostles. In these texts Mary and Peter are apparently proxies for a wider debate about women and their roles in the early Jesus movement, a debate that might have gotten very ugly. In *Pistis Sophia* Mary says, "I am afraid of Peter, for he threatens me and he hates our sex" (72). In the same way, within the circles that cultivated the *Thomas* tradition, there appears to have been a dispute about the presence of women among the apostles. Some were saying, "Women are not worthy of life."

As in those early Pauline communities, it appears that among the *Thomas* Christians women were also recognized as legitimate leaders. The argument for it is a little hard to swallow, though: "Every woman who makes herself male will enter the empire of heaven." This sounds both practically and ethically preposterous. What could the *Thomas* folk have meant by this?

They must have assumed, like many in the ancient world, that women were by nature inferior. For those influenced by Platonic philosophy, this idea had a very natural anthropological correlation. The highest part of the human being—the divine mind—is masculine.

The Greek word for "mind," *nous,* is grammatically a masculine noun. On the other hand, the word for the inferior "soul," *psyche,* is a feminine noun. So the mortal, inferior part of the soul is feminine, while the immortal, superior part is masculine.

In Jewish texts this idea might become clothed in the mythology of Genesis, in which Adam is created first, perfect and immortal, the image and glory of God, while Eve comes second, the "glory of man." These words are Paul's from 1 Corinthians (11:7). Paul favored women as leaders in his communities, but he wanted them to dress and act in a feminine way. That is the context for 1 Corinthians 11:2–16. In Corinth, some were ignoring the etiquette with regard to hair styling during prayer and prophecy (short for men, coiffed for women), and it was difficult to tell the men and the women apart. They had taken seriously a baptismal creed in use among Pauline Christians that declared in Christ there was no longer male and female. In baptism the narrative of Genesis had been reversed, and male and female were no more. Paul disliked the Corinthian prophets' practice of gender-bending in worship, but he agreed with their theology. He writes:

> Nevertheless, in the Lord woman is not different from man, nor man from woman, for just as woman was made from man, now man is born from woman, and all things come from God. (11:11–12)

In Corinth women and men had erased gender distinctions ritually through baptism. It is possible that this was the case also among the *Thomas* Christians. *Thomas* 37 may indicate this—a matter we will take up in Chapter 8. Another scholar has proposed that this was accomplished in the mysterious ritual of the "bridal chamber," mentioned in saying 104. Or it might simply be that women "made themselves male" by doing as Thecla did—cutting their hair short and putting on men's clothing. In any event, Paul's Corinthian prophets are a little less mysterious now than they once were.

The *Gospel of Thomas* and John

But of all the New Testament writings, the closest to *Thomas* in both theology and worldview is the Gospel of John. John, with its dualities of darkness and light and spirit and flesh and its paradoxical and riddling language, has often served as a point of comparison with the *Gospel of Thomas*. And yet, although *Thomas* shares dozens of sayings with the synoptic gospels, it shares only a handful with John. What, then, makes John and *Thomas* sound so much alike?

It is their common rooting in the Jewish wisdom theology we have been describing. They both embrace the fundamental idea that the secret to eternal life lies in Jesus's words. "If anyone keeps my word, he shall not taste death" (John 8:52; cf., e.g., 8:51; 6:63, 68). If this sounds familiar, it is almost a paraphrase of the first saying of the *Gospel of Thomas:* "Whoever finds the meaning of these words will not taste death." The *Gospel of Thomas* works with the categories of "flesh" and "spirit" (see 29), and so does John: "That which is born of the flesh is flesh, and that which is born of the spirit is spirit" (3:6). This comes from the famous exchange between Jesus and Nicodemus in which Nicodemus, being of the flesh, just cannot understand what Jesus is saying to him: if you do not have the spirit, you are lost. This is how *Thomas* gives expression to the same claim:

> Jesus said, "If you bring forth what is within you, that which you have will save you. If you do not have it within you, that which you do not have within you [will] kill you." (70)

Also, both seem to reject the notion of some future consummation of the kingdom of God, enlightenment, or immortality in favor of a present reality that is already here. In John we find: "Truly, truly, I say to you, anyone who hears my word and believes the one who sent me, has eternal life; he does not come into judgment, but has passed (already) from death to life" (5:24). This is John's much discussed "realized eschatology," which *Thomas* also embraces: "That which you anticipate has (already) come, but you do not recognize it" (51:2).

But perhaps most significantly, *Thomas* and John share the idea that Jesus is a divine messenger sent to enlighten a reluctant and recalcitrant humanity. We have already seen *Thomas*'s most significant articulation of this Christological claim; here it is again:

> Jesus said, "I stood in the midst of the world and in the flesh I appeared to them. I found all of them drunk; none of them did I find thirsty. And my soul ached for the human race, for they are blind of heart and cannot see. For they came into the world empty, and empty too they seek to leave the world. But now they are drunk. When they have shaken off their wine, then they will change their minds." (28)

The Jesus who speaks these words is the same Jesus who stands behind the mytho-poetic strains of the Johannine prologue:

> The true light that enlightens everyone was coming into the world. He was in the world, and the world was made through him, yet the world did not know him. (1:9–10)

Here is where *Thomas* and John come nearest to finding a common voice. In both gospels Jesus is a divine emissary sent to sojourn but for a time. Soon he will retreat and be heard from no more. Compare the following:

> Jesus said, "Many times you have desired to hear these words, these that I am speaking to you, and you have no one else from whom to hear them. There will be days when you seek me and you will not find me." (*Thomas* 38)

Jesus then said, "I shall be with you a little longer, and then I go to the one who sent me; you will seek me and you will not find me; where I am you cannot come." (John 7:33–34)

One might be inclined to imagine this highly mythological reflection on Jesus's identity and fate to have required a relatively long gestation period. But actually, no. It is, rather, native to the tradition of collecting Jesus's wise sayings. All wisdom is a gift from God, and the sages are God's chosen ones. Even in Q Jesus takes on this mythic persona in a surprisingly Johannine-sounding voice:

Then he said, "I bless you, Father, Lord of heaven and earth, for you have hidden these things from sages and scholars and revealed them to babes. Yes, Father, for this is what seemed right to you. All things have been entrusted me by my Father. And no one knows the son except the Father, and none the Father except the son, and anyone to whom the son wishes to reveal (him)." (Q 10:21–22)

But in John we also gain an idea of how adaptable this wisdom tradition was to new times and circumstances. Sometimes John's modifications to it are ever so subtle. Recall these two sayings, one from *Thomas*, the other from John:

And he said, "Whoever finds the meaning of these sayings will not taste death." (Thomas 1)

Truly, truly, I say to you, if any one keeps my word, he will never see death. (John 8:51)

What do you do with an aphorism? You think about it. You contemplate its possible meaning. You apply it to your life. This is the heart of the wisdom tradition: "to understand a proverb and a figure, the words of the wise and their riddles" (Prov. 1:6). This is how the *Gospel of Thomas* begins—with an admonition to seek understanding. But notice how the idea is formulated in John. For John it is not *understanding* Jesus's word that matters, but *keeping* it. This assumes that one already knows the meaning of his words—indeed, the singular "word" that is his testimony. Now it is a matter of *keeping*—retaining, believing, remembering his testimony. The issue for John is no longer understanding the teachings of Jesus, but remaining faithful to him.

Scholars of John have long noticed this about the fourth gospel. In John the teaching of Jesus has narrowed. Gone are the proverbs and aphorisms of Jesus, his parables about the kingdom of God, all of the sayings of prophetic critique. Instead, Jesus teaches only about himself. What he teaches is the basic mythic structure of Wisdom's descent and sojourn in the world: "I have not come on my own. But the one who sent me is true, and you do not know him. I know him because I am from him, and he sent me" (John 7:28–29). The issue is not what he teaches, but *who he is*—the very incarnation of Wisdom, God's own Logos. "I and the Father are one" (10:30). "Believe in God; believe also in me" (14:1).

It has all come down to this because of the way the fourth evangelist interprets his circumstances. He believes that his community is under threat because of the things it believes. In the midst of the long Johannine sermon known as the Farewell Discourse (chaps. 14–17), John's version of Jesus pauses to speak to his followers these telling words:

> I have said these things to you to keep you from stumbling. They will put you out of the synagogues. Indeed, the hour is coming when those who kill you will think they are offering worship to God. And they will do this because they have not known my Father or me. But I have said these things to you so that when their hour comes you may remember that I told you about them. (16:1–4)

John's community is under threat. The evangelist thinks that those who believe as he does might even be killed. In this moment he makes a decision. What matters now is not the wisdom of Jesus. What matters now is the claim that Jesus is who they say he is, the Wisdom of God, God's Logos. Will those who read his words be willing to die for this belief? And so he takes up a form that was common and popular among Christians in the latter part of the first century and tells the story of Jesus as martyr. Jesus goes to the cross never wavering in his testimony about himself. Will the evangelist's readers do the same?

THE *GOSPEL OF THOMAS* EAST OF THE EUPHRATES

This focus on Jesus's death—his martyrdom at the hands of his enemies—is, of course, the theme that connects John to the other biblical gospels. They all share this theme, and probably for similar reasons. They were all written by authors who lived out their lives in the Roman Empire, the very imperial power that arrested Jesus and put him to death for sedition. The early followers of Jesus all lived as dissidents within a totalitarian imperial society that did not accept dissidents with equanimity. To follow a criminal as though he were a savior, to proclaim another empire, a new kingdom of God that would soon arrive amid a great judgment in which the powers of this world would be overthrown—these were all things that placed the early followers of Jesus at odds with the imperial powers that controlled their lives.

At first the Jesus movement was so small and inconsequential that the authorities would scarcely have noticed it. The great empire-wide persecutions of Christians still lay centuries in the future, when their numbers had grown enough to pose a significant threat to the order and security of the empire. But even in these early years the followers of Jesus were at risk in an empire that valued conformity and order. Dissidents like Paul of Tarsus, who predicted the overthrow of the empire, who would not even eat the meat that came from the public sacrifices, soon became well acquainted with the inside of an imperial prison cell.

To these dissidents, the fate of Jesus was a comfort. If they were to suffer, they could take solace in the fact that Jesus had suffered too. As he was raised from the dead, so too would they be redeemed in the final hour. That is why the biblical gospels all culminate in the martyrdom and resurrection of Jesus. It is why Paul stressed to his readers the importance of the cross of Christ. He was not sent to preach with a "wisdom of word," he says, "lest the cross be emptied of its power" (1 Cor. 1:17). "I chose to know nothing among you except Jesus Christ— even this crucified one" (2:2). From reading the New Testament, one might readily conclude that Christianity is and always was about the death of Jesus on the cross.

So when the *Gospel of Thomas* appeared in the 1950s, one of the most striking and controversial things about it was the fact that it offered scarcely a word about Jesus's death and resurrection. Could this even be considered a gospel, theologians wondered aloud. Where is the gospel in it? For centuries, the gospel of Jesus Christ had to do with the saving power of his atoning death. Could a document that said virtually nothing about this be a gospel? And yet, here it was, the "*Gospel* According to Thomas." There is, of course, good news in this gospel. It has to do with Jesus's wise words. Whoever understands them "will not taste death" (1). Salvation is here. It just has nothing to do with Jesus's death. It is all about his words, his mysterious saving words. How shall we account for this dramatic conceptual difference in the way the *Gospel of Thomas* presents the meaning of Jesus?

The answer lies in large measure in the simple facts of ancient geography. The *Gospel of Thomas* as we know it today came into being in Edessa, east of the Euphrates River. At the end of the first century the Euphrates River marked the easternmost frontier of the Roman Empire. The emperor Trajan once tried to push that boundary farther east in the early second century, but his efforts failed, and Edessa and its sister cities out there in the Syrian desert remained free of Roman domination for almost another century. Edessa was not a Roman city. Its leaders cared little if an odd band of Jews settled there to meditate on the wise sayings of their slain leader, Jesus. The followers of Jesus likely settled in Edessa among the many other Jews who lived there and gradually came to blend into the multifaceted culture of this lively caravan town. They were not persecuted. They did not fear death—at least violent death. Martyrdom was not to be their fate.

Consequently, their Jesus was not the model martyr. He was the model sage. He spoke to them of how to navigate a meaningful life in the midst of the hustle and bustle of the caravan town. To the well-dressed he said, "Do not worry from morning to evening about what you will wear" (36). To those who watched fortunes gained and lost in the blink of an eye, he said, "Dealers and merchants will never enter the places of my Father" (64). To the worldly he said, "If you do not fast from the world, you will not find the empire" (27). To those who watched the traders come and go, here one day and gone the next, he said, "Become passersby" (42). Real poverty, he said, is when you fail to realize that you are a child of the Living Father (3).

The *Gospel of Thomas,* it turns out, was well suited to its circumstances. Those who read and meditated upon its verses did not fear the violent death of the martyr. They feared the same death that confronts every human being when faced with the fact of mortality. In the wisdom of Jesus, fused now with the wisdom and insight of Plato, they found an answer. Know thyself—that you are an immortal child of God (3). You come from the place of light, and to that place you shall return (50). This was an answer that would one day find its way into the heart of Christianity, when the threat of martyrdom had passed and the Roman Empire had become the Holy Roman Empire, a safe harbor at least for orthodox believing Christians. Persecution and violent death were now a thing of the past. All that remained was the eternal and universal question of human mortality. One day everyone in Christendom would come to believe in Plato's immortal soul and look forward to the heavenly journey home. But in the first century, to find this familiar belief one must look to a very unfamiliar gospel, the *Gospel of Thomas.*

For Further Study

The significance of collecting sayings in early Christianity was first explored by James M. Robinson in a famous article, "LOGOI SOPHON: On the Gattung of Q." Originally published in German in 1964, it later appeared in a revised form in James M. Robinson and Helmut Koester, *Trajectories Through Early Christianity* (Philadelphia: Fortress, 1971), 71–113. Robinson's ideas were inspired by Rudolf Bultmann's treatment of the sayings of Jesus in his *History of the Synoptic Tradition* (New York: Harper & Row, 1976), originally published in German in 1921. For a comprehensive study of such sayings collections in the context of early Christianity, see John Kloppenborg, *The Formation of Q: Trajectories in Ancient Wisdom Collections* (Philadelphia: Fortress, 1987).

The **Edessene origin of the** *Gospel of Thomas* was first asserted by the French scholar Henri-Charles Puech; see "The Gospel of Thomas," in Edgar Hennecke and Wilhelm Schneemelcher, eds., *New Testament Apocrypha*, trans. Robert McL. Wilson (Philadelphia: Westminster, 1963; German original, 1959), 1:286. Since then most scholars have adopted this position. One exception is Michael Desjardins, who thinks it could have been written in Antioch; see his essay "Where Was the Gospel of Thomas Written?" *Toronto Journal of Theology* 8 (1992): 121–330. For a summary of the arguments, see my discussion in *The Gospel of Thomas and Jesus* (Sonoma, CA: Polebridge, 1993), 118–20.

The story of **King Abgar** is told by Eusebius in *Ecclesiastical History* 1.13.10. The story of **Egeria's travels in the east** is found in J. Wilkinson, ed., *Egeria's Travels to the Holy Land*, rev. ed. (Jerusalem: Ariel, 1981). The account of her visit to Edessa is found on 113.

For more on the remarkable city of **Edessa**, see J. B. Segal, *Edessa: The Blessed City* (Oxford: Clarendon, 1970).

That **Judas Thomas is meant to be Judas the brother of Jesus** was the insight of Helmut Koester, who mentions it in his introduction to the critical edition of *Thomas* published in 1989: "Introduction" (to the *Gospel Accord-*

ing to Thomas), in Bentley Layton, ed., *Nag Hammadi Codex II,2–7 together with XIII,2*, Brit. Lib. Or. 4926(1), and P. Oxy. 1, 654, 655*, vol. 1, Nag Hammadi Studies 20, Coptic Gnostic Library (Leiden: Brill, 1989), 38–50 (see 39). For years, however, confusion persisted around the name "Thomas," with the broad assumption that this referred to the well-known "doubting Thomas" of John 20. But this is a mistake. For an explanation, see Stephen J. Patterson, Hans-Gebhard Bethge, and James M. Robinson, *The Fifth Gospel: The Gospel of Thomas Comes of Age*, rev. ed. (London: Clark, 2011), 29–32.

I have explored **the theology and teaching of the *Gospel of Thomas*** in an essay entitled "Jesus Meets Plato: The Theology of the Gospel of Thomas," in *Das Thomasevangelium, Entstehung—Rezeption—Theologie*, BZNW 157, ed. J. Frey, et al. (Berlin: de Gruyter, 2008), 181–205. This essay was reprinted in my book *The Gospel of Thomas and Christian Origins: Essays on the Fifth Gospel*, NHMS 84 (Leiden: Brill, 2013), 33–60. My interpretation of *Thomas* was influenced especially by Elaine Pagels's essay "Exegesis of Genesis 1 in the Gospel of Thomas and John," *Journal of Biblical Literature* 118 (1999): 477–96; and Stevan Davies's essay "The Christology and Protology of the Gospel of Thomas," *Journal of Biblical Literature* 111 (1992): 663–82. A Platonic interpretation of *Thomas* is also explored by Charles Hedrick in *Unlocking the Secrets of the Gospel According to Thomas* (Eugene, OR: Wipf and Stock, 2010).

For more on **Middle Platonism**, see John Dillon, *The Middle Platonists, 80 B.C. to A.D. 220*, 2nd ed. (Ithaca, NY: Cornell Univ. Press, 1996).

The ideas about **the *Gospel of Thomas* and Christian origins** expressed here are argued in more detail in *The Gospel of Thomas and Jesus* and the essays collected in *The Gospel of Thomas and Christian Origins*.

For more on **the relationship between *Thomas* and the synoptic gospels**, see my essay "The Gospel of Thomas and the Synoptic Problem," in *The Gospel of Thomas and Christian Origins*, 93–118. My argument for the autonomy of the *Thomas* tradition was laid out originally in *The Gospel of Thomas and Jesus*, 9–110. Recently two monographs have appeared that take me to task on this issue: Simon Gathercole's *The Composition of the Gospel of Thomas: Original Languages and Influences*, SNTSMS 151 (Cambridge: Cambridge Univ. Press, 2012); and Mark Goodacre's *Thomas and the Gospels: The Case for* Thomas's *Familiarity with the Synoptics* (Grand Rapids, MI: Eerdmans, 2012). An upcoming issue of the *Journal for the Study of the*

Historical Jesus will be devoted to hashing out this issue, with responses back and forth between Goodacre, Gathercole, and Christopher Tuckett, on one side, and myself, John Kloppenborg, and others, on the other.

For more on *Thomas* **and the historical Jesus debate,** see my essay "The Gospel of Thomas and the Historical Jesus," in *The Gospel of Thomas and Christian Origins,* 119–40.

John Dominic Crossan's book is entitled *The Historical Jesus: The Life of a Mediterranean Jewish Peasant* (San Francisco: HarperSanFrancisco, 1993). The ideas of this book were presented in condensed form in Crossan's *Jesus: A Revolutionary Biography* (San Francisco: HarperSanFrancisco, 1994).

I argued for many of these views on **the *Gospel of Thomas* and Paul** in an essay entitled "Paul and the Jesus Tradition: It Is Time for Another Look," *Harvard Theological Review* 84 (1991): 23–41. Subsequently, Simon Gathercole criticized some aspects of my position in his essay entitled "The Influence of Paul on the Gospel of Thomas," in *Das Thomasevangelium, Entstehung—Rezeption—Theologie,* BZNW 157, ed. J. Frey, et al. (Berlin: de Gruyter, 2008), 72–94. In response to his criticisms, I revised the essay for republication in *The Gospel of Thomas and Christian Origins* (237–60). I will say a great deal more about *Thomas* and the ideas expressed in 1 Corinthians in Chapter 8 of this book.

For more on **becoming male** and *Thomas* 114, see Marvin Meyer's essay, "Making Mary Male: The Categories of 'Male' and 'Female' in the Gospel of Thomas," *New Testament Studies* 31 (1985): 554–70; and Jorunn Jacobsen Buckley, "An Interpretation of Logion 114 in *The Gospel of Thomas,*" *Novum Testamentum* 27 (1985): 245–72.

For more on **the *Gospel of Thomas* and John,** one should consult Helmut Koester's *Ancient Christian Gospels* (Harrisburg, PA: Trinity International, 1990), 113–23. Ismo Dunderberg's book *The Beloved Disciple in Conflict? Revisiting the Gospel of John and Thomas* (Oxford: Oxford Univ. Press, 2006) is also helpful.

The significance of *Thomas*'s Edessene origins for its distinctive theology is the subject of my essay "The View From Across the Euphrates," *Harvard Theological Review* 104 (2011): 411–31, now reprinted in *The Gospel of Thomas and Christian Origins,* 61–92.

For more on ***Thomas* and the origins of the Christian concept of an immortal soul,** see my essay "Platonism and the Apocryphal Origins of Immortality in the Christian Imagination, or Why do Christians Have Souls That Go to Heaven?" in Jens Schröter, ed., *Apocryphal Gospels within the Context of Early Christian Theology,* BETL 260 (Leuven: Peeters, 2013), 447–76. It is now reprinted in *The Gospel of Thomas and Christian Origins,* 61–92.

6

THOMAS TRANSLATED

I have created the following translation based on the Coptic text of *Thomas* from Nag Hammadi. The *Gospel of Thomas* was originally composed in Greek, but only a few fragments remain of this original—the result of chance discoveries at the Egyptian archaeological site Oxyrhynchus. The entire text of *Thomas* survives only in a single manuscript, which happens to be a Coptic translation of a Greek original. I will include a few of the Greek fragments from Oxyrhynchus for comparison, but most of the fragments are too spare to be of any real help in reconstructing the original text of *Thomas*.

This serves as a reminder that with only one (or sometimes two) witnesses to this ancient text, we are on relatively thin ice. With most New Testament texts, by contrast, we have dozens of ancient manuscript witnesses. These multiple witnesses enable scholars to reconstruct an original text free (nearly) of the myriad mistakes and idiosyncrasies that fill every ancient manuscript. Our manuscripts of *Thomas* also contain many errors of this sort. But without additional witnesses, we cannot always tell where they are. Sometimes, however, they are obvious and scholars have corrected them. These appear in pointed brackets (< ... >) in the translation. The critical edition of the Nag Hammadi text of *Thomas* used here is work of Bentley Layton, published in Bentley Layton, ed., *Nag Hammadi Codex II,2–7 together with XIII, 2*, Brit. Lib. Or. 4926(1), and P. Oxy. 1, 654, 655,* vol. 1, Nag Hammadi Studies 20, Coptic Gnostic Library (Leiden: Brill, 1989).

In this translation I have given considerable thought to how one should handle the androcentric language of the text, which reflects its ancient time frame. When translating aphorisms or advice addressed to the general audience of the *Gospel of Thomas,* I have generally rendered third-person singular masculine pronouns as third-person plurals, on the premise that since the intended audience would have included both men and women, this is clearly what is meant. Elsewhere I have generally left masculine pronouns in place—where they are integral to the telling of a story or where they express some mythic idea in which gender plays a specific role.

THE TEXT OF THE *GOSPEL OF THOMAS*

Prologue

These are the secret sayings that the living Jesus spoke and Didymos Judas Thomas wrote them down.

Saying 1

And he said, "Whoever finds the meaning of these sayings will not taste death."

Saying 2

[1]Jesus said, "Let all who seek seek until they find, [2]and when they find, they will be disturbed, [3]and when they are disturbed, they will marvel, [4]and they will rule over the universe."

Saying 3

[1]Jesus said, "If those who lead you say to you, 'Behold, the empire is in the sky, the birds of the sky will precede you.' [2]If they

Here is the Greek fragment of saying 2 discovered by Grenfell and Hunt at Oxyrhynchus. It comes from POxy 654, lines 5–9. Notice how the Greek version lacks v. 2 in the Coptic, has a different version of v. 4, and adds v. 5.

¹Jesus said, "Let those who [seek] not rest [until] they find, <v. 2 missing> ³and when they find [they will be astonished, ⁴and when they have been] astonished, they will rule, ⁵and [when they have ruled, they will] rest."

say to you, 'It is in the sea,' then the fish will precede you. ³Rather, the empire is inside you and outside you. ⁴When you come to know yourselves, you will be known and you will realize that you are sons of the Living Father. ⁵But if it happens that you never come to know yourselves, then you exist in poverty, and you are the poverty."

Saying 4

¹Jesus said, "The man old in his days will not hesitate to ask a child of seven days about the place of life, and he shall live. ²For there are many who are first who will become last, ³and they will become a single one."

Saying 5

¹Jesus said, "Come to know what is before your eyes, and what is hidden from you will become clear to you, ²for there is nothing hidden that will not become manifest."

Saying 6

¹His disciples questioned him and said to him, "Do you want us to fast? And how shall we pray? Shall we give alms? And what diet shall we observe?"

²Jesus said, "Do not lie, ³and do not do what you hate, ⁴for all things are revealed before heaven, ⁵for there is nothing hid-

den that will not become manifest, [6]and there is nothing covered up that will remain without being disclosed."

Saying 7

[1]Jesus said, "Blessed is the lion that the human being will eat and the lion will become human, [2]and cursed is the human being whom the lion will eat and the human will become the lion."

Saying 8

[1]And he said, "The human one is like an intelligent fisher, who cast his net into the sea (and) drew it up from the sea filled with small fish. [2]Among them he found a fine large fish. [3]He threw all the small fish back into the sea (and) chose the large fish without difficulty. [4]Whoever has ears to hear should listen."

Saying 9

[1]Jesus said, "Look, the sower went out, filled his hand, and threw. [2]Now some fell upon the road, and the birds came and gathered them up. [3]Some others fell upon the rock and did not take root in the soil and did not send heads of wheat shooting up to the sky. [4]And some others fell among the thorn bushes, and they choked the seed and the worm ate them. [5]And some others fell upon the good soil, and it sent up good fruit. It produced sixty per measure and a hundred and twenty per measure."

Saying 10

Jesus said, "I have cast fire upon the earth, and look, I am guarding it until it blazes."

Saying 11

[1]Jesus said, "This heaven will pass away and the one above it will pass away. [2]And the dead are not alive, and the living will

not die. ³In the days when you consumed what is dead, you made it alive. When you come to dwell in the light, what will you do? ⁴On the day when you were one, you became two. But when you become two, what will you do?"

Saying 12

¹The disciples said to Jesus, "We know that you will depart from us. Who is to become preeminent among us?"

²Jesus said to them, "Wherever you have come from, you are to go to James the Just, the one for whom heaven and earth came into being."

Saying 13

¹Jesus said to his disciples, "Compare me (to someone) and tell me whom I am like." ²Simon Peter said to him, "You are like a righteous angel."

³Matthew said to him, "You are like a wise philosopher."

⁴Thomas said to him, "Teacher, my mouth is utterly unable to say whom you are like."

⁵Jesus said, "I am not your teacher. For you have drunk, you have become intoxicated from the bubbling spring which I have dug."

⁶And he took him (and) withdrew (and) spoke three sayings to him.

⁷Now when Thomas returned to his companions, they asked him, "What did Jesus say to you?"

⁸Thomas said to them, "If I tell you one of the sayings he spoke to me, you will take up stones and throw them at me, and fire will come out of the stones (and) consume you."

Saying 14

¹Jesus said to them, "If you fast, you will bring sin upon yourselves, ²and if you pray, you will be condemned, ³and if you

give alms, you will harm your spirits. ⁴And if you go into any land and walk about in the countryside and they take you in, eat what they set before you and care for the sick among them. ⁵For what goes into your mouth will not defile you. Rather, it is what comes out of your mouth that will defile you."

Saying 15

Jesus said, "When you see the one not born of woman, fall on your faces and worship him. That one is your Father."

Saying 16

¹Jesus said, "Perhaps people think that I have come to sow peace upon the world ²and do not know that I have come to sow conflict upon the earth: fire, sword, war. ³For there will be five in a house: there will be three against two and two against three, father against son and son against father, ⁴and they will stand as solitaries."

Saying 17

Jesus said, "I will give you what no eye has seen, what no ear has heard, what no hand has touched, and what has not arisen in the human heart."

Saying 18

¹The disciples said to Jesus, "Tell us how our end will be."
²Jesus said, "Have you discovered the beginning, then, that you now seek the end? For where the beginning is, there the end will be. ³Blessed are those who will stand at the beginning, and they will come to know the end and will not taste death."

Saying 19

¹Jesus said, "Blessed is the one who existed before coming into being. ²If you become my disciples and listen to my words,

these stones will serve you. ³For there are five trees for you in paradise, which do not change, summer or winter, and their leaves do not fall. ⁴They who come to know them will not taste death."

Saying 20

¹The disciples said to Jesus, "Tell us what the empire of heaven is like."

²Jesus said to them, "It is like a mustard seed. ³It is the smallest of all seeds, ⁴but when it falls on tilled soil, it produces a large branch and becomes shelter for the birds of the sky."

Saying 21

¹Mary said to Jesus, "Whom are your disciples like?"

²He said, "They are like servants who are entrusted with a field that is not theirs. ³When the owners of the field come, they will say, 'Release to us our field.' ⁴They strip (it?) bare in their presence, so as to give it to them and return their field to them. ⁵For this reason I say, if the owner of a house knows that a thief is on the way, he will be on guard before the thief arrives (and) will not let him break into his house, his domain, and carry away his possessions. ⁶But you be on guard against the world. ⁷Gird your loins with great strength, lest the robbers find a way to come to you. ⁸For the situations you are expecting will come. ⁹Let there be a person of understanding among you. ¹⁰When the fruit ripened, he came quickly with sickle in hand (and) harvested it. ¹¹Whoever has ears to hear should listen."

Saying 22

¹Jesus saw little ones receiving milk. ²He said to his disciples, "These little ones being nursed are like those who enter the empire."

³They said to him, "Then shall we enter the empire as little ones?"

⁴Jesus said to them, "When you make the two one and when you make the inside like the outside and the outside like the inside and the above like the below— ⁵that is, in order to make the male and the female into a single one, so that the male will not be male and the female will not be female— ⁶when you make eyes in place of an eye and a hand in place of a hand and a foot in place of a foot, an image in place of an image, ⁷then you will enter the empire."

Saying 23

¹Jesus said, "I will choose you, one from a thousand, two from ten thousand, ²and they will stand as single ones."

Saying 24

¹His disciples said, "Show us the place where you are, for it is necessary for us to seek it."

²Jesus said to them, "Whoever has ears to hear should listen: ³There is light within people of light, and they shed light on the whole world. If they do not shine, there is darkness."

Saying 25

Jesus said, "Love your brother like your soul; protect him like the pupil of your eye."

Saying 26

¹Jesus said, "You see the splinter that is in your brother's eye, but you do not see the beam that is in your own eye. ²When you cast the beam out of your own eye, then you will see clearly to cast the splinter from your brother's eye."

Saying 27

[1]"If you do not fast from the world, you will not find the empire. [2]If you do not observe the Sabbath as a Sabbath, you will not see the Father."

Saying 28

[1]Jesus said, "I stood in the midst of the world and in the flesh I appeared to them. [2]I found all of them drunk; none of them did I find thirsty. [3]And my soul ached for the human race, for they are blind of heart and cannot see. For they came into the world empty, and empty too they seek to leave the world. [4]But now they are drunk. When they have shaken off their wine, then they will change their minds."

Saying 29

[1]Jesus said, "If the flesh came into being because of the spirit, it is a marvel; [2]but if the spirit (came into being) because of the body, it is a marvel of marvels. [3]But I marvel at how this great wealth has come to dwell in this poverty."

Saying 30

[1]Jesus said, "Where there are three gods, they are gods. [2]Where there are two or one, I am with him."

Here is the Greek fragment of saying 30 discovered by Grenfell and Hunt at Oxyrhynchus; it is from POxy 1, horiz. side, lines 23–30. Notice that it makes quite a lot more sense than the Coptic version, which is probably corrupt. Note also how it appends the saying that appears as 77:2 in the Coptic version from Nag Hammadi.

[1][Jesus said,] "Where there are [three], they are without God. [2]But where there is [a single one], I say, I am with [him]. Raise the stone and you will find me there; split the wood and I am there.

Saying 31

¹Jesus said, "No prophet is accepted in his (own) village. ²A physician never heals those who know him."

Saying 32

Jesus said, "A city built upon a high mountain (and) fortified cannot fall, nor can it be hidden."

Saying 33

¹Jesus said, "That which you hear in your ear, preach from your housetops. ²For no one lights a lamp and puts it under a bushel, nor do they put it in a hidden place. ³Rather, they set it on a lamp stand, so that everyone who comes in and goes out will see its light."

Saying 34

Jesus said, "If a blind person leads a blind person, both will fall into a pit."

Saying 35

¹Jesus said, "It is not possible for someone to enter a strong man's house and take it by force unless he (first) binds his hands. ²Then he will loot his house."

Saying 36

¹Jesus said, "Do not worry from morning to evening and from evening to morning about what you will wear."

Saying 37

¹His disciples said, "When will you appear to us and when will we see you?"

²Jesus said, "When you undress without being ashamed and take your clothes (and) put them under your feet like little

Here is the Greek fragment of saying 36 discovered by Grenfell and Hunt at Oxyrhynchus. It is found on POxy 655, col. 1, lines 1–17. Note that it is quite a lot longer than the Coptic version from Nag Hammadi. As such, it stands much closer to the canonical versions of this saying in Luke 12:22–31; Matt. 6:25–33 (from Q).

¹[Jesus said, "Do not worry] from morning [to evening and] from evening [to] morning, neither [about] your [food]—what [you will] eat, [nor] about [your clothing]—what you [will] wear. ²[You are far] better than the [lilies], which [neither] card nor [spin]. ³[And] having one garment, what more [do you need?] ⁴Who might add to your stature? He it is who will give you your garment."

children and trample them, ³then [you] will see the son of the Living One, and you will not be afraid."

Saying 38

¹Jesus said, "Many times you have desired to hear these words, these that I am speaking to you, and you have no one else from whom to hear them. ²There will be days when you seek me and you will not find me."

Saying 39

¹Jesus said, "The Pharisees and the scribes have taken the keys of knowledge and hidden them. ²They have not entered, nor have they allowed those who wish to enter to do so. ³You, however, be as wise a serpents and innocent as doves."

Saying 40

¹Jesus said, "A grapevine has been planted outside the Father. ²And since it is unsound, it will be pulled up by its root and destroyed."

Saying 41

   ¹Jesus said, "Whoever has (something) in their hand, to them will be given (more); ²and whoever has nothing, the little they have will be taken from them."

Saying 42

   Jesus said, "Become passersby."

Saying 43

   ¹His disciples said to him, "Who are you that you should say these things to us?"

   ²"Based on what I am saying to you, do you not realize who I am? ³But you have become like the Jews, for they love the tree (and) hate its fruit, or love the fruit (and) hate the tree."

Saying 44

   ¹Jesus said, "Whoever blasphemes against the Father will be forgiven, ²and whoever blasphemes against the Son will be forgiven. ³But whoever blasphemes against the Holy Spirit will not be forgiven, neither on earth nor in heaven."

Saying 45

   ¹Jesus said, "Grapes are not harvested from thorns, nor are figs picked from thistles, for they do not produce fruit. ²Good people bring forth good from their treasure. ³Bad people bring (forth) evil things from their wicked treasure (which is in their hearts), and say evil things. ⁴For out of the abundance of the heart they bring forth evil things."

Saying 46

   ¹Jesus said, "From Adam to John the Baptist, among those born of women there is no one superior to John the Baptist, so his eyes need not be downcast. ²But I have said, 'Among you the

one who comes to be as a child will know the empire and surpass John.'"

Saying 47

[1]Jesus said, "It is impossible for people to mount two horses or to stretch two bows. [2]And it is impossible for slaves to serve two masters; else they will honor the one and insult the other. [3]No one drinks old wine and immediately desires to drink new wine. [4]And new wine is not put into old wineskins, lest they burst; nor is old wine put into (a) new wineskin, lest it spoil it. [5]An old patch is not sewn onto a new garment, because a tear will result."

Saying 48

Jesus said, "If two make peace with one another in one and the same house, they will say to the mountain, 'Move away!' and it will move."

Saying 49

[1]Jesus said, "Blessed are the solitary, the chosen ones, for you will find the empire. [2]For you come from it and you will return to it."

Saying 50

[1]Jesus said, "If they say to you, 'Where do you come from?' say to them, 'We have come from the light, the place where the light came into being by itself, established itself, and appeared in their image.' [2]If they say to you, 'Is it you?' say 'We are his children, the elect of the living Father.' [3]If they ask you, 'What is the sign of your Father within you?' say, 'It is movement and rest.'"

Saying 51

    ¹His disciples said to him, "When will the rest of the dead take place, and when will the new world come?"

    ²He said to them, "That which you anticipate has (already) come, but you do not recognize it."

Saying 52

    ¹His disciples said to him, "Twenty-four prophets have spoken in Israel and all of them spoke in you."

    ²He said to them, "You have dismissed the living one in your presence and (instead) spoken of the dead."

Saying 53

    ¹His disciples said to him, "Is circumcision beneficial or not?"

    ²He said to them, "If it were beneficial, their father would beget them out of their mother already circumcised. ³But the true circumcision, in the spirit, brings profit in every way."

Saying 54

    Jesus said, "Blessed are the destitute, for the empire of heaven is yours."

Saying 55

    ¹Jesus said, "Those who do not hate their father and mother cannot become my disciples. ²And those who do not hate their brothers and sisters and take up their crosses in my way will not be worthy of me."

Saying 56

    ¹Jesus said, "Whoever has come to know the world has found a corpse, ²and whoever has found a corpse, of them the world is not worthy."

Saying 57

¹Jesus said, "The empire of the Father is like someone who had [good] seed. ²His enemy came in the night and sowed weeds among the good seed. ³The man did not allow them to pull up the weeds. He said to them, 'Not yet, lest you go to pull up the weeds and pull up the wheat with it. ⁴For on the day of the harvest the weeds will be visible and they will be pulled up and burned."

Saying 58

Jesus said, "Blessed is the one who has struggled and found life."

Saying 59

Jesus said, "Observe the Living One while you live, lest you die and try to see him and are unable to see."

Saying 60

¹<He saw> a Samaritan carrying a lamb while going to Judea.
²He said to his disciples, "The (person) is holding tight to the lamb."
³They said to him, "So that he may kill and eat it."
⁴He said to them, "As long as it is alive, he will not eat it. But only if he kills it and it becomes a corpse."
⁵They said to him, "Otherwise he cannot do it."
⁶He said to them, "You too look for a place for yourselves in rest, lest you become a corpse and be eaten."

Saying 61

¹Jesus said, "Two will rest on a bed. The one will die and the other will live."
²Salome said, "Who are you, mister? You have climbed up onto my couch <as a stranger> and eaten from my table."

³Jesus said to her, "I am the one who exists from the one who is (always) at one with himself. I have been given some of the things of my Father."

⁴"I am your disciple."

⁵"Therefore I say, if someone is <at one with himself>, he will be filled with light, but if he is not at one with himself, he will be filled with darkness."

Saying 62

¹Jesus said, "I tell my secrets to those who [are worthy] of [my] secrets. ²Whatever your right hand does, do not let your left hand know what it is doing."

Saying 63

¹Jesus said, "There was a rich man who had much money. ²He said, 'I will invest my money so that I may sow, reap, plant, and fill my storehouses with produce so that I might lack nothing.' ³These were the things he was thinking in his heart, but that very night he died. ⁴Whoever has ears should listen."

Saying 64

¹Jesus said, "A man had guests. And when he had prepared the dinner, he sent his servant so that he might invite the guests. ²He came to the first (and) said to him, 'My master summons you.' ³He said, 'I have bills (to present) to some merchants. They are coming to me this evening. I ought to go (and) give them instructions. Please excuse me from the dinner.' ⁴He came to another (and) said to him, 'My master has summoned you.' ⁵He said to him, 'I have bought a house, and I have been called (away) for a day. I will not have time.' ⁶He went to another (and) said to him, 'My master summons you.' ⁷He said to him, 'My friend is going to marry, and I am the one who is going to prepare the meal. I will not be able to come. Please

excuse me from the dinner.' ⁸He came to another (and) said to him, 'My master summons you.' ⁹He said to him, 'I have bought a village. Since I am going to collect the rent, I will not be able to come. Please excuse me.' ¹⁰The servant went away. He said to his master, 'Those whom you invited to dinner have asked to be excused.' ¹¹The master said to his servant, 'Go out on the roads. Bring (back) whomever you find, so that they might dine.' ¹²Dealers and merchants [will] not enter the places of my Father."

Saying 65

¹He said, "A [greedy] man had a vineyard. He leased it out to some farmers so that they would work it (and) he might receive its fruit from them. ²He sent his slave so that the farmers might give him the fruit of the vineyard. ³They seized his slave, beat him (and) almost killed him. The slave went (back and) told his master. ⁴His master said, 'Perhaps he did not know them.' ⁵He sent another slave, (and) the farmers beat that one as well. ⁶Then the master sent his son (and) said, 'Perhaps they will show respect for my son.' ⁷(But) those farmers, since they knew that he was the heir of the vineyard, seized him (and) killed him. ⁸Whoever has ears should listen."

Saying 66

Jesus said, "Show me the stone that the builders have rejected. It is the cornerstone."

Saying 67

Jesus said, "Those who understand the universe but are lacking in themselves are lacking everything."

Saying 68

¹Jesus said, "Blessed are you whenever you are hated (and) per-

secuted. ²But no place will be found wherever you have been persecuted."

Saying 69

¹Jesus said, "Blessed are those who have been persecuted in their hearts. They are the ones who have truly come to know the Father. ²Blessed are those who go hungry, so that the belly of the needy will be satisfied."

Saying 70

¹Jesus said, "If you bring forth what is within you, that which you have will save you. ²If you do not have it within you, that which you do not have within you [will] kill you."

Saying 71

Jesus said, "I will [destroy this] house, and no one will be able to build it [. . .]."

Saying 72

¹A [man said] to him, "Speak to my brothers so that they might divide my father's possessions with me."
²He said to him, "Mister, who made me a divider?"
³He turned to his disciples (and) said to them, "I am not a divider, am I?"

Saying 73

Jesus said, "The harvest is great, but the workers are few. So beg the Lord that he might send workers into the harvest."

Saying 74

He said, "Lord, there are many around the <well>, but there is nothing in the <well>."

Saying 75

Jesus said, "There are many standing at the door, but it is the solitary ones who will enter the wedding hall."

Saying 76

¹Jesus said, "The empire of the Father is like a merchant who had merchandise and found a pearl. ²That merchant is a wise one. He sold the merchandise (and) bought the single pearl for himself. ³So also with you, seek the treasure that never perishes, which endures where no moth ever comes to eat it and no worm ever destroys."

Saying 77

¹Jesus said, "I am the light that is above them all. I am the Universe. From me did the Universe come forth, and to me did the Universe reach. ²Split a piece of wood and I am there, ³lift the stone and there you will find me.

Saying 78

¹Jesus said, "Why have you come out to the countryside? To see a reed shaken by the wind, ²and to see someone dressed in soft clothing [like your] rulers and your aristocrats? ³These people wear soft clothing, but will not be able to recognize the truth."

Saying 79

¹A woman in the crowd said to him, "Hail to the womb that bore you and to the breasts that fed you."

²He said to [her], "Hail to those who have heard the word of the Father (and) have truly kept it. ³For there will be days when you will say, 'Hail to the womb that has not conceived and to the breasts that have not given milk.'"

Saying 80

¹Jesus said, "Those who have come to know the world have discovered the body. ²But those who have discovered the body, of them the world is not worthy."

Saying 81

¹Jesus said, "Those who have become rich, let them rule, ²and those who have power, let them renounce (it)."

Saying 82

¹Jesus said, "Whoever is near me is near the fire, ²and whoever is far from me is far from the empire."

Saying 83

¹Jesus said, "Images are visible to people, but the light within them is hidden in the image. ²The light of the Father will reveal itself, but his image is hidden by his light."

Saying 84

¹Jesus said, "When you see your likenesses, you are full of joy. ²But when you (pl.) see your (pl.) images which came into existence before you—they neither die nor become manifest—how much will you bear?"

Saying 85

¹Jesus said, "Adam came from great power and great wealth. But he did not become worthy of you. ²For had he been worthy, [he would] not [have tasted] death."

Saying 86

¹Jesus said, "[Foxes have] their dens and birds have their nest. ²But a human being has no place to lay his head down (and) rest."

Saying 87

¹Jesus said, "Wretched is the body that depends on a body, ²and wretched is the soul that depends on these two."

Saying 88

¹Jesus said, "The messengers and the prophets are coming to you, and they will give you what is yours. ²And you, in turn, give to them what you have in your hands (and) say to yourselves: 'When will they come (and) take what is theirs?'"

Saying 89

¹Jesus said, "Why do you wash the outside of the cup? ²Do you not understand that the one who made the inside is also the one who made the outside?"

Saying 90

¹Jesus said, "Come to me, for my yoke is easy and my lordship is mild, ²and you will find rest for yourselves."

Saying 91

¹They said to him, "Tell us who you are that we might believe in you."
²He said to them, "You examine the face of the sky and earth, but the one who is in your presence you have not recognized, and you do not know how to examine this moment."

Saying 92

¹Jesus said, "Seek and you will find. ²But the things you asked me about in past times, and what I did not tell you then, now I am willing to tell them, but you do not seek them."

Saying 93

¹"Do not give what is holy to the dogs, lest they throw it upon

the dunghill. ²Do not throw pearls to swine, lest they make <them> [muddy]."

Saying 94

¹Jesus [said], "The one who seeks will find. ²To [the one who knocks], it will be opened."

Saying 95

¹[Jesus said,] "If you have money, do not lend (it) at interest. ²Rather, give [it] to someone from whom you will not get it back."

Saying 96

¹Jesus [said], "The empire of the Father is like [a] woman. ²She took a little yeast, [h]id it in some dough, (and) made it into large loaves of bread. ³Whoever has ears should listen."

Saying 97

¹Jesus said, "The empire of the [Father] is like a woman who is carrying a [jar] filled with flour. ²While she was walking on [the] road, (still) far (from home), the bottom of the jar sprang a leak (and) the flour spilled out [on] the road. ³(But) she did not know (it); she had not noticed a problem. ⁴When she had reached her house, she put the jar down on the floor (and) found it empty."

Saying 98

¹Jesus said, "The empire of the Father is like someone who wanted to kill a great man. ²He drew the sword in his house (and) thrust it into the wall to test whether his hand would be strong enough. ³Then he killed the great one."

Saying 99

¹The disciples said to him, "Your brothers and your mother are standing outside."

²He said to them, "Those here who do the will of my Father, they are my brothers and my mother. ³They are the ones who will enter the empire of my Father."

Saying 100

¹They showed Jesus a gold coin and said to him, "Caesar's people demand taxes from us."

²He said to them, "Give to Caesar what belongs to Caesar, ³give to God what belongs to God, ⁴and that which belongs to me, give it to me.

Saying 101

¹"Whoever does not hate his [father] and his mother as I do will not be able to be my [disciple]. ²And whoever does [not] love his [father and] his mother as I do will not be able to be my [disciple]. ³For my mother [. . .], but my true [mother] gave me life."

Saying 102

Jesus said, "Woe to them, the Pharisees, for they are like a dog sleeping in a manger, for it neither eats nor [lets] the cattle eat."

Saying 103

Jesus said, "Blessed is the man who knows in which quarter the brigands are going to enter, so that [he] might arise, mobilize his [empire], (and) arm himself before they invade."

Saying 104

¹They said to [Jesus], "Come, let us pray today and let us fast!"

²Jesus said, "What is the sin I have committed, or how have I

been overcome? ³Rather, when the bridegroom comes out of the bridal chamber, then let them fast and pray."

Saying 105

Jesus said, "Those who will come to know father and mother will be called the child of a whore."

Saying 106

¹Jesus said, "When you make the two into one, you will become children of Adam, ²and when you say, 'Mountain, move away,' it will move away."

Saying 107

¹Jesus said, "The empire is like a shepherd who had a hundred sheep. ²One of them, the largest, went astray. He left the ninety-nine (and) sought the one until he found it. ³After he had toiled, he said to the sheep, 'I love you more than the ninety-nine.'"

Saying 108

¹Jesus said, "Those who drink from my mouth will become like me. ²I myself will become them ³and what is hidden will be revealed to them."

Saying 109

¹Jesus said, "The empire is like a man who had a treasure hidden in his field, although he did not know about it. ²And [after] he had died, he left it to his [son]. (But) the son did not know (about it either). He took over that field (and) sold [it]. ³And the one who bought it came and, while he was plowing, [found] the treasure. He began to lend money at interest to whomever he wished."

Saying 110

Jesus said, "Let those who have found the world (and) become wealthy renounce the world."

Saying 111

[1]Jesus said, "The heavens and the earth will roll up before you, [2]and whoever is living from the Living One will not see death."

[3]Does not Jesus say, "Those who have found themselves, of them the world is not worthy"?

Saying 112

[1]Jesus said, "Woe to the flesh that depends on the soul. [2]Woe to the soul that depends on the flesh."

Saying 113

[1]His disciples said to him, "The empire—*when* will it come?"

[2]<Jesus said,> "It will not come by watching for it. [3]They will not say, 'Look, here!' or 'Look, there!' [4]Rather, the empire of the Father is spread out upon the earth and people do not see it."

Saying 114

[1]Simon Peter said to them, "Let Mary leave us, for females are not worthy of life."

[2]Jesus said, "Look, I will guide her along so as to make her male, so that she too may become a living spirit similar to you males. [3]For every woman who makes herself male will enter the empire of heaven."

FOR FURTHER STUDY

The following are also excellent **translations of the *Gospel of Thomas*.** Comparing them can sometimes be quite helpful.

Antoine Guillaumont, et al., *The Gospel According to Thomas: Coptic Text Established and Translated* (Leiden: Brill; New York: Harper, 1959). This was the first authorized publication of the *Gospel of Thomas.*

Ron Cameron, *The Other Gospels: Non-Canonical Gospel Texts* (Philadelphia: Westminster, 1982), 23–37. An excellent translation, this is part of a collection that brought *Thomas* to a wider audience for the first time.

Thomas O. Lambdin, "Translation [of the Gospel of Thomas]," in Bentley Layton, ed., *Nag Hammadi Codex II,2–7 together with XIII,2*, Brit. Lib. Or. 4926(1), and P. Oxy. 1, 654, 655,* vol. 1, Nag Hammadi Studies 20, Coptic Gnostic Library (Leiden: Brill, 1989), 53–93. Lambdin's translation is standard among scholars.

Marvin Meyer and Stephen J. Patterson, in John Kloppenborg, et al., eds., *The Q-Thomas Reader* (Sonoma, CA: Polebridge, 1990), 129–55. This translation was undertaken for a project called Scholars Version Gospels sponsored by the Westar Institute and Polebridge Press. This was the translation used by the Jesus Seminar and later printed in Robert J. Miller, ed., *The Complete Gospels* (Sonoma, CA: Polebridge, 1992). Polebridge made these translations available to the public and so many of them, including our translation of *Thomas,* later made their appearance on the Internet. This is probably the most commonly found version online.

Uwe Karsten Plisch, *Gospel of Thomas: Original Text with Commentary* (Stuttgart: Deutsche Bibelgesellschaft, 2008). Plisch, one of the most knowledgeable Coptologists in the world today, prepared an excellent translation in German for the German original of this work, which was translated into English by Gesine Schenke Robinson, who is also an excellent scholar of Coptic.

7

THE FIRST GOSPEL

In the Bible, the Gospel of Matthew is the first gospel. As every Sunday school child knows, the order goes: Matthew, Mark, Luke, and John. But as we learned earlier, this is misleading. Of these gospels, Mark was actually written first, around the year 70 CE. Matthew and Luke were written later, by authors who used the Gospel of Mark as a source. This, recall, is the Hypothesis of Markan Priority, one of the basic tenets of critical biblical scholarship. No one knows exactly when the Gospel of John was written, but a reasonable best guess would be in roughly the same time frame as Matthew, that is, fifteen to twenty years after Mark. *Thomas?* Also about the same time. Q? A little earlier than Mark, perhaps, but—and this is also a reasonable best guess—not a lot earlier, say, 50–60 CE. Luke may have been the latest of these gospels. Some scholars now place its companion volume, Acts, in the mid-second century.

Now, Jesus was active in the Galilee in the late 20s and early 30s CE, when Pilate was the Roman prefect in Judea. Our earliest gospels, then, were written twenty, forty, sixty, or more years after Jesus roamed the Galilee. This raises a number of questions. Why did it take so long for anyone to write down anything about Jesus? Before Matthew, Mark, Luke, and John, before *Thomas,* before Q—before all these later gospels, in all their diversity, what did the Jesus tradition look like? What form did the memory of Jesus take in those early years? And is there any way to dig behind the known gospels into that relatively unknown period when the Jesus tradition was nascent and fresh?

THE GOSPEL BEFORE THE GOSPELS

Why did it take so long for someone to write something down about Jesus? In the ancient world books were rare, and the skills necessary to read or write a book very rare indeed. Literacy rates in the Roman Empire were in the neighborhood of 5–10 percent; in Galilee and Judea scholars put that figure at around 3 percent. The materials needed to make a book or scroll were just too expensive to make literacy a practical technology for everyday use. And with 90 percent of people living at subsistence level, almost no one had the time or leisure to learn to read and write. Mass education, in which the neighborhood children would trundle off to school to learn their 3 R's, lay centuries in the future. So the answer to our first question is fairly simple. No one wrote down the Jesus tradition, because almost no one could read or write. It was a long time before someone happened to join with the followers of Jesus who could write, who had the wherewithal to purchase the necessary materials, and who had the time to devote to the actual production of a text. Gospels, it turns out, were a luxury almost no one could afford.

Let us not imagine, however, that the followers of Jesus sat around pining away for gospels to come along. In a world where books were rare and almost no one had the skill to use a book, cultural life generally did not center on books. This is a little hard for moderns to grasp. Books are everywhere in our world. Modern culture lives through literature and its modern derivatives, like movies, TV, and the Internet. And most of what we study from the ancient world also comes to us in the form of literature. Literature—what little there was—survived. But we must remember that almost no one in the ancient world actually experienced culture *textually*. Almost all of what we think of as culture was delivered and experienced *orally*. The Jesus tradition was originally an oral tradition.

Our first instinct may be to think of oral tradition as though it were just like textual tradition, only without the text. It was once assumed, for example, that sages of old must have been virtuosos of memorization, committing to memory the equivalent of hundreds of pages of text for ready presentation or recall whenever the occasion demanded. But it turns out this is all wrong. It isn't that a person could not, if motivated, memorize a lot of material. The problem is the motivation. This older model presumes that ancients knew about texts, valued them for what they could do, and in their absence tried to do what texts could do by an act of memorization. But this is a little like imagining people in the 1960s hearing about computers for the first time and then setting off to accomplish with a typewriter or slide rule what they imagined they might be able to achieve thirty years hence with a personal computer. Math was different in 1960. Correspondence was different. Databases were different. Before texts, culture was different.

Oral culture was more fragile. Texts endure; the spoken word does not. Oral tradition relied for survival on constant repetition and use. It had to be useful. If something was not useful, it was not repeated, and if not repeated, it very soon vanished. Now, things that are useful in one context are not always useful in another. Repetition of a saying or story in a new and different setting doesn't always deliver the desired result. The skilled sage was one who was able to render things useful in new and ever-changing settings. Oral tradition was malleable. It had to be.

One may see this even in the *literature* of early Christianity. Literature that comes from a predominantly oral culture behaves more or less like oral tradition itself. So when one compares a saying or parable of Jesus as it appears in two or more gospels, it is often striking how differently it has been rendered. This is true of the stories about Jesus as well. In sorting out the literary relationships between the gospels, we have before stressed the similarities that extend across these texts. But that is only half the story. Each of the gospel writers also exercised great liberty and creativity with the tradition. This reflects quite simply the oral mentality of the ancient world. Things were never simply repeated; they were repeated and interpreted.

Here is a good example of what I'm talking about. Matthew 20:16 preserves an old Q saying that goes like this: "So the last will be first, and the first last." In the Gospel of Mark the saying also crops up, but notice that now it is a little different: "But *many* that are first will be last, and the last first" (10:31). Ah! It seems that a few "first" people have now joined the Jesus movement. *Many* of the first will be last, but apparently there will be exceptions. In Luke, finally, there is yet another version of the saying: "And behold, *some* are last who will be first, and *some* are first who will be last" (13:30). In Luke's community—or perhaps just in Luke's own mind—the whole first and last reversal just won't hold water as a general principle. So he reformulates the saying to refer only to "some," presumably those "first" who are truly callous and—let us be fair—those "last" who are truly deserving. If malleability characterizes the Jesus tradition even in its textual form, this is all the more true for its oral form.

So before the gospels there was oral tradition, a lively exchange of stories about Jesus, of remembered sayings and parables from him, and more, all of it ever changing in response to the infinite permutations of particular circumstances that could arise among the followers of Jesus. Each of the gospels is, in a sense, an elaborate instance of this. Each evangelist rendered the Jesus tradition into a form that would bring Jesus to life for those in his particular community. And once these written gospels were created, did the oral tradition cease and give way to these new, written instantiations of it? Of course not. How could it? Who was there to tell all those sages and teachers, wandering apostles and prophets to cease and desist, learn to read, and buy a gospel? Absurd. No, for centuries to come the Jesus tradition would live primarily in oral form.

But all of that died centuries ago. What we have are the calcified remains of that tradition—written gospels—oral tradition frozen in time. But that is something. Could the gospels offer us a passageway, of sorts, into the broader world of oral tradition from which they derive? Yes, to an extent. Consider the saying about first and last that we just saw in Q and Mark and later in Matthew and Luke. There are several different versions of this saying spread out among the gospels: Mark 10:31, Matthew 19:30 and 20:16; Luke 13:30; and the *Gospel of Thomas* 4:2. There is also an echo of it in the *Letter of Barnabas* 6:13—another early Christian writing from about this same time frame. With a little analysis and comparison, one may quickly identify a Q version (Matt. 20:16; Luke 13:30), a Markan version (Mark 10:31; Matt. 19:30), and a *Thomas* version (*Thomas* 4:2). From these three separate instances of the saying in written form, we may safely conclude that before the authors of these texts wrote it down, this saying also circulated in oral form. That is how each of them came to know the saying independently of one another—they all encountered it in the oral tradition.

In what form did it circulate orally? Probably many forms—dozens even. Oral tradition was malleable. But we can easily catch the gist of it: the first will be last, and the last first. In that very earliest period of the Jesus movement, before texts, before gospels, people remembered Jesus saying something like this: the first will be last, and the last first. This short, memorable saying must have sparked a lot of conversation in those early years. *That* will always be lost to us, but the saying itself remains.

We will never be able to transport ourselves back in time to experience in fullness the rich conversation that was going on about Jesus in the first twenty years after his death. But from the gospels we can get a sense of the gist of what they were talking about. The key is something we have just seen in the case of the first-and-last saying: independent multiple attestation. When two or more texts share a saying, parable, or story in common, either the authors of these texts knew one another's work or they shared a source. We have seen in earlier chapters that Matthew and Luke share lots of material. Some of it comes from Mark, one of their shared sources. Some of it comes from Q, their second source. Their use of Mark and Q is indicated by a very distinctive pattern of agreement; the material they share agrees both in specific words, phrases, and sentences and in order (their shared stories unfold in a common plot or sequence). It is this shared wording and order that indicates Matthew and Luke used Mark and Q as sources.

But what about Mark and Q themselves? Each had a version of the first-and-last saying. But there is no evidence that Mark used Q, that Q used Mark, or that Mark and Q drew from another written source. Mark and Q do not share a common order, and they do not agree verbatim as Matthew and Luke do. For this reason, most scholars assume that Mark and Q are independent of one another. Their overlaps come not from a written source, but from shared oral tradition. The reason we could recover the first-and-last saying from the oral tradition was the fact that it is attested independently in two or more gospels—*independent multiple attestation.*

So how common is independent multiple attestation? Mark and Q overlap some, but recognizing these overlaps poses considerable technical problems. How can we know, for example, that Matthew and Luke drew a saying from Q when there is a Markan version that could just as easily have been their source? There are ways, but clear-cut cases of Mark-Q overlap are relatively few. John sometimes offers independent attestation, when its stories overlap with Q, with Mark, and a few times with just Luke. But John is on the whole such a different gospel, these too turn out to be relatively few in number. If we were to rely upon the canonical gospels and their sources for instances of independent multiple attestation, our window into the oral tradition would be very small. But the canonical gospels are not our only sources. We also have the *Gospel of Thomas*. That changes everything.

One of the most interesting and historically useful things about the *Gospel of Thomas* is the fact that it shares so much material with the synoptic gospels, and yet it does not seem to have been part of that complex web of literary relations known as the Two-Source Hypothesis. It was not a source for any of these gospels; its author did not use Q; nor did he use Mark, Matthew, or Luke as a source. And yet there are close to a hundred parallels between *Thomas* and the synoptics. So where before there were a dozen or so instances of independent multiple attestation, now there are about a hundred. Where before our glimpse into the murky world of oral tradition that preceded the gospels was so minuscule as to be insignificant, now we really have something to look at.

Before we turn to this material, however, I must add that none of what I have just said has gone undisputed. Some scholars have argued that *Thomas* is in fact not independent, that the author of *Thomas* used Matthew, Mark, and Luke as sources. *Thomas* did not draw these dozens of shared sayings from oral tradition, but from the canonical gospels themselves. Earlier I offered a brief explanation of my own view—that *Thomas* is an independent (or "autonomous") gospel. Now perhaps a more thorough discussion of this important point is in order. But before I begin, I must warn you: if your tolerance for scholarly tedium is low and you are willing to trust where this is going, you may wish to skip the next few paragraphs.

There are many conservative scholars whose Christian convictions simply will not allow them to include a nonbiblical gospel in the conversation about the origins of Christianity. The biblical gospels were chosen because they are the original and most reliable gospels, written by eyewitnesses even. *Thomas* and all others are late and heretical and therefore to be discounted. For many biblical scholars, this is all a matter of faith and not really negotiable. For them, *Thomas* is a fake, a knockoff of the more original true gospels, a deliberate perversion of a tradition whose more original form is to be found in the Bible. Needless to say, this is simply a different approach to history and scholarship, one that is far removed from the approach taken in this book. I will therefore lay those arguments aside and turn instead to the issues that critical scholars are debating.

How do you know when one author has used the work of another? In the case of the synoptic gospels, we think that Matthew and Luke used Mark because they agree both in how they word specific sayings and in their respective ordering of events. The Two-Source Hypothesis rests on the evidence of common wording and common order. If one takes that standard and applies it to the question of *Thomas* and the synoptics, it soon becomes clear that here is a very different situation. Unlike Matthew, Mark, and Luke, *Thomas* does not share in the high degree of verbatim agreement and the common order that link the synoptic gospels together and suggest the Two-Source Hypothesis. *Thomas* is not a fourth synoptic gospel. It clearly represents another effort, autonomous from the synoptics.

Others disagree. They point out that sometimes one finds a detail in *Thomas* that Matthew or Luke appears to have added to Mark, their source. How, they ask, if the author of *Thomas* did not know the synoptics, did he just happen to include details that turn up specifically in the editorial work of Matthew or Luke? An example will make the point clearer. In Mark 7:15 Jesus is heard to say, "There is nothing outside a person that by going in can defile him, but the things that come out of a person are what defile him." The context in Mark is the question of whether it might be acceptable to eat unclean foods, a significant question in ancient Judaism. The author of Matthew, as usual, borrowed this story from Mark, including it in his chapter 15 and changing details as he saw fit. When he came to this saying of Jesus, he apparently decided to reword it as follows: "It is not what goes into the mouth that defiles a person, but what comes out of the mouth, this defiles a person" (15:11). Notice that in rewording the saying, the author of Matthew added "mouth" (into *the mouth*, out of *the mouth*), presumably for clarity. Now, the same saying of Jesus occurs in the *Gospel of Thomas:* "For what goes into your mouth will not defile you. Rather, it is what comes out of your mouth that will defile you" (14). As one can see, this version is a little closer to Matthew's than to Mark's. But notice that Matthew and *Thomas* share the specific addition of "mouth." Is this just a coincidence? Or is this evidence that the author of *Thomas* borrowed this saying from Matthew?

If this sort of thing were relatively common in *Thomas*, one would have to assume that the author must have known one or more of the synoptic gospels. So how common is it? There are roughly 95 sayings shared by *Thomas* and the synoptics. This seems like a lot. *Thomas*, after all, is conventionally divided into 114 sayings. Ninety-five would be nearly all of them. But in reality, each of the numbered sayings in *Thomas* contains two, three, or more discrete sayings. Saying 14, for example, actually contains three sayings, and two of them have synoptic parallels. All told, there are about 200 actual sayings in *Thomas* (depending on how you count) and roughly half of them—95—have synoptic parallels. Close scrutiny of these 95 parallels reveals possibly 16 instances where *Thomas* has a telltale detail from one or another of the synoptics. In each of these cases, the evidence is slight—a single word, a grammatical detail, a pair of sayings in the same order, and so on. The rest of them—the other 79 sayings with synoptic parallels—show no trace of the various synoptic versions.

This is more striking than it may at first seem, for each of the synoptic evangelists placed a fairly strong and distinct stamp on the Jesus tradition. None of that shows up in the *Gospel of Thomas.* Even in those 16 cases where scholars believe they have found evidence of influence, *Thomas* never reproduces the bold interpretive moves that make each of the synoptic versions distinctive. Those who assembled the *Gospel of Thomas*, to be sure, often placed their own stamp on the material. But the synoptic signatures are completely absent. This would be very hard to explain if *Thomas* were actually dependent on the synoptic gospels. When we bear in mind that virtually all of this Jesus tradition would also have circulated orally, the chances that *Thomas*'s author knew it from reading the synoptic gospels are fairly slim anyhow. Written gospels were all small craft sailing in a sea of oral tradition. Under such circumstances, we can assume one author copied another only when there is strong evidence to suggest it. This is not the case with *Thomas* and the synoptic gospels.

So where does this argument currently stand among scholars? Recently one scholar has argued that the evidence summarized above indicates that *Thomas* is a case of wholesale plagiarism and that virtually all of the *Thomas*-synoptic parallels come from the synoptic gospels. The lack of evidence is simply testimony to the skill with which the plagiarist covered his tracks. But most are sobered by the relative paucity of the evidence for such borrowing and advocate more of a piecemeal approach. Where there is evidence that a saying in *Thomas* has come from a synoptic source, this must be considered a possibility. After all, the collection of sayings that we know as the *Gospel of Thomas* was not created all at once. It is a list, and probably grew incrementally over time. That a scribe remembered a synoptic saying and copied it into *Thomas* at some point is possible, even likely. But for most of the *Thomas*-synoptic parallels, we have to assume two independent witnesses drawing from a common source—in most cases, oral tradition. And that brings us back to where we started this long digression. Most of the *Thomas*-synoptic parallels are instances of independent multiple attestation. Before the discovery of the *Gospel of Thomas,* there were perhaps a dozen or so sayings with independent multiple attestation. With *Thomas* in the mix, there are now about 100. They are our window into the oral tradition—a much larger window than we ever had before.

If we are interested in the earliest period in which oral traditions about Jesus were being formed, *Thomas* and Q offer a unique opportunity. Q is the oldest known gospel. *Thomas* offers independent attestation for many of its sayings. Therefore, we may safely assume that all of these multiply attested sayings actually predate Q and derive from the oral tradition. In other words, the Q-*Thomas* parallels offer a window into the earliest oral traditions about Jesus, traditions that circulated in the twenty years between the death of Jesus and the first written forms of Q. That, for all practical purposes, is the first gospel.

EXCAVATING THE FIRST GOSPEL

There are about 50 sayings attested independently in Q and *Thomas* (I count 53—see my list of parallels in figure 10 on pages 215–216). These sayings represent a cross section of the earliest oral traditions about Jesus. It is a cross section only—not a complete account of the oral tradition. The oral tradition itself was a wide-ranging conversation. Not everything in that conversation found its way into Q and *Thomas.* To the contrary, we should assume that only a small part of it did. Most of it was never written down; and some of it was ignored by these gospels, only to gain a hearing later in Mark or even decades later in Matthew or Luke. But it is a cross section of material that we *know* was there at the beginning—or as close to the beginning as we'll ever get. So if you want to begin at the beginning, this is it.

First, some general characteristics. Out of these 50 sayings, 26 of them—so a little more than half—appear in both Q and *Thomas* as straightforward proverbs, aphorisms, parables, or sayings of social critique. That is a telling baseline. The tradition they share is largely a wisdom tradition. Another 13 of these parallel sayings are used by Q in the service of its overall "judgment" theme. But when we encounter these same sayings in *Thomas,* it is clear that they too appear originally to have been wisdom sayings or parables and sayings of social critique. Another 5 of these sayings *Thomas* reworks in the service of that nascent Platonic theology so characteristic of the *Gospel of Thomas.* But in Q these same sayings appear as wisdom sayings, social critique, or advice. So, out of 53 sayings, at least 44 of them appear originally to have been simple wisdom sayings, parables, and social criticism. In other words, the oral tradition that predates Q and *Thomas* was largely a wisdom tradition.

Q appears to have brought to this material a certain apocalyptic sensibility and in many cases has rendered the tradition to reflect that predilection. *Thomas* brought a Platonizing agenda to the tradition and sometimes appears to have worked the tradition accordingly. Now, wisdom texts from ancient Judaism often include apocalyptic scenarios and Platonic speculation, and so we should not be surprised to find these ideas in Q and *Thomas*. But if the cross section offers a glimpse of the earlier tradition from which these texts drew, it appears to have been on the whole neither Platonic nor apocalyptic, but mostly a wisdom tradition consisting of proverbs, aphorisms, parables, and sayings of social critique.

THE EMPIRE OF GOD

When we look at specific sayings contained in this tradition, some themes and ideas emerge with great clarity. First, this early wisdom tradition makes repeated reference to a striking and curious concept: the *basileia tou theou*, the "kingdom of God." As we have seen, this is a very common phrase in Q and *Thomas*. Naturally, one also encounters this phrase everywhere in this corpus—in parables, beatitudes, aphorisms. Everywhere.

Most Christian believers have come to take this phrase for granted. The kingdom of God is that heavenly realm to which the faithful go when they leave this earth for a better place. The Gospel of Matthew almost always calls it the "kingdom of heaven." And that is how most people think of it—"heaven." But that is mistaken. The author of Matthew didn't actually mean "heaven." He just used the word "heaven" because he was Jewish and generally shied away from using the word *theos* ("God") out of respect for the deity. "Heaven" (in Greek *ouranos*, literally "sky") is simply a circumlocution for God. The kingdom of God/heaven in this corpus is actually not very heavenly. There is only one instance in either Q or *Thomas* where the kingdom of heaven probably means "heaven" in that specifically Platonic sense of another place up above the sky: *Thomas* 49–50. But this is most likely a "*Thomas*" spin on things.

The kingdom of heaven (or of God) in the first gospel is an earthly thing, where tenants scheme, sowers sow, the hungry are fed actual food, and itinerant prophets sometimes knock on the door—as we shall see presently. But we should also probably now notice that this term "kingdom of God" is also generally not used with reference to the coming judgment, the apocalypse. Even in Q, where many sayings speak of the coming judgment, the kingdom of God is never used in this way. The kingdom of God is not heaven and it is not the coming apocalypse. It is something else. Here is how the matter is addressed in the first gospel:

> But when he was asked when the kingdom of God is coming, he answered them and said, "The kingdom of God is not coming with signs. Nor will anyone say, 'Look, here!' or 'There!' For, look! The kingdom of God is in the midst of you!" (Q 17:20–21)

> His disciples said to him, "The kingdom—*when* will it come?"
> <Jesus said,> "It will not come by watching for it. They will not say, 'Look, here!' or 'Look, there!' Rather the kingdom of the Father is spread out upon the earth and people do not see it." (*Thomas* 113:1–4)

"In the midst of you." "Spread out upon the earth." The kingdom, it turns out, is all about the here and now.

I have always preferred to translate *basileia* using the word "empire," rather than "kingdom," and in the translations of Q and *Thomas* provided in this volume I have done this. In Jesus's day, the Greek word *basileia* would have been used primarily in reference to various earthly kingdoms, especially the currently reigning kingdom, Rome. But we don't usually refer to Rome as a kingdom. We call it an empire—the Roman *Empire*. Why did the followers of Jesus choose this word and this phrase to signify their project? For one, using *basileia* like this is more than just a little bold. Why speak of empire, an ideal empire, God's empire, unless one wished to register a complaint about *the* empire, Rome? There was no "suggestion box" in the Roman Empire. Complaints and complainers were generally crushed with little ado.

But more than this, the use of *basileia* to frame things says something about the focus of this wisdom tradition. It was religious, to be sure. The Roman Empire was itself a religious crusade. The Romans believed that they were the most pious people on earth and that the gods had chosen them to bring peace to the world, even if it meant waging war. Jesus lived and died during the celebrated *Pax Romana*—the Roman Peace. But the *basileia* of Rome was more than this. It was also an economic system, an ever-expanding network of provinces and colonial cities established to extract wealth and resources from its conquered lands and to enrich the Roman aristocracy. And of course the Roman *basileia* was a political force. When the followers of Jesus chose the word *basileia* to frame their conversation, they meant to speak of something that was at once religious, economic, and political. In the ancient world these things did not fall into separate categories. Religion and politics and economics—they were all intertwined.

Curiously, however, our nascent Christian sages seldom speak *directly* about religion, politics, or economics. Perhaps this was because Jesus and his companions were peasants who experienced the empire only locally, close in. They probably knew nothing about the Roman Senate, how Rome's military forces were organized, or the difference between a *propraetor* and a *procurator*. Their knowledge of the empire was limited to the way it impacted their daily lives. It was the "surround of force" that imposed itself on them in the form of taxes and tribute. So there is a story in *Thomas* (100) and the Gospel of

Mark (12:13–17) in which Jesus's foes try to entrap him with a question about whether to pay the Roman tax. That is the sort of question that occupied the members of the early Jesus movement. They knew the empire in the form of oppressive taxes and tribute. They knew the empire in the form of tenancy, the result of scores of peasants losing their claim to ancestral lands through debt and bankruptcy. So they told and retold a story about tenant farmers who try to take over their rental property, but end up getting in over their heads by killing the owner's son (*Thomas* 65; Mark 12:1–12). They knew the empire as an everyday presence in their lives, and they remembered Jesus teaching people to imagine another empire, an empire *of God*. That, by the way, was what got them all into trouble.

In the first gospel Jesus appears as a close observer, a clever critic, a skilled raconteur with a penchant for planting odd ideas, many of them about this new empire. One image that endured through the oral tradition was the empire as "mustard." Jesus apparently used to say something like this:

> [The empire of God] is like a mustard seed, which a person took and threw into his garden. And it grew and became a tree, and the birds of the sky nested in its branches. (Q 13:18–19)

As we observed earlier, this idea is truly odd. Mustard was a weed in the ancient world. Why sow weeds in your garden? And who wants birds in a garden? Is the empire of God weedlike? Is it a nuisance? Does it attract unwanted pests?

The oral tradition captured another, similar image for the new empire: "leaven," that is, yeast. In Q these images were paired (13:18–21), but in *Thomas* they arrived from the oral tradition separately (20; 96). Here, again, is the Q version:

> And again, to what shall I compare the empire of God? It is like yeast, which a woman took and hid in three measures of flour until the whole batch was leavened. (13:20–21)

This doesn't seem so odd on the surface. If you mix yeast into flour, add a little water, and bake it, you have bread. But these ancient Jews were not baking Wonder Bread in the Galilee. The normal meal consisted of unleavened bread—pita bread. In that context, leaven had a different metaphoric flavor altogether. One can see this elsewhere in the New Testament itself, where it always signifies something bad, rotten, corrupt (see, e.g., Mark 8:15: "Beware of the leaven of the Pharisees . . ."). That is true generally in the Mediterranean world. Leaven is more like mold. Who puts mold in flour? Who would *hide* mold in flour? Imagine someone trying to use that flour. Whatever she expected to happen, she's in for a big surprise. Is the new empire a big surprise? Does it corrupt the expectations of ordinary peasants? The precise meaning of this image is not really clear.

It is provocative, though. This wisdom tradition is nothing if not thought provoking. You have to think about these images, consider them, meditate upon them. If you don't, nothing happens. Wisdom requires effort.

In the first gospel Jesus generally uses common ingredients to give expression to what he was imagining. Mustard. Leaven. A shepherd:

> Jesus said, "The empire is like a shepherd who had a hundred sheep. One of them, the largest, went astray. He left the ninety-nine (and) sought the one until he found it. After he had toiled, he said to the sheep, 'I love you more than the ninety-nine.'"
> (*Thomas* 107)

What shepherd leaves ninety-nine sheep unattended to look for one single sheep? In the corresponding passage in Q (15:4–5a, 7) it is worse: he leaves them alone "in the mountains." Is the empire of God about bad shepherding? If we were to mull it over, perhaps something like this would emerge: a single one can matter even more than the herd. In the Gospel of Luke this Q passage is modified to refer to "sinners" (see Luke 15:4–7). God cares about one sinner more than ninety-nine righteous people. Fair enough.

But Matthew understands it better, I think. In Matthew (18:12–13) the errant sheep is a "little one." The Matthean context is a street scene in which little children try to approach Jesus. Unattended children must have been part of the cityscape anywhere you went in the ancient world. Women died in childbirth, leaving orphans by the thousands. Jesus warns those around him not to try to corrupt them, for God cares for them just like the shepherd cares for that one sheep. In *Thomas* the shepherd has a reason to love the lost sheep more than all the others. It is the biggest, after all. In Matthew it is a stand-in for the smallest, the least, the lowest rung in the social order of antiquity, the street urchin. In the empire of God no one is lost. Now, is that a religious sentiment? Or is it an economic principle? Or is it a new kind of politics? It's a new *basileia*.

LISTEN TO THE BEGGARS

The beatitude, like the parable, is a common wisdom form. It begins "Blessed are . . . ," and the sage fills in the blank with an example of true happiness, fortune, or favor. There are many beatitudes in the first gospel. In *Thomas,* for example, we have "Blessed is the one who has struggled and found life" (58) and "Blessed are the solitary, the chosen ones, for you will find the empire" (49). In Q we find "Blessed is the one who is not offended by me" (7:23). This was, apparently, a favored form for the teacher Jesus. There are four very ancient beatitudes that occur in both *Thomas* (54, 68, 69) and Q—in the latter, assembled into a list that is used to introduce Jesus's inaugural sermon. Here they are as listed in Q:

Blessed are you beggars, for yours is the empire of God.
Blessed are you who hunger, for you shall be filled.
Blessed are you who mourn, for you shall be comforted.
Blessed are you when they insult and persecute you and utter

every sort of evil against you because of the Son of Man. Be glad and rejoice, for so they persecuted the prophets who came before you. (6:20–23)

The first requires a word about the translation. For those familiar with the Bible, this is a very well-known verse: "Blessed are the poor . . ." (Luke 6:20) or "Blessed are the poor in spirit . . ." (Matt. 5:3). But "poor" does not quite capture the spirit of the saying. The Greek word in question is *ptochos* (pl. *ptochoi*). In the Roman Empire most people were poor by modern standards. They lived at subsistence level, earning enough in a day to live for a day. *Ptochos,* though, is a notch or two below that. The *ptochoi* are the truly destitute, the beggars in the street. There is nothing noble here, no joys of the simple life. *Ptochos* indicates grinding, desperate poverty. It is often translated "beggars" or "the destitute."

So destitute beggars are blessed because the empire of God belongs to them. What could this possibly mean? In the Roman Empire they were the dregs of society, worthless, expendable. They had no place, no role in the Roman imperial system. But in the empire of God they are central. They belong—or, rather, the empire belongs to them. That would truly be a new and different *basileia*. But is there more to it than this? Do beggars know things, pertinent things in the empire of God? Is this why they are essential to it? They might know, for example, that the world is not as it seems. It wants to offer everything, but to some it offers nothing. They know that the world is not fair. They know that most people really don't care. They also know that some really do, that grace and mercy are real. They must know that we need others to survive. Is this why the empire of God belongs to them?

And why are the hungry blessed? Do they know things? Real hunger—starvation—is a singularly disturbing experience. It is physically painful, but it also brings profound humiliation and leaves behind a deep pool of unspoken rage. The truly hungry are blessed by nothing but food, which is what the beatitude promises. But the sages who cultivated this tradition wanted more. In the Gospel of Matthew "hunger" is transformed into a metaphor: "Blessed are those who hunger and thirst for righteousness," or perhaps "for justice" (Matt. 5:6). That is ennobling, and true. In *Thomas* hunger becomes a cause, a sacrifice for others: "Blessed are those who *go* hungry, so that the belly of the needy will be satisfied" (69:2). That is not original, but it too expresses a truth worth voicing. The beatitude is a simple form and, in its simplicity, malleable. Wisdom sayings unfold in a multiplicity of meanings, each to be judged by its distinctive claim.

What of those who mourn? Who are they? Much learned opinion places the third beatitude in the long tradition of those who mourn Israel's sins; others assume that these mourners bewail Israel's fate at the hands of its enemies. There is indeed a long tradition of this stretching back to the prophet Isaiah (see 1:1–3). But the first two beatitudes do not assume such a grand theological-historical arc. They are personal. The third is too. Mourning and grief literature in the ancient world is plentiful. Understandably so. Consider the life of Veturia, the subject of a grave inscription well known to students of ancient Roman social life:

> Here I lie, a woman named Veturia. My father was Veturius, my husband Fortunatus. I lived for twenty-seven years, and I was married for sixteen years to the same man. After I gave birth to six children, only one of whom is still alive, I died. Titus Fortunatus, a soldier of Legion II Adiutrix, provided the memorial for his wife who was incomparable and showed understanding devotion to him.
>
> *CIL* 3.3572

Veturia's life was not unusual. Married at eleven. Six children, five dead. Then death, probably while giving birth to the sixth. One can well imagine hers as a life filled with mourning. Ancients knew loss and grief. Did they also know that loss is easier borne in the company of others? Did they know that mourning itself brings comfort? Is comfort a religious concern? Economic? Political? It is a human concern.

The final beatitude in our list is different. The persecuted are not blessed by the promise of relief, only reward "in heaven." Persecution is, in this tradition, its own earthly reward. Why? It makes one a prophet. It is a badge of honor to be worn by only the most principled of critics. Among their companions, John the Baptist had been persecuted, and Jesus of course. "Wisdom is justified by *all* her children (prophets)," they said (Q 7:35). So these two must have had company. Why? To speak of a new empire—an empire in which "the last will be first, and the first last" (Q 13:30; *Thomas* 4:2), an empire that will come "as a thief in the night"—would surely have brought down the wrath of Rome's watchmen. We have called this a wisdom tradition, but there is plenty of prophecy in it as well. The followers of Jesus remembered something like this: "I have cast fire upon the earth, and look, I am guarding it until it blazes" (*Thomas* 10; Q 12:49). Jesus and his companions must have raised a ruckus. Q says that Jesus baptized with a holy spirit and "fire" (3:16). Theirs was a "baptism by fire"—this is where the saying comes from.

CARE FOR ONE ANOTHER

But this tradition is not all about the critique and the promise. It also contains advice that, when placed in its ancient context, sometimes turns out to be quite practical and constructive. Recall, for a moment, a Q saying we encountered first in Chapter 3. We saw it there as part of the Mission Discourse, a speech in the heart of Q offering instruction on how people were to spread the word about the new empire. Here is that speech (with our saying italicized):

He says to his disciples, "The harvest is plentiful, but the workers are few. So ask the lord of the harvest to send out workers into his harvest. Go. Look, I am sending you out like sheep in the midst of wolves. Carry no bag, no pack, no shoes, no staff and greet no one on the road. As for any house that you might enter, first say 'Peace to this house!' And if a child of peace is there, let your peace come upon him. But if not, let your peace return to you. And stay at that house, eating and drinking whatever they offer, for the worker is worthy of his reward. (Do not move from house to house.) *And whenever you enter a town and they take you in, eat what is set before you and care for the sick there and say to them, 'The empire of God has come to you.'* As for any town you might enter that does not receive you, as you are leaving that town, shake the dust from your feet. I say to you, on that day Sodom will fare better than that town. (Q 10:2–12)

Here is another version of that saying (again, in italics) in another context entirely, in the *Gospel of Thomas*. Notice that now it is part of a cluster of sayings dealing with dietary issues, but it is the same saying:

Jesus said to them, "If you fast, you will bring sin upon yourselves, and if you pray, you will be condemned, and if you give alms, you will harm your spirits. *And if you go into any land and walk about in the countryside and they take you in, eat what they set before you and care for the sick among them.* For what goes into your mouth will not defile you. Rather, it is what comes out of your mouth that will defile you." (14)

Eat what is given you, and care for the sick. It seems that as Jesus's followers moved around, they found themselves in many situations where this piece of advice proved helpful. But what was its origin?

Consider again the circumstances of someone who lives at subsistence level. There wasn't much margin for error in the lives of ancient peasants. A bad year on the farm meant falling into debt. Debt meant foreclosure. Soon you were working as a day laborer, that is, when there was work. If there was no work, you didn't eat. So, "Will I eat today?" is the first question every peasant wakes to each day in the ancient world. Now, what if you should get injured or sick? If you're sick, you can't work. If you don't work, you don't eat. You get sicker. You weaken. Before long you're circling the drain. So, "Will I get sick today?" is the second question hanging in the air each and every day. If only there were a way to secure daily bread, in spite of ever-changing personal circumstances. If only there were someone to nurse you back to health when you got sick. This is what John Dominic Crossan sees in this little piece of advice. Eat what is set before you and care for the sick there. It is a program: an exchange of food for care. Everyone is given food, and everyone is cared for when they get sick. Those who receive give in return. Those who give eventually receive their share. But it all begins with a gambit, a daring knock on the door, and an equally daring host who says, "Come in."

Crossan theorizes that this may have been the origin of the small communities we eventually detect emerging from the misty beginnings of the Jesus movement. Communities like the ones Paul created in Corinth, where "brothers (and sisters)" came together regularly to share a meal in which all were to participate as equals. Communities like the one that lived by the rules of the *Didache,* where beggars were to be welcomed and fed, but if they wanted to stay for more than a few days, they had to work (12:1–8). For such a system to function, everyone had to pitch in and work. Here, then, is a kind of lived wisdom at the heart of the new *basileia.* Is it political? It's practical. Eat what is set before you, and care for the sick you find there. Q adds: "And say to them, 'The empire of God has come to you.'"

If we follow this program forward into the various communities that tried to live by it, we encounter all the concerns and pitfalls one might expect. In the *Gospel of Thomas* participants have begun to fret about the food they might receive. What if it is unclean food? This means, probably, that the *Thomas* people had taken this program into Gentile lands and were trying to implement it in mixed Jewish and Gentile communities. Indeed, Edessa, where the *Thomas* folk were at home, was just such a place. They addressed the concern with another wisdom saying that was widely known among the followers of Jesus: "What goes into your mouth will not defile you. Rather, it is what comes out of your mouth that will defile you" (*Thomas* 14:5; Q 13:30).

The apostle Paul also famously tried to gather Jews and Gentiles around a common table in several locations in the wider Greco-Roman world—all of them urban, where ethnic enclaves lived side by side, but not always peacefully. In Antioch the experiment blew up in his face (see Gal. 2:11–14). In Corinth he was negotiating the terms in 1 Corinthians 10, where we last saw our saying. It was fine to eat meat that had been obtained from a pagan sacrifice, Paul thought, but only in private and only if no one takes offense (10:23–30). Sensitivity, compromise, bending to larger goals when principles might bring conflict—these are the hallmarks of wisdom.

With the Q people another kind of problem arose: rejection. They knocked on a few doors and apparently got run out of town (Q 10:10). It seems that at first they adapted with a new greeting: "Peace" (Q 10:5). But finally they turned their backs, shook the dust from their feet, and called down judgment upon those who must have been wary of this new, intrusive empire (Q 10:10–11). That is a little disappointing. Wisdom can easily wither under fire.

LET THE WORLD COME IN

The Jesus people seemed to have pondered the power of eating together quite a lot. The ability of the table to transform strangers into a community is considerable. Sharing food is one of the most common and intimate things human beings do. It demands generosity on one side and trust on the other. That is why most of our dinner parties are with family and friends. But the wisdom prophets played with this idea of open tables and open doors and pushed it to the edge of what civilization will tolerate.

Consider this simple story, attributed to Jesus, but told and retold in many different venues and forms:

> A certain person prepared a great banquet and invited many (guests). And at the appointed time for the banquet he sent his slave to say to the invited guests, "Come, for it is already prepared!" But one declined in order to tend to his farm. And another declined in order to tend to his business. And another declined because he was newly married. So the slave reported these things to his master. Then the householder became angry and said to the slave, "Go out on the roads and invite whomever you find, so that my house might be filled!" (Q 14:16–21, 23; *Thomas* 64)

The story is an odd one, to be sure. Like many of Jesus's parables, it starts out in familiar enough territory. A person throws a party and invites his several friends. But alas, none is inclined to come. They make various excuses, one after another, until the slave must go home and tell the master the bad news: you haven't any friends. You ran the flag up the pole, and nobody saluted. You asked for the honor of their presence, and no one granted you the honor. In fact, this is a classic honor/shame situation. Honor comes from knowing one's place in the world and having a certain ability to function successfully in that place. Our host does not know his place. He thinks he belongs at a table with these, his chosen peers, but they do not agree. So they shame him—the universal human sanction against such a misstep. If you don't know your place, the world will help you find it soon enough. And so our host feels the sting of social rebuke. He threw a party and nobody came. Now what?

It is here that the story begins to venture into uncharted territory. The host might be expected to do any number of things at this point—withdraw, hide out, sulk, quietly close the shutters and lay low for a while. But instead, he doubles down on the party. He tells his slave to throw open the doors to his house and welcome anyone who will come in. "Go out on the roads and invite whomever you find there." Who will he find? The poor? The rich? Friend? Foe? The young and the old, the clean and the unclean, the deserving and the rogue, the Jew and the Greek, the slave and the free, the male and the female—anyone and everyone is out there on the street.

They are all to come in to sit at table? In Luke's version the host tells his slave to go out and *compel* people to come in. That's about right. One should not expect that all or any of these disparate types would care to sit at table with strangers so different from themselves. Will the rich sit with the poor? Will the poor sit with the rich? The philosophers sometimes dreamed of a table with equal place for slave and free, but it was a dream. Table fellowship was then, as it is now, a thing for friends and family and peers. Eating together makes of individuals a community and offers to each an identity that derives from the whole. You are what you eat and the company you keep. Can a family be so diverse? Can a community exist without boundaries? Can you really open your doors to the whole world?

It is a disturbing enough tale to evoke sympathy from each of the literate scribes who wrote it down. *Thomas*'s author tweaked the excuses to sound a little more commercial—commerce being the chief threat to wise living in the caravan town, Edessa, his home. He concludes the story on a resentful note: "Dealers and merchants [will] not enter the places of my Father" (65:12). So there.

Luke's author took a higher road (14:15–24). He sets the story up with this advice: "When you give a feast, invite the poor, the maimed, the lame, and the blind, and you will be blessed, because they cannot repay you" (14:13–14). And so, alas, in Luke the host tells his slave, "Go out quickly to the streets and allies of the city and bring in the poor, the blind, and lame" (14:21). If your friends and peers stiff you, you can always win back your honor by assuming the role of benefactor. You may not have friends, but at least you'll have admirers.

In Matthew (22:1–14) the story takes a bizarre and gruesome turn. Now it is a wedding banquet. But the invited guests turn out to be murderous fools who not only refuse to come, but even go so far as to kill the servants sent to invite them. What does the host (now a king) do? He sends in troops to kill the would-be guests and destroy their city. What begins as a wedding party ends in slaughter! Matthew might be forgiven for this narrative miscarriage when we realize that his version is really an elaborate allegory for the destruction of Jerusalem at the end of the Judean revolt in 70 CE, an event that lay heavily on Matthew's heart. But the point of the allegory is far from edifying. It suggests that Jerusalem was destroyed in the war because its inhabitants had rejected Jesus, or perhaps the prophets before or after him. Either way, the host/king is God—a God who wipes out cities. The terror of wide open doors is replaced by the terror of a vengeful God. It's a poor trade.

JUDGE NOT

But Matthew was not alone. The temptation to judge others and call for vengeance is everywhere in early Christianity. As we have seen, the Q people succumbed to it with a vision of the coming judgment in which the "Son of Man" would come to vanquish all their enemies, as in the days of Noah, when "the flood came and took everyone" (17:27). Paul, the apostle of grace and mercy, also envisions a coming judgment from which "there will be no escape" (1 Thess. 5:3). "Love your enemy," says Paul. "Give him food and drink," for, as the saying goes (in Prov. 25:21–22), by doing so "you will heap burning coals upon his head" (Rom. 12:20). Love your enemy—love him to death. Kill her with kindness. But Q also preserves quite a different insight: love your enemies, *really* love them:

> Love your enemies and pray for those who persecute you, so that you may become sons of your Father, for he raises his sun on the bad and the good and makes it rain upon the just and the unjust. (6:27–28, 35)

Nature itself teaches the basic truth that God does not distinguish between the good and the evil, the just and the unjust. The sun shines and the rain falls on the just and the unjust alike. And yet the New Testament concludes with an apocalyptic vision in which the wrath of God is unleashed against the evil and the unjust with unparalleled fury. And who are the unjust, the evil? From the opening chapters of Revelation it would appear that they are other Christians, some of whom admit Gentiles into their company (2:9; 3:9), eat meat that has been offered to pagan gods (2:14, 20), and recognize women as leaders and prophets in their midst (2:20). The author of Revelation hated these rivals. They are "synagogues of Satan," he says, who "say they are Jews, but are not" (3:9). But these errant churches sound remarkably like the communities begun by Paul, who admitted Gentiles, allowed eating meat from a pagan sacrifice (if done privately), and welcomed women as his "fellow apostles" and "co-workers in Christ." How did these churches react to John's bitter vilification? Perhaps they would have followed Paul's advice and offered him food and drink—thereby heaping burning coals upon his head!

So those whose voices inhabit the pages of Christian scripture were not immune to the temptation to judge others. And yet, in spite of this, there is a maxim in Q that tries to raise the bar: "Do not judge, lest you be judged. For with the judgment you give out, you will be judged" (6:37). This saying is not in *Thomas*, but it is so widely attested, we may well assume that it too is part of this early corpus.

In Q it is integrated into Jesus's inaugural sermon, and within that sermon is an extended reflection on the Golden Rule, stated thus in Q: "Just as you want people to treat you, treat them likewise" (Q 6:31; *Thomas* 6:2). The point is not, by the way, that one should judge justly rather than unjustly. The maxim simply says, "Do not judge." In Q it follows another maxim: "Be merciful, just as your Father is merciful." The point is to refrain from judging others. Why? Because no one is perfect. Sooner or later you too will be caught up short, and "with the judgment you give out, you will be judged." In other words, don't consider yourself better than others. "Why do you see the speck in your brother's eye, but fail to notice the beam that is in your own eye?" (Q 6:41; *Thomas* 26). All are equally blind. "Can the blind lead the blind? Won't they both fall into a pit?"(Q 6:39; *Thomas* 34). We are all blind guides. It was an idea, a piece of wisdom that drew a good deal of reflection from the Q folk.

Even though one might say that nascent Christianity in the Roman Empire grew up as a cult of judgment, with the hope that God would soon intervene and rain apocalyptic fire down upon the enemies of the church, the principle "judge not" proved to be remarkably enduring as a minority report. There is an elegant statement of it in *1 Clement,* a letter to the Christ communities in Corinth written near the end of the first century. It turns out that these communities were as contentious at the end of the century as they were in the middle of it, when the apostle Paul first wrote to them. The author of *1 Clement* thinks that their problems stem from arrogance, conceit, anger, and a failure to be gracious to one another. To calm things down the author turns to a small collection of wisdom sayings that includes some of the sayings we've been discussing from Q. He introduces it like this: "We should especially remember the words (*logoi*) the Lord Jesus spoke when teaching about gentleness and patience," for he said:

Show mercy, that you may be shown mercy. Forgive, that you may be forgiven. As you do, so will it be done to you. As you give,

so will it be given to you. As you judge, so you will be judged.
As you show kindness, so will kindness be shown to you. The
amount you measure out will be the amount you receive. (13.2)

Little catechisms like this must have circulated widely in early Christianity. They are the legacy of a wisdom tradition that began with
Jesus and his companions, who eventually created longer collections
like Q and *Thomas.*

"Do not judge, lest you be judged." "Show mercy, that you may be
shown mercy." Roman rule in the eastern provinces was rarely merciful. When, after forty years of iron-fisted rule, Herod the Great finally
perished from the earth, the Jews rose up and begged Caesar Augus-
tus to spare them from more of the same from Herod's sons, who
were set to inherit his kingdom. In Galilee, a certain Judas (the son of
a famous bandit whom Herod had executed) seized the moment to
gather around himself a small following of bandit-rebels. Judas and
his band stormed the royal palace in Sepphoris, raided its treasury,
armed themselves with weapons from its armory, and began foment-
ing rebellion around the city. Jesus's family lived in Nazareth, just
a few kilometers from Sepphoris. They would have witnessed what
happened next. The Roman governor, Varus, marched from Antioch
with two legions to put things back in order. When he arrived at Sepphoris, he burned the city to the ground and sold its inhabitants into
slavery. Later he rounded up two thousand of the rebels and crucified them. Jesus would have spent his youth and young adulthood
rebuilding that ruined city from the ashes. If he was to imagine a new
empire, it would be an empire of mercy.

THE SEEKERS

That is a taste of what is in this tradition. But it is only a taste, a sampling. And it is *my* sampling, *my* taste. It may not be yours. But the

interesting and compelling thing to me about this early wisdom tradition is its malleability: it does not mean one thing; the meaning of its various sayings and parables is negotiable. What would it mean in some concrete situation to refrain from judgment? Why are beggars blessed? What will you do when you hear the story of a rich man who dies sitting on a pile of money? Will you snicker in delight, or will you wring your hands and worry about your own accounts? It depends. It depends on your place in life, your experience, your own wisdom and insight. This tradition makes meaning only when people hear and contemplate it for themselves. It does not state the Truth. It provokes you to seek for truth. In that seeking, everyone is on equal footing. The sayings, parables, and prophetic criticisms we see in this tradition all begin in a place where everyone is in the same boat—life itself. There is to be no special pleading. If you would have truth, you must seek the truth, and when you find it, you must advocate for it.

It all begins with the seeking. There is a wisdom saying picked up from the long tradition of Jewish wisdom theology that captures the spirit of these sages quite elegantly. Here is the version of it that appears in *Thomas*. There is no "original" in this case—the thing is *uralt*. It is, however, to my ears the best rendition:

> Let all who seek seek until they find, and when they find, they
> will be disturbed, and when they are disturbed, they will mar-
> vel, and they will rule over the universe. (2)

Seeking—it is the heart of the wisdom tradition. Pay attention. Think about things. Think about things that disturb you. Marvel at what you have not understood. Take in the whole universe. If you want to know the truth of something, you have to search for it. The sages who cultivated this tradition were seekers.

So who were they, these seekers? Do we know anything about them? Jesus was one of them. But there must have been others too, for when he was executed, the tradition did not die with him. It continued and grew. There must have been others. Who were they, and what were they like?

FIGURE 10. A LIST OF *THOMAS-Q* PARALLELS

KEY:

Regular text indicates simple wisdom sayings or sayings of social criticism in *Thomas* and Q.

Italics indicates sayings used in the service of apocalyptic in Q, which appear as wisdom sayings or sayings of social criticism in *Thomas*.

Bold indicates sayings interpreted Platonically in *Thomas,* which appear as simple wisdom in Q.

	THOMAS	*Q*
Seek and Find	**2:1**	**11:9–10**
The Empire Within	**3**	**17:20–21**
First Last, Last First	4:2	13:30
Hidden Things Revealed	**5:2**	**12:2**
The Golden Rule	6:3	6:31
Hidden Things Revealed	6:4	12:2
Fire on Earth	*10*	*12:49*
Heaven and Earth	11:1	16:17
Eat What Is Before You	14:4	10:8
No Peace on Earth	*16:1–3*	*12:51, 53*
What Eye Has Not Seen	17	10:23–24
The Mustard	20	13:18–19
Beware the Thief	21:5	12:39–40
The Person of Light	*24*	*11:34–35*
Speck and Beam	26	6:41–42
Preach from Your Housetops	33:1	12:3
Lamp Under a Bushel	33:2–3	11:33
Blind Leading the Blind	34	6:39
Strong Man's House	*35*	*11:21–22*
On Cares	36	12:22b–31
The Keys of Knowledge	*39:1–2*	*11:52*
Whoever Has Receives	*41*	*19:26*
Love the Tree, Hate the Fruit	43:3	6:43
Blaspheming the Holy Spirit	*44:1–3*	*12:10*
No Figs from Thorns	45	6:44b–45
Greater than John	*46:1*	*7:28*
Serving Two Masters	47:2	16:13

FIGURE 10. A LIST OF *THOMAS-Q* PARALLELS

	THOMAS	*Q*
Move a Mountain	48	17:6
Blessed Are the Poor	54	6:20
Hating One's Family	55:1–2a	14:26
Take Up Your Cross	55:2b	14:27
Two on a Bed	61:1	17:34
Jesus and the Father	61:3b	10:22
The Great Feast	*64:1–11*	*14:16–21, 23*
Blessed Are the Persecuted	68:1	6:22
Blessed Are the Persecuted	**69:1**	**6:22**
Blessed Are the Hungry	69:2	6:21
The Harvest Is Great	73	10:2
Treasure in Heaven	76:3	12:33
Why Go into the Wilderness	*78*	*7:24–25*
Foxes Have Holes	86	9:58
Washing the Outside	*89*	*11:39–40*
Reading the Times	*91:2*	*12:56*
Seek and Find	**92**	**11:9–10**
Seek and Find	94	11:9–10
Do Not Lend at Interest	95	6:34
The Leaven	96:1–2	13:20–21
Hating One's Family	**101:1**	**14:26**
Where Thieves Enter	*103*	*12:39, 41*
Move a Mountain	106:2	17:6
The Lost Sheep	107:1–2	15:4–5a, 7
Heaven and Earth	111:1	16:17
The Empire Within	113	17:20–21

FOR FURTHER STUDY

The classic study of the **oral tradition** from the last century, still widely consulted today, is Rudolf Bultmann, *History of the Synoptic Tradition*, rev. ed. (Peabody, MA: Hendrickson, 1994), originally published in German in 1921. Today's discussion is influenced strongly by the mid-century study of Serbo-Croatian oral cultures by Albert Lord in *The Singer of Tales* (Cambridge, MA: Harvard Univ. Press, 1954); the theoretical work of Walter Ong, especially his book *Orality and Literacy* (London: Methuen, 1982); and Werner Kelber's study of how oral tradition is transformed by writing, *The Oral* *and Written Gospel* (Philadelphia: Fortress, 1979). The chief antagonist to this approach was Birger Gerhardsson, whose book *Memory and Manuscript* (Lund: Gleerup, 1961) is championed by those who would hope for greater historical reliability in oral tradition. Ong's work, however, is fairly devastating to this approach. Richard Bauckham's *Jesus and the Eyewitnesses* (Grand Rapids, MI: Eerdmans, 2008) is similarly lauded among conservatives. For criticism of Bauckham, see Stephen J. Patterson, "Can You Trust a Gospel? A Review of Richard Bauckham's *Jesus and the Eyewitnesses,*" *Journal for the Study of the Historical Jesus* 6 (2008): 194–210.

On **literacy rates in the ancient world,** see William V. Harris's revolutionary study *Ancient Literacy* (Cambridge, MA: Harvard Univ. Press, 1989). For literacy in Roman Judea, see M. Bar-Ilan, "Illiteracy in the Land of Israel in the First Centuries CE," in S. Fishbane and S. Schoenfeld, eds., *Essays in the Social Scientific Study of Judaism and Jewish Society* (Hoboken, NJ: Ktav, 1992), 46–61; and C. Hezser, *Jewish Literacy in Roman Palestine* (Tübingen: Mohr Siebeck, 2001).

Is the *Gospel of Thomas* dependent on the synoptic gospels? The question is surveyed by Nicholas Perrin in "Recent Trends in Gospel of Thomas Research (1991–2006), Part 1: The Historical Jesus and the Synoptic Gospels," *Currents in Biblical Research* 5 (2007): 191–98. My arguments for an autonomous *Thomas* tradition were laid out originally in *The Gospel of Thomas and Jesus* (Sonoma: Polebridge, 1993). Recently two books have taken up the other side of the issue: Simon Gathercole, *The Composition of the Gospel of Thomas,* SNTSMS 151 (Cambridge: Cambridge Univ. Press, 2012); and Mark Goodacre, *Thomas and the Gospels: The Case for Thomas's Familiarity with the Synoptics* (Grand Rapids, MI: Eerdmans, 2012). The latter argues that *Thomas* plagiarized virtually all of its synoptic parallels from the synoptic gospels. Their views and mine are debated in the *Journal for the Study of the Historical Jesus,* vol. 36, number 3.

Sorting out the Q-*Thomas* overlaps was the subject of my essay "Wisdom in Q and Thomas," which was originally published in Bernard Brandon Scott and Leo G. Perdue, eds., *In Search of Wisdom: Essays in Honor of John G. Gammie* (Louisville: Westminster John Knox, 1993), 187–221. It has now been reprinted in my book *The Gospel of Thomas and Christian Origins: Essays on the Fifth Gospel,* NHMS 84 (Leiden: Brill, 2013), 141–74.

Most of **the interpretations of the parables and aphorisms** of Jesus that appear in this chapter are worked out in more detail in my book *The God of Jesus: The Historical Jesus and the Search for Meaning* (Harrisburg, PA: Trinity International, 1998). My reading of the parables is often influenced by Bernard Brandon Scott, *Hear, Then, the Parable* (Philadelphia: Fortress, 1980).

Again, John Dominic Crossan's interpretation of **"eat what is set before you and care for the sick"** is in his book *The Historical Jesus: The Life of a Mediterranean Jewish Peasant* (San Francisco: HarperSanFrancisco, 1991), 341–45.

8

THE FIRST CHRISTIANS

One fine afternoon in the early 50s CE an itinerant teacher sailed into
the Greek town of Cenchreae, a small port on the Saronic Gulf side of
the Isthmus of Corinth. His name was Apollos. He was coming from
Ephesus, where he had made the acquaintance of two young companions, Priscilla and Aquila. Like him, they were Jewish and shared his
interest in a martyred Jewish teacher, Jesus of Galilee. But as much as
he shared their interest in Jesus, Apollos was more interested in the
teacher of Jesus, John the Baptist. From the account of Apollos found
in the biblical book of Acts, we learn that he "spoke and taught accurately the things concerning Jesus, though he knew only the baptism
of John" (18:25). Perhaps Priscilla and Aquila argued with him about
this. Acts says that they set him straight (18:26). But this is probably
wishful thinking, for when Paul the apostle came later to Ephesus, he
found disciples of Apollos who had been baptized "into John's baptism" (19:3). In spite of their efforts, Apollos was still baptizing people
as John had taught. Jesus, after all, had been baptized by John. If it was
good enough for Jesus, Apollos must have thought, who were Priscilla
and Aquila to dispute its adequacy.

But by the time Paul arrived in Ephesus, Apollos had already left
for Corinth, where he expected a warm welcome from the Jesus fol-

lowers there. Whatever disagreement Apollos had had with Priscilla and Aquila, it apparently had not disqualified him in their eyes, for it must have been on their recommendation that Apollos had set off for Achaea (see Acts 18:27). The leader of the Jesus community in Cenchreae was Phoebe (see Rom 16:1). It was perhaps she who met Apollos at the harbor and escorted him the six kilometers up the road to the ancient capital of the Achaean League, Corinth. By the middle of the first century Corinth was a large, bustling city, the capital of the Roman province of Achaea. It was also home to several communities of Jesus followers organized by Paul only a few years earlier. Apollos soon settled in and began to teach.

Where had he come from, Apollos? Acts says he was a native of Alexandria, "an eloquent man, well-versed in the scriptures" (18:24). We might assume that he had been educated in Alexandria as well, perhaps in one of the academies that flourished around the great library, the preeminent center of learning in the ancient world. There his scriptural training would have included a good deal of Plato. This was the heyday of Philo, the great Jewish Middle Platonist, who read Moses in one hand and Plato in the other. Here the most sophisticated school of ancient Jewish wisdom was flourishing, and Apollos could not have missed it.

But his hero, John the Baptist, and John's protégé, Jesus of Nazareth, never got to Alexandria. Just how an Alexandrian Jew like Apollos might have become acquainted with the teachings and practices of these Galilean rustics is hard to say. Perhaps he made a pilgrimage to Jerusalem and there heard about them from Jesus's brother, James. Perhaps followers of Jesus and John had by then come to Alexandria and initiated Apollos into their ways. Reasonable guesses, all. In any event, by the time he arrived in Corinth he counted himself among the followers of Jesus, practiced the baptism of John, and taught a wisdom theology that would have been right at home among the educated Jews of Alexandria. He was eloquent and charismatic and quickly built a following among the Corinthians. No wonder Paul was threatened by his presence there.

No written record of what Apollos taught in Corinth managed to survive the sands of time. But because of the argumentative tone Paul assumes in the letter known as 1 Corinthians and his direct engagement of Apollos as a rival there, we can surmise that much of what Paul says in this letter was meant to roll back the effects of Apollos's teaching. Paul, after all, was in as good a position to know what Apollos taught as anyone. Later the two met in Ephesus (1 Cor. 16:12)—perhaps in the Hall of Tyrannus, where Paul held forth as a teacher for a few years (Acts 19:9). One can well assume that they exchanged views, perhaps on many occasions. So what did he teach, this itinerant teacher who carried on in the tradition of John the Baptist and Jesus?

THE WISDOM OF APOLLOS

Apollos taught wisdom (1 Cor. 1:18–25), a "wisdom of words" (1:17). If it reflected the sophistication and subtlety of the Jewish Platonism of Alexandria, Paul might well have accurately described it as "worldly" (1:20). At the center of his teaching would have been ideas about the human being—that we consist of flesh (*sarx*), soul (*psyche*), and spirit (*pneuma*; see 2:14–3:4). He would have taught that when the spirit reigns, it pours forth in spiritual gifts like ecstatic speech and prophecy (see 1 Cor. 12–14). He might have taught that the spirit is from God, and that just knowing this could lift one above whatever lowly station one began in and produce such pride that someone like Paul could mistake it for "boasting" (see 1:26–31).

Knowing all of this might have prepared one for baptism (see 1 Cor. 1:13–17). If administered by Apollos, this would have been the baptism of John, in which Jesus himself had been baptized, at which the heavens were said to have opened and the Spirit descended like a dove upon him (Matt. 3:13–17; Luke 3:21–22; Mark 1:9–11; John 1:32–34). In that moment, it was said, Jesus became "a son of God" (Matt. 3:17; Luke 3:22; Mark 1:11; John 1:34). This would explain how Apollos's baptism was understood as somehow conveying already the reality of immortal life, so that any idea of a future resurrection of the dead was superfluous (see 1 Cor. 15:12). For Paul, Jesus became the Son of God when he was raised from the dead (see Rom. 1:4). For Apollos, this would have happened at baptism. Apollos might have even taught that you could baptize the dead vicariously and thereby bring about their transition into immortality (see 1 Cor. 15:29). The followers of Apollos were not waiting for a future time when God would raise the dead. Already they were fulfilled, already they were rich, already they were "reigning" (see 4:8). For them, the empire of God would not to come to pass in some distant time or place. It was already here.

Where could Apollos have gotten this wisdom? Some of it was his own. But when we look closely at Q and *Thomas,* it soon becomes clear that Apollos was not alone. As exotic as he sounds, it turns out that most of the things we can see reflected in 1 Corinthians are evident in Q and *Thomas* as well. His wisdom theology must have been taking shape among those who collected and cherished the wisdom of Jesus of Nazareth (and John the Baptist). How similar is the theology of Q and *Thomas* to the teachings of Apollos?

Q, *Thomas,* and the Wisdom of Apollos

First, there is the very notion that Jesus's significance could be captured in his wise words. Paul, of course, disputes this with Apollos. The significance of Jesus for him, and for most of Christendom since, lay in Jesus's death and resurrection. But Q and *Thomas* are wisdom gospels, which focus on Jesus's words. Neither narrates or speculates about the significance of his death. Both are intent upon Jesus's wise words as the secret to life and salvation. In *Thomas* the one who discovers the meaning of Jesus's words "will not taste death" (1). In Q the idea is less dramatically put, but in one of the oldest parts of Q, the inaugural sermon—the bones of what would later become the Sermon on the Mount in Matthew—it is there at the conclusion of the entire speech: "Everyone who hears my *sayings* and does them is like the person who built his house upon the rock" (6:47–48). The words of Jesus are bedrock in Q and *Thomas*.

Jesus and John

But Apollos was a follower first of John, not Jesus. Was this just an odd thing about Apollos, or is there evidence in Q and *Thomas* that in this tradition there might have been room for more than one teacher, one hero, one sage? Indeed, there is. In Q, Jesus is not the only prophet of Wisdom. Q 7:31–35 is also a very old Q tradition. In its present Q context it forms the conclusion to a section discussing Jesus and John the Baptist, the gist of which is that John was great, a prophet, and more than a prophet, but Jesus is greater. But in this remarkable concluding paragraph Jesus is actually not greater than John. John and Jesus are different, but they are the same in one important respect. Here is the Q text:

> Jesus said to them, "To what shall I compare this generation? What is it like? It is like children sitting in the marketplaces calling to others, saying, 'We piped for you but you would not dance, we wailed but you would not cry.' For John came neither eating nor drinking, and you say he has a demon. The Son of Man came eating and drinking and you say, look, a glutton and a drunkard, a friend of tax collectors and sinners. Even so, Wisdom (Sophia) is justified by her children."

That is the passage as the IQP reconstructed it. But in Luke the final verse reads, as I would guess it originally did in Q: "Indeed, Wisdom is vindicated by *all* her children" (7:35). John and Jesus in this tradition are *both* children of Wisdom. They have different styles—John the ascetic, Jesus the libertine—but they are both cast in the same role. In this very old portion of Q, John and Jesus are not seen as precursor and successor, but equals. They were both prophets of Wisdom who experienced the fate of all of Wisdom's prophets.

Elsewhere in Q we hear the familiar lament:

[34]Ah, Jerusalem, Jerusalem, who kills the prophets and stones the messengers sent to her! How many times have I wanted to gather your children together, like a hen gathers her chicks beneath her wings, and you were unwilling! (13:34)

The words belong to Jesus in Q. But beneath this text, with its "mother hen theology," are the words of Wisdom herself. She sends her prophets, like John and Jesus, but the world does not listen. It turns a deaf ear.

This equal pairing of John and Jesus as prophets of Wisdom is striking and quite surprising. Every extant gospel bears witness to a cordial but clear parting of ways between John and Jesus. Jesus begins as a disciple of John and is baptized by him, but then breaks out on his own. John becomes the precursor, who paves the way for the real savior to come, Jesus (see, e.g., Mark 1:2–8; John 2:19–42). The Q folk would eventually adopt this notion (see 3:16), as did those who used the *Gospel of Thomas* (see 46). But was this the real story? Was John really the precursor to Jesus? John's followers did not see it that way. They continued baptizing in the Jordan Valley for a very long time, from which various offshoots eventually sprang. One of them, the Mandaeans, still survives today.

But even in the Jesus tradition there are indications that the precursor idea was a conceit later conceived. In Q 7:18–23 there is a story in which John hears about Jesus. It is a story that clearly predates its present setting in Q, for it seems to presuppose that John and Jesus had not yet met—in spite of the fact that Q opens with Jesus's baptism by John. In this story, John sends disciples to Jesus to inquire of him, "Are you the one who is to come, or shall we look forward to someone else?" Jesus tells them to go to John and say that the lame walk, lepers are cleansed, and the dead are raised—and "blessed is the one who is not offended by me." In this story one can clearly hear someone negotiating the relationship between Jesus's followers and John's, but presupposed is the fact that well after Jesus began to gather his own following, John continued to gather and teach disciples who were loyal to him. In this Q tradition the followers of John and Jesus are depicted as friendly and working toward the same goals. This would explain how, twenty years after the deaths of both John and Jesus, Apollos could show up in Ephesus and be greeted as a follower of Jesus who practiced the baptism of John. Both John and Jesus were Jewish prophets of Wisdom. Apollos honored them both. Why wouldn't he?

The Meaning of Baptism

The wisdom theology that Apollos taught clearly included baptism, the practice initiated by John the Baptist. In Q we actually hear about John's baptismal practice for the first time. In fact, Q begins with an account of the baptism of John's most famous disciple, Jesus (Q 3:1–22; Matt. 3:3–17; Luke 3:1–22). There are other accounts of this event as well (see Mark 1:9–11; John 1:32–34), which actually complicate our efforts to reconstruct Q's account. But the basic elements of the story, and the practice, are clear enough. All the versions of this story involve baptism in water, the descent of the Spirit on Jesus, and the proclamation that he is now a "son of God." These stories stem from about the time when Apollos was traveling around and baptizing people in the Johannine manner. His was, then, probably a baptism in water, in which the recipient was said to receive the Holy Spirit and by which he or she was recognized as a child of God.

Baptism in the *Gospel of Thomas* is a little harder to spot, but for scholars who know a little about early Christian baptismal practice, it pops out clearly in saying 37:

> His disciples said, "When will you appear to us and when will we see you?"
>
> Jesus said, "When you undress without being ashamed and take your clothes (and) put them under your feet like little children and trample them, then [you] will see the son of the Living One, and you will not be afraid."

The first thing that catches our eye in this saying is the act of disrobing. The only activity in ancient Judaism and Christianity that involved cultic nudity was baptism. This is clearly a saying about baptism among the *Thomas* Christians.

But scholars also notice a little tick in the saying that communicates another of its important valences: "when you undress *without being ashamed.*" This is a reference to the story of Adam and Eve in the garden, who, when they ate of the fruit, became ashamed of their nakedness (see Gen. 3:7). Initially they covered their nakedness with fig leaves. But later Genesis says that God made for them garments of skin and clothed them (3:20). For philosophically minded Jews, this was an account of how Adam and Eve, originally immortal, acquired mortal bodies of flesh. The garment of skin is the mortal body that clothes the immortal spirit dwelling within. For *Thomas* Christians, steeped in this Hellenistic Jewish reading of Genesis, the act of disrobing for baptism would have had special significance. To "undress without being ashamed" was to enact ritually a return to that original, spiritual state of immortality before Adam and Eve fell from perfection and acquired their "garments of skin."

This is not the only nascent Christian tradition that draws upon the story of Adam and Eve to interpret the significance of descending into baptismal waters. In another of Paul's letters, the Letter to the Galatians, Paul also makes reference to baptism. It is a passing remark, made in the context of a dispute that does not involve baptism at all. But in this brief statement, Paul pulls back the curtain on what may have been the earliest creedal formulation of the movement that would eventually become Christianity. Paul is trying to convince the Galatian followers that it is not necessary for Gentiles to become Jewish in order to become part of their movement—that circumcision is not necessary for them. In the midst of making his case, Paul quotes to them a baptismal formula with which they must have been familiar. Perhaps Paul had used it when he baptized them into the new faith. But Paul had not invented it. For various reasons, scholars think that it was a pre-Pauline formula that Paul himself had learned from others. Here is the formula as Paul quotes it:

> In Christ you are all children (sons) of God (through faith).
> For as many of you as were baptized into Christ have put
>   on Christ.
> There is no longer Jew nor Greek;
> There is no longer slave nor free;
> There is no longer male and female;
> For you are all one in Christ Jesus. (3:26–28)

Paul's interest in this formula is in the first clause of the three—"There is neither Jew nor Greek." But our interest is in the third clause. Scholars have noticed that it is formulated ever so slightly at odds with the first two. It is not, as would be expected, that in Christ there is "no longer man nor woman," but rather "no longer male and female." Why the oddity? It is because the words "male and female" mimic directly the words of Genesis 1:27 in the Greek version available to most Greek-speaking Jews of the time. This, then, is another baptismal reference to Genesis and the legend of how Adam and Eve came to be. The formula means to say that in baptism the gendered nature of human beings, which goes back to Genesis, is overcome.

In another early Christian gospel the baptismal traditions of *Thomas* 37 and Galatians 3:28 are brought together in a way that reveals more clearly how this tradition works. This gospel is the lost *Gospel of the Egyptians,* known to us only through snippets of it that survive in quotations found in other works. This quotation is found in a work of Clement of Alexandria, a second-century Christian philosopher:

> When Salome asked when the things that she had asked about would be made known, the Lord said, "When you have trampled on the garment of shame, and when the two become one, and the male together with the female are neither male nor female." (*Stromateis* 3.13.92)

Salome, a woman who was a disciple of Jesus, has asked him about certain hidden teachings. When will they be revealed? Jesus replies that they would be revealed at baptism, when "you have trampled on the garment of shame." This must refer, on the one hand, to the actual clothes worn by initiates as they arrived to be baptized. But as they disrobed to be immersed in the baptismal waters, the shedding of these garments would be at once the shedding of their old lives, their old selves. Part of that self was, of course, the gendered self. The new self that emerged from those primordial waters was different. No longer male and female, the initiate was said to be "neither male nor female."

The somewhat later *Gospel of Philip* reveals the interpretation of Genesis that was presupposed in such traditions. In this gospel, Jesus teaches, "When Eve was in Adam, there was no death. But when she separated from him, death came into being" (68.22–24). In other words, the separation of Eve from Adam in Genesis 2:18–24 was the beginning of sin and death. But Christ has come, by this account, to heal this separation: "Christ came to correct the separation that existed from the beginning and to unite the two, to give life to those who died because of the separation and unite them" (70.13–17). In the *Gospel of Philip*, this reunification is achieved in a ritual known as the "bridal chamber," a mysterious ceremony about which very little is known. But in the earliest communities, this was the meaning of baptism.

If this was the meaning of baptism in *Thomas* and even in the nascent Christian communities from whom Paul learned the baptismal formula in Galatians 3:27–28, could this have been the meaning of baptism for Apollos as well? Perhaps. In one very well-known passage, 1 Corinthians 11:2–16, Paul argues against a practice that can best be described as ritualized gender-bending. Traditionally, it has been read to mean that women must worship with their heads covered by a veil—a practice that persists in many churches even to this day. But the Greek word for "veil" never actually appears in this passage. Instead, the issue seems to have been how men and women were wearing their hair (see vv. 13–15).

When they prayed or prophesied in the spirit men were wearing their hair long, against custom, and women were wearing their hair—already long by custom—down about their shoulders instead of up on their heads in a knot or bun or under a fancy headdress, as respectable women did. In other words, both men and women were praying and prophesying in long, flowing hair. You couldn't tell them apart. In appearance, they were "neither male nor female." They must have justified this practice with a reading of Genesis similar to what we have seen in *Thomas* and Galatians 3:28.

This is indicated by the tack Paul takes in opposing them. He admits that "in the Lord" men and women are now equal—"for as woman was made from man, now man is born of woman" (vv. 11–12). But blurring the distinction between male and female was messing with the order of creation (see vv. 2–3), and this just bothered Paul.

He says it's "because of the angels," but no one knows what this cryptic remark means. In any event, the Corinthians were messing with the order of creation. Who taught them to do this? Not Paul. It must have been Apollos, who baptized them.

Spiritually, Children of God

The role played by the spirit in Apollos's theology cannot be overstated. Those who were baptized by Apollos in Corinth apparently thought of themselves as "spirituals" (*pneumatikoi*) as opposed to people of flesh (*sarkinoi;* 1 Cor. 3:1–4). This juxtaposition of spirit and flesh was one that the readers of *Thomas* would have understood (see 29), indeed, as it would have had a broad resonance in Jewish wisdom theology wherever Platonic thinking had come into play. The spirit is always the presence of the divine in humanity, the God dwelling within. It makes sense then that blaspheming the Spirit is the unforgiveable sin in both *Thomas* (44) and Q (12:10). In Q, after the Spirit descends upon Jesus at his baptism, it then plays a decisive role in his prophetic transformation, first driving him into the wilderness to prepare through ordeal for the life of prophetic calling (Q 4:1). Later in Q, it is said to help those facing ordeal find the words to defend themselves (12:12).

Paul, of course, is also well acquainted with the Spirit and experienced the same spiritual gifts that were manifested by those whom Apollos had baptized, such as speaking in tongues and prophecy (1 Cor. 14:18). But in a later letter, to the Romans, he mentions another practice that was apparently common enough that Paul could assume these Roman communities, which he had never visited, knew it. This is what he says: "For all who are led by the Spirit of God are children of God. . . . When we cry 'Abba! Father!' it is the Spirit bearing witness with our spirit that we are children of God" (8:14–15).

This, then, was another feature of this early wisdom theology: the truly wise know that they are children of God. Baptism signaled it; spiritual gifts bore witness to it. When Paul introduced that baptismal formula in Galatians 3:28, it was to show in part that all who are baptized have become "children (sons) of God" (see Gal. 3:26). In Q the baptism of Jesus by John conveys sonship upon Jesus (Q 3:22)—a claim one might assume was unique and associated with Jesus alone. But this would be to overlook the relatively common way in which ancients used the "son of a god" phrase. In Q itself, in the inaugural sermon, those who follow the wisdom of Jesus, love their enemies, treat others as they would be treated, and lend without expectation of any return are said to be "sons (children) of your Father" (6:35). Perhaps the clearest and most programmatic expression of this idea is in the opening lines of the *Gospel of Thomas:*

> Jesus said, "If those who lead you say to you, 'Behold, the empire is in the sky,' the birds of the sky will precede you.' If they say to you, 'It is in the sea,' then the fish will precede you. Rather, the empire is inside you and outside you. When you come to know yourselves, you will be known and you will realize that you are sons (children) of the Living Father. But if it happens that you never come to know yourselves, then you exist in poverty, and you are the poverty." (3)

In the *Gospel of Thomas,* the quest for wisdom is cast in terms of the Hellenistic ideal of self-knowledge, but the thing individuals discover about the self is the truth that they are children of God.

Messengers from God

If in this tradition all are said to be children ("sons") of God, is there anything left for its leading figures, John and Jesus? Is there a "Christology" here? Yes, in a sense. John and Jesus were messengers sent by God into the world to reveal Wisdom's ways to the children of God. That this way of thinking about Jesus was around from the very first days of the Jesus movement is evident from elsewhere in the Pauline correspondence. In Paul's letter to the Christ community in Philippi there is found a hymn to Christ composed around this very theme. The so-called Philippians Hymn is widely regarded by scholars as a pre-Pauline hymn that Paul felt moved to incorporate into this letter. It is one of the oldest traditions in the New Testament:

> [Christ Jesus,]
> Who, though he was in the form of God,
> Did not try to be equal with God,
> But emptied himself,
> And took the form of a slave,
> And was born in human likeness.
> And being found in human form,
> he humbled himself,
> and became obedient unto death—death by crucifixion.
> Therefore, God has highly exalted him
> And given him the name that is above every name,
> That at the name of Jesus every knee should bow,
> In heaven and on earth and under the earth,
> And every tongue confess that Jesus Christ is Lord,
> To the Glory of God the Father. (2:5–11)

This highly mythological view of Jesus is found also in the *Gospel of Thomas,* where Jesus speaks in the first person as the descending and ascending messenger from God:

> Jesus said, "I stood in the midst of the world and in the flesh I appeared to them. I found all of them drunk; none of them did I find thirsty. And my soul ached for the human race, for they are blind of heart and cannot see. For they came into the world empty, and empty too they seek to leave the world. But now they are drunk. When they have shaken off their wine, then they will change their minds." (28)

This is often seen as an element of "Gnostic" mythology in *Thomas,* but one should bear in mind that this mytheme was at home in Jewish wisdom theology long before it was found useful among later so-called Gnostics (see, e.g., Prov. 8; *1 Enoch* 42; Sir. 24). What is more, Q also indulges in this kind of mythic speculation about Jesus, again, as in *Thomas,* in the first-person voice of Jesus himself:

> I bless you, Father, Lord of heaven and earth, for you have hidden these things from sages and scholars and revealed them to babes. Yes, Father, for this is what seemed right to you. All things have been entrusted me by my Father. And no one knows the son except the Father, and none the Father except the son, and anyone to whom the son wishes to reveal (him). (10:21–22)

One wonders if Apollos taught that Wisdom's second child, John the Baptist, was also a messenger sent from God. Paul doesn't say anything about this in 1 Corinthians. Perhaps Apollos did teach this, and Paul raised no objection because he had none. On the other hand, Paul does say in 1 Corinthians that no one under the Spirit's influence could ever say "Jesus be cursed" (12:3). To what could Paul be referring? Who would say such a thing, and why? Could the followers of Apollos have said this, because they did not believe that Jesus was the divine messenger sent from God? But if not Jesus, then who? If Apollos did not see John as precursor for, but simply as a predecessor to Jesus, then perhaps he would have seen John in this role instead. Perhaps John was his descending and ascending messenger. If this sounds unlikely, one should remember that some twenty years later it was precisely such a dispute that prompted the author of the Gospel of John to insert a disclaimer into the poetry of the Johannine prologue clarifying, explicitly, that Jesus, not John, was the Logos sent into the world to bring light and life (see 1:6–8). Are these texts the remnants of a quarrel that broke out among the Wisdom prophets about who, really, was the true prophet sent from God?

The larger view here is of a movement of prophets who understood their heroes and themselves in terms of a wisdom tradition with deep roots in Hellenistic Judaism. In the period of Christian origins this idea had blossomed into a rich spiritual tradition in which Sophia, a mythological figure, the divine personification of Wisdom, was thought to bridge the gap between God and mortals. Through her aegis, people could explore the secrets of the universe, plumb the depths of human experience, and become wise in the ways of God. A contemporary version of it is found in the Wisdom of Solomon, a Jewish wisdom book from slightly earlier in the same time frame as Q and *Thomas*. In it the sage sings the praises of Sophia, who teaches him everything: the universe and all its elements, the times and the seasons, the nature of animals and of plants, "the virtues of roots" (7:20). He says, "I learned what is secret and what is manifest, for Sophia, the fashioner of all things, taught me" (7:21). Thereupon follows a remarkable passage that is something like a hymn to Sophia:

For in her there is a spirit that is
intelligent, holy, unique, manifold, subtle, mobile,
clear, unpolluted, distinct, invulnerable,
loving the good, keen, irresistible,
beneficent, humane, steadfast, sure,
free from anxiety, all-powerful, overseeing all,
and penetrating through all spirits
that are intelligent and pure and most subtle.

For Wisdom is more mobile than any motion;
because of her pureness she pervades and penetrates all things.

For she is a breath of the power of God,
and a pure emanation of the glory of the Almighty;
therefore nothing defiled gains entrance into her.

For she is a reflection of eternal light,
a spotless mirror of the working of God,

and an image of his goodness.
Though she is but one, she can do all things,
and while remaining in herself, she renews all things;
in every generation she passes into holy souls
and makes them friends of God, and prophets;
for God loves nothing so much as the one who lives with
 Wisdom.

For she is more beautiful than the sun,
and excels every constellation of the stars.
Compared with the light she is found to be superior,
for it is succeeded by the night,
but against Wisdom evil does not prevail. (7:22b–30)

The spirituality of this tradition is rooted in Jewish wisdom theology. This tradition was eclectic, taking in a contemporary Platonism of the sort we have seen in the *Gospel of Thomas*. The spirit of Wisdom (Sophia) passes into every spirit that is "intelligent and pure." She finds her way into holy souls and makes them friends of God and prophets. Their role is to make known that which Wisdom would teach. Here is the basis for a spirituality of teaching and learning that informs both Q and *Thomas*. This is also the theology that animated the opponents of Paul in 1 Corinthians and their teacher, Apollos, who followed not just Jesus, but John the Baptist, another of Sophia's children.

THE FIRST CHRISTIANS?

Sophia's children. If we encounter them in such an early portion of Q, in the *Gospel of Thomas,* and even in the background of one of Paul's earliest letters, are these prophets and sages the first known "Christians"? In one sense no—for none of them, or few, were anything if not Jewish. It would be decades before anyone would use the term *Christianoi* to designate the followers of Jesus, and even centuries before Christians and Jews can be seen as truly distinct religious communities. But if we are looking for nascent Christianity, for people who very soon after the death of Jesus developed a distinctive self-understanding based on things they believed Jesus had revealed to them, well, here they are. They don't look anything like what we thought they would look like. But here they are. They revered the words of Jesus, but practiced the baptism of John. Baptism signified that they were the children of God, filled with the Spirit of Wisdom, immortal, neither male nor female, and truly wise.

So what happened to Sophia's children? Why have we not met them before? In Galilee, where Q gave them voice, they were soon overwhelmed by events that demanded answers to questions that wisdom alone could not provide. In 66–70 CE the Jewish homeland erupted into violence and chaos when the Jews tried to throw off Roman rule and were crushed in the attempt. The followers of John and Jesus were caught up in the fray, just like everyone else. Their most urgent questions now were not about the meaning of life, but the meaning of death—violence, suffering, betrayal, and destruction. Q itself was probably edited in the prelude to the war to include themes of apocalyptic judgment and reckoning. Ultimately it did not survive as an independent document. The authors of Matthew and Luke used it to supplement the basic outline of the Jesus story provided them by the Gospel of Mark, a story of martyrdom. Martyrdom was the right story for this time.

Would the followers of Jesus remain faithful even in the face of violence and death? The Gospel of Mark created the Christian narrative, a story of suffering, death, and resurrection. The Gospel of John also adopted this martyrological form, submerging within it its own distinctive elements of wisdom theology, fragments of which can still be seen in the prologue and many of its long sermonlike speeches. When the world seems to be ending, the questions of life and death become more urgent. Wisdom must have seemed quaint in that day and time.

As for Apollos, he disappears as quickly as he appears. We've made much of him here, but in reality his presence is so fleeting and ghostlike that we scarcely grasp his outline. Someone still remembered him half a century after Paul sparred with him in 1 Corinthians, or else the author of Acts would have not mentioned him at all. And yet the things Acts says about Apollos are so strange and incongruous that we must credit them with some historical reality. In 1 Corinthians 16 we learn that he made his way back to Ephesus and stayed there awhile with Paul. Did they get along? Did they part ways? Did he return to his native city and find a following there? We don't know.

And what of the many people who must have received the baptism of Apollos in Corinth? What became of them? We don't know. It is striking that some of the practices that Apollos inspired in Corinth were undertaken by women as well as men. Women in Corinth engaged in asceticism and did not marry (1 Cor. 7). And women were among the prophets who engaged in the gender-bending worship practices Paul addresses in 1 Corinthians 11:2–16. This has caused one scholar to wonder whether the prophets of Wisdom in Corinth might have been primarily women. This is possible. That some were women is beyond dispute. This fact alone, however, did not inspire Paul's opposition to them. In chapter 11 he does not tell the women to keep silent, but only to pray and prophesy with their hair done up "ladylike." This, of course, belies the often assumed idea that Paul was opposed to women leaders in these communities. In fact, the early Pauline communities appear to have had as many female leaders as male.

But as Pauline Christianity continued to develop into the second century, the issue of women's roles became a matter of dispute. So long as these communities were small and confined to private spaces, women leaders were acceptable. But as they became larger and better known, acquiring a public face, some became nervous. Public space was male space, and women leaders marked the church as countercultural. In the second century letters were forged (1 Timothy, 2 Timothy, and Titus), and authentic letters of Paul were doctored (the addition

14:33–36 to 1 Corinthians is a notorious example) to make it seem as though Paul had opposed women leaders. On the other side, texts like the *Acts of Paul and Thecla* show that women continued to champion their own cause in these churches. Who prevailed? Who today has heard of Thecla? And the forged letters? They are now read as scripture in churches everywhere.

But, ironically, in the Pauline communities the tradition of secret and hidden wisdom eventually found a home and flourished. In refuting Apollos in 1 Corinthians, Paul had promised that he too could offer "secret and hidden wisdom" to those who were ready for it (2:6–10). Later, students of the apostle picked up on this and ran with it. In the forged Pauline letter known as Colossians, the author promises his readers that they shall have "all the riches of the fullness of consciousness, into the higher knowledge of the mystery of God, of Christ, in whom are hidden all the treasures of wisdom and knowledge" (2:2–3). Later still, in the second century, the Roman teacher of higher knowledge, Valentinus, developed a Platonic Christian theology, which he claimed had been part of the secret and hidden wisdom to which Paul refers in 1 Corinthians. So Apollos disappeared from history, but Paul, who opposed him, became the font of secret wisdom teaching and higher knowledge in the second-century church. History is full of such ironies. Of course, not everyone embraced the Valentinian interpretation of Paul. In fact, most opposed it, and so it passed into the history books as heresy. Paul became the apostle of justification by faith, not wisdom. It was Jesus's faithful death on the cross that brought salvation to the world, not his wise words. Apollos would be footnoted and forgotten along with the (male and female) prophets he baptized.

And what about the *Gospel of Thomas*? The wisdom theology of *Thomas* seems to have flourished in the east, where it made its home in Edessa. Edessa, recall, was not a city of the Roman Empire. The struggles that Jesus followers like Paul had in following the crucified messiah were not the struggles of those who moved east and settled in

Edessa. Paul was a dissident in the empire, and the death of Jesus on the cross inspired him to acts of great heroic defiance, as it did many Christians who lived in lands ruled by Rome. But this was not the case in Edessa, which lay beyond Rome's imperial reach. Neither did the Jewish war affect the Edessene Christians in the same way that it did the author of Mark and his readers. The questions that inspired him to see Jesus as an apocalyptic warrior in the final cosmic battle— the meaning of violence, death, and destruction, the meaning of war itself—these were not questions that burned hot for the Edessenes.

Their questions, for the most part, remained wisdom questions: What is a human being? Where do we come from? Where are we going? How do we lead meaningful lives amid the pressing concerns of the everyday world of work and family? When people come and go, and fortunes are gained and lost, where is the enduring worth of a human being to be found? The Edessene followers of Jesus found answers to these questions in the wisdom of Jesus—supplemented by insights from philosophy, especially Plato. This was probably true of Edessene Christianity through the end of the second century.

But in the early third century, the emperor Caracalla made Osrhöene a province of Rome, with Edessa as it capital. When we encounter eastern Syrian theology after that in the works of its great fourth-century theologians, Ephraem and Aphraat, for example, it has much more in common with the theology being worked out elsewhere in the Roman Empire than with the early wisdom theology of *Thomas*.

The wisdom theology of Q and *Thomas* and early teachers like Apollos disappeared from view in the centuries that followed along with its roots in the early days of the Jesus movement. But did it cease to exist? No. It disappeared in part because it was not distinctive enough to show up against the backdrop of wider Judaism and Hellenism in the ancient world. Christians eventually became visible as Christians because they insisted on exclusive loyalty to Jesus as the Christ. They became committed to the claims they made about Jesus—that he was the only Son of God, that he was truly divine, he and no other, and that his death and resurrection were cosmic events that changed everything for all time. These claims made Christians stand out in the ancient world over against Jews and Greeks alike. But the children of Sophia did not make such claims. To be sure, they thought of Jesus and John as messengers from God, but this was a common thing for ancient teachers. Their focus was on the teaching of their messenger, Jesus. What he taught—whether about the ethics of turning the other cheek or about the immortal spirit that makes one a child of God—these things did not make them unique in their world. They shared these ideas with many other Jews and Greeks. The real reason this early form of nascent Christianity disappeared—probably—was that it eventually was simply reabsorbed into the Hellenistic Jewish world of which it was always a part.

To recover this early wisdom theology is to rediscover ways in which early Christianity was an expression of the world of its origins. Christianity is a religion that stresses its exclusive claim to the Truth. Over the centuries, it has not lived comfortably with the notion of being common. The issue of our common humanity has typically given way to the issue of our uncommon claims. But the extraordinary faith claims that Christians make about the death and resurrection of Jesus, about his unique relation to God, about his divinity and our salvation are not the whole story. If you tread back into the unexplored terrain of these gospels you encounter wisdom and insight that is not so unique, but no less extraordinary. It is not unique precisely *because* it is wisdom. Wisdom is not the special claim of an individual, but the common heritage of humanity.

When, in the Gospel of Mark, Jesus asks his disciples what people are saying about him, they tell him that some say he is John the Baptist, or Elijah, or some other prophet. But then Jesus asks them to say what *they* believe about him. Peter, their spokesperson, says, "You are the Christ" (8:27–29). *The* Christ. There is no other. This scene is repeated in the *Gospel of Thomas,* but here it has a very different outcome. Jesus asks the disciples to say what he is like. Peter says he is like "a just angel." Matthew answers "a wise philosopher." But then Thomas says, "Teacher, my mouth is utterly unable to say what you are like." So, then, is Jesus completely beyond compare? No. For this is what Jesus says in response to Thomas's high compliment:

> I am not your teacher. For you have drunk, you have become intoxicated from the bubbling spring, which I have dug. (13:5)

"I am not your teacher." The intoxicating wisdom of God is there for anyone to discover. Jesus has dug this well, but the water was already there. No one owns the water. It is a gift from God.

FOR FURTHER STUDY

For an early take on **the role played by wisdom theology in earliest Christianity**, see Elizabeth Schüssler Fiorenza, *In Memory of Her: A Feminist Theological Reconstruction of Christian Origins* (New York: Crossroad, 1983); and *Jesus: Miriam's Child, Sophia's Prophet* (New York: Continuum, 1995). Also helpful and interesting is James M. Robinson's essay "Jesus as Sophos and Sophia," in Robert Wilken, ed., *Wisdom Tradition in Judaism and Early Christianity* (South Bend, IN: Univ. of Notre Dame Press, 1975) as well as other essays in this volume.

Relatively little has been written about **Apollos**. Two recent works begin to fill this gap in scholarship: Patrick Hartin, *Apollos: Paul's Partner or Rival?* (Collegeville, MN: Liturgical Press, 2009); and Corin Mihaila, *The Paul-Apollos Relationship and Paul's Stance Toward Greco-Roman Rhetoric*, LNTS 402 (New York: Clark, 2009). Both see Paul and Apollos as colleagues and minimize their conflict. My view is informed more by Niels Hyldahl, "The Corinthian Parties and the Corinthian Crisis," *Studia theological* 45 (1991) 19–32, who senses more of a rivalry between them.

The question of **what Apollos taught** is a matter of educated speculation. I follow the line laid out by Richard Horsley in a series of essays originally published in the 1970s and 1980s, now collected in his book *Wisdom and*

Spiritual Transcendence at Corinth: Studies in First Corinthians (Eugene, OR: Cascade, 2008).

The relationship of Apollos's teaching to the *Gospel of Thomas* is discussed in my essay "Paul and the Jesus Movement: It Is Time for Another Look," originally published in *Harvard Theological Review* 84 (1991): 23–41, now revised and reprinted in my book *The Gospel of Thomas and Christian Origins: Essays on the Fifth Gospel*, NHMS 84 (Leiden: Brill, 2013), 237–60. The connection between Apollos's teaching and the *Gospel of Thomas* was first suggested by Helmut Koester in an essay entitled "One Jesus and Four Primitive Gospels," *Harvard Theological Review* 61 (1968): 203–47, later reprinted in James M. Robinson and Helmut Koester, *Trajectories Through Early Christianity* (Philadelphia: Fortress, 1971), 158–204 (see esp. 186). He discusses the idea more fully in *Ancient Christian Gospels: Their History and Development* (Philadelphia: Trinity, 1990), 55–62.

The ideas about **baptism and androgyny** explored in this chapter are inspired by Wayne Meeks's article "The Image of the Androgyne: Some Uses of a Symbol in Earliest Christianity," *History of Religions* 13 (1974): 165–209.

The idea that in the earliest years of the *basileia* movement **Jesus might have shared the spotlight with others, like John the Baptist**, is explored by Melanie Johnson-Debaufre in her Harvard dissertation *Jesus Among Her Children: Q, Eschatology and the Construction of Christian Origins*, Harvard Theological Studies 55 (Cambridge, MA: Harvard Univ. Press, 2006).

For the insight that **the empire (kingdom) of God is a concept found also in Jewish wisdom theology**, see Burton Mack, *A Myth of Innocence* (Philadelphia: Fortress, 1988), 69–74.

Antoinette Wire proposed **the theory that Paul's opponents in 1 Corinthians were female prophets** in *The Corinthian Women Prophets* (Minneapolis: Fortress, 1990).

The **pseudonymous authorship of the Pastoral Letters** (1 Timothy, 2 Timothy, and Titus) is the standard critical judgment of scholarship. The venerable and conservative Catholic scholar Raymond Brown guesses: "About 80–90 percent of modern scholars would agree that the Pastorals were written after Paul's lifetime" (*Introduction to the New Testament* [New York: Doubleday, 1997], 668; he summarizes the evidence on 662–68). Brown would never call the letters "forgeries"; he prefers "pseudonymous writings."

The forged nature of Colossians is much more disputed. **That 1 Corinthians 14:33b–36 is a later addition** to the letter is also a commonplace position among critical scholars. For a discussion with bibliography, see Wire, *Corinthian Women Prophets*, Appendix 11, 229–32.

On the shifting role of women in the second-century church, one should consult Karen Torgeson, *When Women Were Priests* (San Francisco: HarperSanFrancisco, 1995); and a fascinating study by Dennis MacDonald, *The Legend and the Apostle: The Battle for Paul in Story and Canon* (Louisville: Westminster John Knox, 1983).

For **the Valentinian interpretation of Paul,** see Elaine Pagels, *The Gnostic Paul: Gnostic Exegesis of the Pauline Letters* (Philadelphia: Trinity, 1975).

On **the *Gospel of Thomas* at home in Edessa**, see Stephen J. Patterson, "The View From Across the Euphrates," *Harvard Theological Review* 104 (2011): 411–31, now reprinted in *The Gospel of Thomas and Christian Origins*, 9–32.

9

THE LOST WAY

Today Christianity stands under the sign of the cross. Islam has its crescent, Judaism its Star of David. Christianity is the religion of the cross. The significance of Jesus lies in the story of his death on the cross. The biblical gospels tell this story in fourfold completeness. The apostle Paul insists that the true gospel is the cross, the symbol of Christ crucified. Catholics wear crosses; Protestants wear them; Orthodox too; even Hutterites wear crosses. From this, one could easily gain the impression that this was all there is and ever was to Christianity. But we have seen that this is not so. When Paul in 1 Corinthians insisted that the gospel of Christ crucified is all there is, he was taking explicit aim at another version of the gospel. It came to Corinth through the teaching of Apollos, a wandering disciple of Jesus and John the Baptist, whose credentials were just as deep and credible as Paul's. Paul was opposed to the teaching of Apollos, so the Bible is opposed to it, and thus it became an obscure early chapter in the story of odd heresies that from time to time have plagued the church. But history's judgments are sometimes hasty. The fact is that in earliest Christianity the cross was not all there ever was. There, staring back at us through the words of Paul meant to discredit it, is another gospel. What was the content of this *other* gospel?

It was wisdom—*sophia*. Paul refers to it as *sophia tou logou,* or "word wisdom." By this he probably means wisdom that came in the form of words, or sayings of Jesus. This was part of the Jesus tradition that Paul only rarely touched. Fortunately, and largely by chance, we have two texts that come from this lost and submerged side of Christian origins, Q and the *Gospel of Thomas.* These two early gospels were the handiwork of sages and disciples who revered the words of Jesus as words of wisdom. Q itself did not (so far as we know) really survive. It lay buried in Matthew and Luke, whose authors used it as a source. Like Apollos, Q could be detected only by peering through the surface of the texts to reveal a reality that lay beneath them, and before them, before there was a Bible, a church, or a single version of "the gospel." The survival of the *Gospel of Thomas* was just pure chance.

The wisdom contained in these two lost gospels is odd. It seems to lack a basic ingredient of wisdom: prudence. It did not simply counsel love of God and neighbor. It taught love your enemies, turn the other cheek, make bad loans, forgive debts, knock on a door and care for the sick inside, dine with a stranger, take leave of home and family and become, as it were, passersby. This wisdom tradition spoke of a new "empire," an empire of God, dawning in the lives of those who embraced it. They were already living it. *This* empire belonged to the destitute. In it the hungry were to be fed, the sad made happy, and the persecuted prophets honored, just as memory honors the prophets of old.

This wisdom was profoundly spiritual. Its prophets, like John the Baptist and Jesus, were prophets of Sophia, the divine embodiment of God's wisdom in the world. Their ritual of baptism was thought to convey the Spirit and to make those who embraced it children of God. Or perhaps they were to *realize* that they were already children of God. Among the children of God the distinctions by which human beings draw up and divide, order and rank were to be swept away. There would be no more Jew or Greek, no more slave or free, no more male and female. Ethnicity, class, and gender—the three great illusions by which human beings order the world—would no longer divide them one from another. The long story of fallen humanity, the story that began with Genesis, had now turned a corner.

What should we call the people who were devoted to this sort of wisdom? When we first encounter Apollos in the Acts of the Apostles, it is said that he had been instructed in "the Way of the Lord" (18:25). The author of Acts offers no explanation for this phrase, as if he already expected his audience to know what it meant. Earlier in his account of Christian origins he drops a similar term—also without explanation, as if it were a term he had used a hundred times before. Here is the text. It is the beginning of the account of Paul—in this archaic story referred to as "Saul"—and his initial opposition to the Jesus movement. Notice especially what he calls it:

> But Saul, still breathing threat and murder against the disciples of the Lord, approached the high priest and asked him for letters to the synagogues in Damascus, authorizing him to bind and bring to Jerusalem any members of the Way he might find there, both men and women. (9:1–2)

"The Way," in Greek *he hodos*. What does it mean? Our author uses the term here, and then not again until Acts 19—also just as abruptly and without explanation. Altogether the term appears in just four episodes, each time crying out for a footnote. What is the Way? Why haven't we heard of it before? Is it like the time I remarked to my teenage son that Paul McCartney had always been my favorite Beatle? He knew who Paul McCartney was, but wondered why I would call him a beetle. "You know," I said. "The Beatles—the band that started it all." But, of course, he did not know, because he is not of that generation. I get the same feeling when I see "the Way" pop up in Acts. Was "the Way" where John, Jesus, and Apollos all got their start?

The truth is, no one really knows where this odd phrase comes from and what it means. By one account it came from John the Baptist, who preached about preparing "the way of the Lord," in imitation of Isaiah. That explains why Acts would say that Apollos had been instructed in "the Way of the Lord." His teacher, recall, was John. The Way, by this account, was a later, shortened form of this primitive designation for the movement that included John and Jesus and later disciples like Apollos. Later still, Paul and everyone else would call this movement "the church," in Greek *he ekklesia*. But way, way back, before there was the church, there was the Way. If the author of the Acts of the Apostles had not absently dropped the term a few times into his narrative of Christian origins, we would never have heard of it. When Paul first encountered the church, it was not yet the church, but the Way.

Do we not know about the Way for the same reason we would not know about Q and the *Gospel of Thomas,* save for the accidents of history and the scholarly elbow grease that eventually restored them to life? Q, *Thomas,* the Way—why did they not catch on and spread so dramatically as the gospel of Jesus's death on the cross?

It is useful to remember that Christianity was born in the Roman Empire, a totalitarian regime with little tolerance for rival empires, however great or small. Naturally the followers of Jesus were dissidents within it. Their story soon became one of resistance and eventually persecution. Its leading heroes, John the Baptist and Jesus, were executed by the empire, as were Peter and Paul, and many others, unnamed and anonymous. Their story of resistance against the empire would soon merge with the larger Jewish struggle against Roman rule. With the outbreak of open rebellion in 66 CE, the Jewish people of the Roman East embarked on an extended quest for freedom that would last for seventy years. During that time the Jewish temple would be destroyed, thousands of Jews would be killed, and thousands more enslaved. Jerusalem, the Holy City, would become a Roman military encampment, and later rebuilt as a Roman city with a new name, Aelia Capitolina. All of the books of the New Testament, save for the authentic letters of Paul, were written during the period bracketed by the Judean revolt (66 CE) and the Bar Kokhba rebellion (135 CE). This was one of the most violent and tragic periods in the history of the Jewish people in antiquity. The New Testament is a collection of books written by Jewish dissidents negotiating their tender existence in a very hostile environment. Its earliest texts show resistance; later texts, accommodation. Through all of them, though, the cross remains central. They tell the story of Jesus as the story of the cross because this was *their* story. Jesus died by the hand of the empire. Thousands of Jews did. And many Christians, most of them Jews, did as well. This is why the cross became the church's story. It remained so for a very long time, centuries.

The Way—if that's what we shall call the people who created Q and the *Gospel of Thomas*—focused elsewhere. To be sure, they must have taken stock of the fate of John and Jesus and noted their passing as prophets in the long line of persecuted prophets. But their fate was not the point—their message was. It was a useful message for dissidents: "I came not to bring peace, but a sword" or "The first shall be last and the last first." This was provocative and brash, and much of it was folded into the synoptic gospels. Some of it, though, was hard. Love your enemies? The apostle Paul taught this too, but only with the caveat that by doing so you would heap burning coals upon their well-deserving heads. In the synoptic gospels, the spirit of "Love your enemies" and "Be impartial just as your heavenly Father is impartial" is overshadowed by another hope: the coming apocalypse, in which the enemies of the struggling church would all be destroyed— the Romans who had sacked the Holy City as well as the Jews who had brought this calamity upon them by rejecting the true messiah (see Mark 12–13). God is not impartial after all. We can see this idea beginning to dawn already in Q. By the time Q was swallowed up by the canonical gospels Matthew and Luke, it had already incorporated the idea so clearly expressed in their other source, Mark—that the troubles with Rome were God's punishment for the Jews' refusal to welcome the new empire of God. Under the pressures of the war, the

Way and its ideals did not hold up so well. It was not a teacher they needed, but a savior who could do battle with demons and drive evil from the earth.

But in our other wisdom gospel, *Thomas,* these ideas did not take hold. For the sages who created this gospel, the Way lead east, to the caravan towns that lay out along the desert highways, beyond the eastern frontier of the Roman Empire. They must have heard about the troubles back west in Jerusalem. Perhaps it was the war or its threat that sent them packing in the first place. But once they crossed the Euphrates River, the Roman Empire was no longer their problem. The cross was Jesus's fate, but it would not be their own. Theirs was a different kind of struggle. They did not face the wrath of a totalitarian state. Their foes were more personal, individual, interior demons. They lived in Edessa, a caravan town, with all the temptations such a place could offer. They saw fortunes won and lost, experienced the ecstasy and agony of the body of flesh, and saw life lived at its short-term shallowest. Everything is temporary in the caravan town. There the Way intensified into a kind of asceticism, a withdrawal from the world to focus on the inner life of the spirit.

In this the people of the Way found an ally in Plato. They might have brought Plato with them. Back in Corinth, Apollos had already espoused a good deal of Plato's philosophy alongside "the Way of the Lord." In any event, Plato's anthropology gave them a new way to articulate the experience of the spirit of God within them. Plato's divine spark, the "mind," became their "spirit." The Platonists spoke of the "image of God" dwelling within—language the followers of the Way could well understand from their own creation story, in which God creates the human being in His own "image." Plato's universe gave them a place to imagine their new empire, as hopes for it on earth began to fade: heaven. And so the Way became the way home, the way back to God, Plato's God, the creator from whom they had come and to whom their destiny now propelled them.

Some of these ideas that took root out in Edessa would eventually make their way into the mainstream of Christian thought in the West. That human beings have bodies and souls, souls that come from God and return to God; that the kingdom of God is a heavenly kingdom, the place where souls go to rest—these would all find their way into Christianity through other readers of Plato: Clement of Alexandria, Origin, and Augustine. When the Roman Empire became the Holy Roman Empire and the dissidents of Christianity became its saints, the problem of death changed. The question was no longer what happens when good people are killed, but what happens when people, generally, die. Plato had an answer for that: the eternal soul. So, ironically, ideas that first found expression in a gospel initially rejected by the church in the West eventually became central. Of all the gospels from that early period, only one, *Thomas,* holds the central idea that most of Christianity embraces today: when you die, your soul goes to heaven.

So the Way was lost. Q was swallowed by Matthew and Luke. *Thomas,* like a black-sheep cousin, moved out east, got all sophisticated, and was seldom heard from again. There must have been other texts too. But they, like 90 percent of the Christian literature that once existed, were completely lost and forgotten.

Is the Way worth remembering? I think it is. For centuries Christians have built a religion around the death of Jesus, his resurrection, and his eventual return to destroy our enemies in a great apocalypse. As helpful and cathartic as these themes might have been to the early church as it struggled to survive in the hostile environs of the Roman Empire, when saints were still martyrs and the kingdom more than a utopian dream, they have proved their limitations over time. The apocalypse never came, and it's not going to come. This idea belongs to the world of ancient mythology, and it wasn't a very good idea to begin with. In it the Jewish God of *shalom* becomes a violent overlord, and the Prince of Peace becomes a supernatural warrior, a fire-breathing monster who lays waste the earth, its forests, its animals, and all but a remnant of its people—the chosen few. How many have believed they were the few!

In our time we have developed the capacity to make this mythology come alive. We can destroy worlds with the flip of a switch. Our drones, angels of death, hover over the alleys of distant cities we count as seats of evil. We could, if our enemies become too mighty in our estimation, destroy the world itself. Somehow, I believe, imagining a God who will certainly one day do this himself has made it easier to excuse our own hubris in assuming this power ourselves. The Sons of Light always get to participate in the final battle. The apocalypse is a common New Testament idea we should finally give up on. It wasn't true; it did not come to pass. God, it turns out, is not as our forebears imagined him. Even if John, or Jesus, or Paul, or Apollos entertained such thoughts, they were wrong. When, in a few billion years, fire at last consumes the earth, it will be an act of nature, not of God, and the whole human race will perish—no chosen few.

The cross is a multivalent symbol with much more to recommend it than the violent drama of apocalyptic. Martyrdom is still an issue somewhere. People still do face the question, "What am I willing to die for?" This may not be a bad thing to hang on to, so long as it is not confused with another question: "What am I willing to *kill* for?" These two questions, it turns out, lie very close to one another in our history. Under the sign of the cross Crusaders marched across Europe slaughtering Jews and Muslims by the millions. In our own place and time, just a moment ago in the great sweep of history, the stench of burning crosses and burning bodies beat the flames of passion for a Christian nation, a flame that burns still in the heart of a people that has never really taken account of its violent, Christian past. Since the moment Constantine made the cross his personal talisman, the sign under which his troops would always win, the cross has been the symbol of both martyrdom and murder. Soldiers' declaration that they are willing to die for the cause always also buys them a license to kill for it.

But before the followers of Jesus asked the question, "What would I die for?"—before Jesus himself asked this question, before John the

Baptist asked it—they all asked another question: "What would I live for?" The empire of God was a way of life. It was not a future or distant reality. It was already spread out upon the earth for people to see. It was only a matter of embracing its wisdom. Turn the world on its head, be the leaven, be the weed, value the least, listen to the beggars, feed the hungry. Eat what is put before you and care for the sick, the stranger, even your enemy. Open your doors to the world, judge not, and above all seek—look, see, don't turn away, even when the sights are unsettling. Living the way of wisdom means living with eyes wide open and brain switched on. This is timeless advice and worth remembering.

Q and *Thomas* remind us that this was once the Way. But it is not as though Christianity completely walked away from the Way. It is still there, of course, embedded in the New Testament. Seeing it is only a matter of focus. There is no clearer statement of this wisdom tradition than Luke 6:20–45, the Sermon on the Plain. This was Jesus's inaugural sermon in Q, and perhaps an early epitome of the whole Jesus tradition, the Way. It is overshadowed by its bulked-up brother, the Sermon on the Mount. But the Sermon on the Plain is about as close to the voice of these early prophets as we can get:

> Blessed are the destitute, the hungry, the sad . . .
> Blessed are the prophets . . .
> Love your enemies . . .
> Give to anyone who begs from you . . .
> Judge not . . .
> Take the log from your own eye . . .

And Paul? We have seen him mostly in conflict with one of our prophets, Apollos. But Paul was not unaffected by this tradition. As far as we know, Paul was one of the few who went the whole nine yards—who pulled up stakes, left house and home and all his social capital behind, and became a wandering apostle spreading his own wise words. He once despised the Way, but eventually he embarked upon it. He says that it's all about the cross—in 1 Corinthians—but that was not really true. Throughout his letters he sprinkles his own wise words, words composed—so many scholars suppose—in his own school of wisdom. A good example of this is found in 1 Corinthians itself. This is what Paul calls "the highest form of the Way" (*kath' hyperbole hodon;* 1 Cor. 12:31):

> Love is patient and kind.
> Love is not jealous or boastful or arrogant or rude; it does not seek its own interests; it is not irritable; it does not calculate wrong; it does not celebrate injustice, but rejoices in the truth.
> It bears all things, trusts all things, hopes in all things, endures all things. (13:4–7)

This little gemstone of rhetorical flourish sits at the center of one of scripture's most beautiful texts, the encomium to love in 1 Corinthians 13. Paul and his sages probably workshopped it in the Hall of Tyrannus in Ephesus, where Paul held forth in the months after leaving Corinth. By including it in the Corinthian letter he wished to show the Corinthian faithful that he too had a little wisdom in him. Indeed, he did.

And lest one underestimate Paul's devotion to the fruits of his labors in the service of Wisdom, note well what he says at the end of 1 Corinthians 13:

> So faith, hope, and love remain, these three things, but the greatest of them is love.

These are the words of the apostle of *faith,* who argued that one is justified by faith in Jesus Christ, Christ crucified. He was the apostle whose *hope* resided in an imminent return of the Son of Man, who would bring judgment and destruction upon the earth. But faith and hope are secondary, he says, to *love*. Love is "the highest form of the Way." So says Paul.

So what is Christianity? Christianity was and is many things. There was much ado about Jesus's death, to be sure. He was a martyr. From this so many other things flow—the story of Jesus's life, the idea that his death would atone for the sins of others, the claim that he was raised from the dead. The resurrection claim meant for some that the time of God's visitation was near. Jesus had not really died like other people. He had gone to heaven, his original home, and from there he would return one day to finish what he started. These are all still part of Christianity today.

But before all of this—before anyone would have taken notice of Jesus, decided to kill him, or mourned his death—Jesus was saying and doing things that moved people. He was a sage and a prophet. In Q and the *Gospel of Thomas* we recover something of that original modality of Jesus—wisdom. This was the lost Way. When you see it in texts that feature it, like the wisdom gospels Q and *Thomas,* it is easy to see. But these texts also make it possible to see this wisdom modality reflected in other texts, in more familiar gospels and in Paul, where it is often overwhelmed by other themes. That is why scholars are eager to shine a light on these ancient texts, these lost gospels. Their discovery and presence now are changing the way we tell the story of how Christianity began. Jesus was more than a martyr. He was a teacher—and not *merely* a teacher, for there is nothing "mere" about a teacher of wisdom. In antiquity, the sage was a prophet, the philosopher, a messenger from God. This tradition had its own spirituality and a theological claim to rival that of the canonical scriptures. God can be present in the world shaped by our words. The empire of God is not going to come with signs, with earthquake, fire, and war. It is already here—"spread out upon the earth." It is only a matter of seeking it out and finding it.

FOR FURTHER STUDY

The Way is truly an odd and mysterious phrase. The theory that it is **a short-ened form of John the Baptist's "way of the Lord"** comes from S. Vernon McCasland, "The Way," *Journal of Biblical Literature* 77 (1958): 222–30.

The irony that the doctrine of Christian souls that go to heaven appears in apocryphal literature is explored in my essay "Platonism and the Apocryphal Origins of Immortality in the Christian Imagination, or Why Do Christians Have Souls That Go to Heaven?" in Jens Schröter, ed., *Apocryphal Gospels Within the Context of Early Christian Theology*, BETL 260 (Leuven: Peeters, 2013), 447–476; now reprinted in Patterson, *The Gospel of Thomas and Christian Origins: Essays on the Fifth Gospel*, NHMS 84 (Leiden: Brill, 2013), 61–92.

For more on how **martyrdom** could generate much of the early Christian claims about Jesus death, see my book *Beyond the Passion: Rethinking the Death and Life of Jesus* (Minneapolis: Fortress, 2004), esp. chap. 2, "Martyr."

That the Sermon on the Mount/Plain might have been an early epitome of the Jesus tradition was argued by Hans Dieter Betz in an essay entitled "The Sermon on the Mount (Matt. 5:3–7:27): Its Literary Genre and Function," in his *Essays on the Sermon on the Mount* (Philadelphia: Fortress, 1984), 1–16.

I argued that **1 Corinthians 13:4–7 is the product of a Pauline wisdom school** in the essay "A Rhetorical Gem in a Rhetorical Treasure," *Biblical Theology Bulletin* 39/2 (2009): 87–94.

The idea **that Paul founded a wisdom school** and that it may have been housed in the Hall of Tyrannus in Ephesus belongs to the mid-century German scholar Hans Conzelmann, whose commentary on 1 Corinthians has been translated into English as *1 Corinthians*, Hermeneia (Philadelphia: Fortress, 1975).

ACKNOWLEDGMENTS

To acknowledge and thank everyone in whose debt I labor would take another book-length manuscript. But there are a few without whom this book would not have seen the light of day. First, thanks to Michael Maudlin, who agreed to read a finished manuscript from a stranger, and to Marc Borg and Dom Crossan, who convinced him with a word that it might not be a waste of his time. Mickey Maudlin's deft handling of the initial work and editor's instinct about what would strengthen the work made it a much better book than the one I sent to him. Thanks to Marc for planting the idea that perhaps I should write something people could read. Thanks to Ann Floto, who gave the manuscript her expert attention and helped straighten out the many little tangles. Thanks also to the editorial team at Harper-One: Kathryn Renz, Suzanne Quist, and Natalie Blachere, for their patience and respect for the work. What a pleasure to work with these professionals. And finally I offer my utmost appreciation and respect to Jim Robinson, Helmut Koester, John Kloppenborg, and Elaine Pagels, from whom I have learned so much about Q, Thomas, and the hidden histories these texts represent.

INDEX